SHATTERED LENS

A Tale of Domestic Violence and
Redemption through Love

By

Mary Alice Beasley

authorHOUSE®

AuthorHouse™
1663 Liberty Drive
Bloomington, IN 47403
www.authorhouse.com
Phone: 1-800-839-8640

© 2010 Mary Alice Beasley. All rights reserved.

No part of this book may be reproduced, stored in a retrieval system, or transmitted by any means without the written permission of the author.

First published by AuthorHouse 9/30/2010

ISBN: 978-1-4520-2787-6 (e)
ISBN: 978-1-4520-2785-2 (sc)
ISBN: 978-1-4520-2786-9 (hc)

Library of Congress Control Number: 2010907805

Printed in the United States of America

This book is printed on acid-free paper.

Because of the dynamic nature of the Internet, any Web addresses or links contained in this book may have changed since publication and may no longer be valid. The views expressed in this work are solely those of the author and do not necessarily reflect the views of the publisher, and the publisher hereby disclaims any responsibility for them.

DEDICATION

"MOM"   "ELIZABETH"

To my beloved mother, Mattie Beasley, who taught me that I would never be bored if I sought to learn something new every day; and to my big sister, Elizabeth Beasley Vaughn who dreamed for me even before I could imagine.

SPECIAL THANKS

An author writes for the readers. I was blessed with three people who served as my audience. My soror and good friend, Fredericker Rolle Rhodriquez, helped me through the process, refreshed my memory of events and encouraged me to complete this memoir after it had been on the bookshelf for fifteen years; Melinda Armstrong, a life coach and organizer of the "Butterfly Circle Women's Network" with whom I'd recently become acquainted; and Donna Craig of Chicago, Illinois.

To these sisters of Delta Sigma Theta Sorority, Incorporated
who demonstrated unconditional support:
Dr. Luvernice Hooks Croskey, Ph.D.
Linda Darden Bellamy
Joan Pullum Duckworth
Gwendolyn L. Bryant
Cecilia Lawrence Hunter
Karen Bullard - Jordan
Constance Thornton
Mona Bethel Jackson
Parthenia Days
Marsha Sims

Fredericker: friend, mentor and confidant

TABLE OF CONTENTS

DUSK: PSYCHOGENESIS	1
The Inner Child	5
Hindsight	12
Blind Faith	66
THE FIRST DAY: ON THE SEA	79
The Teacher	81
The Professional Class	84
The Line	88
The Passover Plot	91
THE SECOND DAY: ON THE SEA	97
The Exodus	99
Crimestoppers	106
Passing the Word	110
Wearing White	115
Black on White	123
Discipleship	126
THE THIRD DAY: PUERTO RICO	131
The University	133
The Entourage	139
The 70th Floor	150
Crisis Investing	157
THE FOURTH DAY: ST. THOMAS	163
The Sacrificial Lamb	165
Marked for Death	170
Getting My "House" in Order	174
The Crucifixion	177
The Death Wish	180
In the Tomb	182
THE FIFTH DAY: ST. MAARTEN	185
The Tarot Reading	187

Close Encounters	193
Julius	193
Job	195
THE SIXTH DAY: ON THE SEA	**201**
The Agate	203
The Healing Process	215
Reprogramming	218
SUNDOWN	**221**
The Dream	223
The Resurrection	227
THE ELEVENTH HOUR	**231**
A New Name – A New Teacher	233
Blossom	243
DAWN	**249**
Insight	251
No Coincidences	255
Realization	258
THE SEVENTH DAY: SUNRISE	**265**
The Upper Room: A Higher Order of Thinking	267
Self Actualization	270
HOME: MY DEBUT	**273**
The Cotillion: A Dream Fulfilled	277
BLESSINGS	**283**
My Beloved: The Rock	283
20 / 20 Vision	298
Post Script	319
CONTACT INFORMATION	**320**

Overview

Throughout this narrative, I symbolically emphasize my visual impairment, initially sustained as a toddler, as a metaphor for the blindness from which we all occasionally suffer as we journey along the path of life. Our perceptions of life's events are almost always influenced by our attitudes which are based on prior external conditioning. We either believe what we see, or we see what we believe.

This book is based on the premise that most of us: find strength while facing fear; learn the correct way to proceed after making mistakes; build perseverance while attempting to overcome obstacles; develop a desire to love unconditionally after experiencing loss or rejection; and learn to live happily and spiritually after confronting death.

All of my experiences, propelled by my insatiable quest for knowledge through relentless questioning, and my need for healing the emotional and physical wounds inflicted during attacks of domestic violence in my marriage, ignited a raging fire within me to know the true essence of my being.

This journal was written: to help me understand the causes of the thought processes which governed my behavior; to explain why I repeated experiences; to focus attention on the devastating effects of unresolved inner conflicts; and finally to break the years of silence and give voice to my story.

This publication is not an endorsement or a condemnation of any doctrines, beliefs, creeds or of any persons with whom I have associated in the past. It is simply a chronology of my levels of thinking and stages of spiritual development as I traveled through various religious institutions and studied different philosophies.

Perhaps there are those with whom I have interacted on my journey to self actualization that possibly have different views, opinions and memories of the events that are expressed. Their stories are also true; but this tale represents my perception of how my personal, professional and social life was profoundly impacted by the decisions and choices that I made and for which I take full responsibility.

Two names have been changed to protect privacy.

SEVEN DAY
EASTERN CARIBBEAN CRUISE

Carnival Cruise Lines
"Celebration"

DUSK: PSYCHOGENESIS

The feeling of fluttering butterflies in my stomach makes me want to change my mind and stay home but it's too late to cancel. After a most demanding school year, I should be jumping with joy anticipating a relaxing seven day Eastern Caribbean cruise to San Juan, Puerto Rico; St. Thomas, Virgin Island; St. Maarten, and Antigua aboard the M.S. Celebration, one of Carnival Cruise Lines' most impressive ships. What a paradox! What should be a joyous occasion is going to be a very somber one for me.

This is my first vacation alone. I'm so accustomed to traveling with family, close friends or groups. I don't know anyone in any of the ports of call and I don't even know the identity of my cabin mate. That's what happens when you book as a single passenger. I'm so anxious.

"Ok girl, get it together," I voice loudly talking to myself. Double check your list. Make sure you haven't forgotten anything important. Identification cards, travelers' checks, credit cards and tickets are in my purse. Vitamins, camera, sunglasses, tape recorder and books are in my handbag. My books are so important. Without them I'll find it difficult to appear preoccupied. For so long I've used them as props to isolate myself in social settings.

I force a smile when my kids, Renee, Juanita and Lonnie and two of their friends, Damon and Kristy approach me.

"Got everything?" Lonnie asks. He knows me so well he can almost read my mind.

"Yes, and I'm ready to go."

"I'll put your baggage in the trunk of the car."

"Thanks Damon."

"And I'll drive," Lonnie announces as he chivalrously opens the car doors. "All aboard for the Port of Miami!"

Lonnie senses my anxiety and kisses me on the cheek as I get into the car. Then bowing as if he were a chauffeur he says, "At your service, ma'am."

"You are so funny," I chuckle.

The girls get into Renee's car and follow.

I sit quietly staring out of the window at the beautiful scenery as we ride across the causeway to the port. Seeing the ocean has a calming effect on my nerves. I glance over at fabulous Bayside in downtown Miami and see the skyline of the wonderful attractions and realize how little time I've spent enjoying the amenities in my own city.

We arrive at the port in twenty minutes. It takes another thirty minutes to get through the procedures for boarding. Finally we enter the gangplank and stop briefly to pose for the traditional picture.

Damon and Lonnie carry my bags to the cabin. My anonymous roommate has already been in the room and declared squatter's rights by placing her luggage on the lower bunk. I look around the cabin and think, "Why didn't I pay for an upgrade, a bunk bed?" I sigh.

"Just place the bags against the wall. I'll unpack later. Let's take a tour of the ship before departure."

"This ship is beautiful," Renee remarks.

"It sure is. It's a floating luxury hotel."

Knowing that I might not ask strangers to snap my picture, I say in a commanding tone, "Let's hurry! I want you to take lots of pictures of me on board in various locations."

As we stroll from deck to deck, I think, "I wish that they were going with me. It's so obvious that I'm the one holding on; but this is one phase of my life's journey that they cannot help. I'll have to do this alone."

An announcement from the public address system interrupts my thoughts: "Attention all visitors. Please return to shore immediately. The ship is preparing to set sail promptly at 5:30 p.m. Thank you for being our guests."

"Ok everybody. Come quickly and give me a hug."

Sensing my separation anxiety, Renee says, "Relax and have a good time."

I hurry to the upper deck to catch a glimpse of them and wave goodbye until they are completely out of view. I sigh as my thoughts quickly revert to my cabin mate. Will she be much younger or older; Black, White or Hispanic; friendly or reclusive?" It's time to meet her. I slowly return to the cabin.

Beth, a Jewish legal secretary from New York, is warm, friendly and a seasoned passenger. This is her fourteenth cruise. She dates one of the co-captains and sails often, using her vouchers, to spend time with him. We are the same age and have lots in common.

Dusk: Psychogenesis

"Other than being in the room to shower and redress, you will practically have the room to yourself Mary," she states.

I think, "Great!" I earnestly want to be alone so that I can concentrate. I have to find solutions to some major personal problems and I want to think clearly without being distracted.

After dinner, I'll look for a quiet spot on the lower deck where I can begin introspecting. I must get myself together without any advice from relatives, friends or the clergy concerning relationships and biblical interpretations, my two major areas of concern.

I don't wish to go on like this any longer. I've been looking at life through a shattered lens for too long. I must begin to see people and situations as they really are, not as I want them to be.

The sun is beginning to sink below the horizon. It is now dusk, like my past, dim and unfulfilling. I quickly explore the ship in search of a place to meditate. Great! I see the perfect spot near the life boats. Armed with books, notepads and pens, I position the lounging chair so that I can put my feet up on the railing.

As I sit down, lie back and stare at the darkening sky, the smell of the ocean's breeze and the motion of the waves begin calming my agitated mind. How do I begin my self analysis? How can I adequately reflect on more than thirty years in just seven days and come to some reasonable decisions about how to proceed in the future?

As I look up at the stars, the creation story in the book of Genesis overwhelms me. As I recite the verse, "In the beginning God created the heavens and the earth," I realize that thoughts are things that are brought into existence. My mind has created my dark world of despair. If I want a better brighter world, I must recreate it by thinking more rationally. I smile as the word "psychogenesis" comes to mind. Yes, I must go back to the beginning of my childhood and remember any incidents that affected my way of thinking positively about life and its possibilities.

Knowing that this was not going to be an easy task, I remember the story of Nicodemus's clandestine meeting with Jesus and his comments. I laugh aloud as I also think, "It would be easier if I could just reenter my mother's womb and be born again," as he suggested.

My laughter quickly turns to prayer. "Oh God, please help me through this process. I want to be happy now, in this life. I want to love and be loved unconditionally."

As I begin to cry, I sense the Spirit of Truth moving upon the face of the waters. The concept judgment day permeates my mind. Yes! This is my day of reckoning. I wipe the tears away and close my eyes. Amazingly I see sparkling particles of light as my mind is flooded with colorful images of the past. It's as if a video recording of my life has been projected onto a screen and someone has pressed the play button.

My memory is enhanced as I ease into a state of reflection. Sensing that someone is whispering in my ear, I place my fingers behind the lobe and listen. I smile knowing that my prayer is being answered. I relax, confidently pick up the pen and begin to write.

THE INNER CHILD

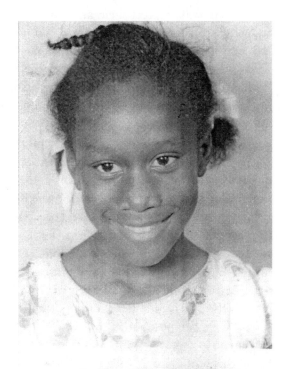

School Days 58-59

"Mary at age 9"

I was in the fifth grade at Holy Redeemer Roman Catholic School. Every day was pretty much routine. We gathered on the basketball court and played until the nuns arrived. Then we lined up by classes, there was only one class per grade level, and followed our teachers to the devotional area in front of the flagpole.

Once assembled, the entire student body simultaneously greeted the faculty of all white priests and nuns, recited the Pledge of Allegiance, prayed and performed other prescribed rituals. Mother Superior would end with special announcements for the day. A standard of excellence was instilled in us every morning. We were required to speak correctly and in complete sentences at all times, but we could not talk unless we raised our hands and was recognized. Our behavior was to be in accord with a strict code of moral conduct. The consequence of disobedience was immediate expulsion.

Whenever priests, nuns or any adults entered our classrooms, we were required to stand immediately to greet them and would remain standing until prompted to be seated. Usually the visitors would just motion with their hands in a downward move to indicate permission.

Our daily class schedule was highly structured and followed strict protocol. Prayer was performed before and after each subject; when we left the room for lunch; when we arrived in the cafeteria; and when we returned to the classroom after recess.

We attended Mass every day. We prayed fervently for the service to be over quickly as we had to kneel on unpadded prayer benches for a very long time while the priest went through the liturgy in Latin, the Stations of the Cross or the Rosary. Our knees were so sore when Mass was over that we even prayed for them to stop aching as we hobbled back to class.

We recited a prayer of safety and protection at the close of the school day and were reminded to pray before dinner, before bed and when we awakened in the morning. We prayed a lot. I also prayed as I walked home from school alone. The public school kids joked about the yellow and white uniform that I wore, the cap on my head and yes, the black and white saddle-oxford shoes. They laughed, called me unkind names and teased me all the way home.

If I responded to their criticism, they would mock my speech, grammar and pronunciation. "She talk so white and proper don't she. Who you thank you is? You thank you bettuh than us, don't chuh?" they taunted.

However, one day there was a slight change in our school's daily routine. Even before Sister Justella told the class what was going to happen, we knew that this day was different. We saw uniformed nurses from the public health department in the building. Small groups of children from each class followed the nurses to the school's clinic across the street from the basketball court. We could see them walking in a single file line from the windows of our classroom on the second floor. Soon it was our turn.

This was exciting. We were being given vision and hearing screening tests. We had not had this service at our school since my enrollment. As we waited in line, I carefully observed the nurses. When it was my turn I followed the procedure exactly as the others had until it was time for the vision examination.

"Close your left eye and read the letters as I point to each one," said the nurse.

"E,G,K,P,T," I proudly read. I was doing fine.

"Now close your right eye and read the letters."

This was just too easy I thought. As I attempted to follow her directions the lighting changed, images became blurred, colors faded, and the letters seemed to merge on the chart. Some letters completely disappeared. What was happening to me? I squinted and refocused again and again.

"Read the letters please," she reiterated.

"They are all blurred, ma'am. I can't see them clearly."

She stopped the test and directed me to another nurse who looked into my eyes with a lighted object, then handed me a note to take home.

"Give this letter to your parents to read," she instructed.

"Yes, ma'am," I answered. As I took the paper, I knew immediately that something was wrong with my left eye.

At the age of six, my older sister Elizabeth took charge of my rearing. I was born during Liz's freshman year in college. After graduating with a degree in Nursing, she returned to Miami to care for the family because mother was stricken with polio, placed in an iron lung for treatment and confined to an isolation ward at Variety Children's Hospital in South Miami for several months. At that time, I was attending Liberty City Elementary School. Liz, who had converted to Catholicism in college, decided to enroll me in Holy Redeemer Roman Catholic School.

The letter was given to Liz who took me to "Historic Overtown" on 3rd Avenue to Dr. Brown, an ophthalmologist. After the examination, the doctor looked disturbed, then asked, "When did this injury occur and what medical treatment did Mary receive?"

Liz replied, "I'll have to call mom on the phone for the answers. I was away in college during her early years." As she dialed the number, I listened.

"Mom, what happened to Mary's eye?" she inquired.

"She was hit with a soda bottle after her first birthday. The eye was bloodshot for months so I put some salve on it and kept it covered. When it cleared up, I thought it was all right," she reported.

"Did you ever take her to see a doctor?"

"No, I didn't."

Liz looked upset as she relayed the information to Dr. Brown. "What's the diagnosis?"

"She has suffered a blow so severe that a traumatic cataract has formed on the lens of her left eye," he explained. "There is lots of scar tissue around the injury. Her lens is so shattered that surgery will not reverse nor improve the condition. In that eye, she is legally and medically blind; her vision will always be blurred. She'll have to wear glasses for the rest of her life just to protect her better eye."

"Why didn't we know something was wrong before now?"

"The injury happened so early in her development that the brain adjusted to the difference very quickly. It shut down most of the signals of the left eye and her right eye compensated. To her, everything is normal."

When we returned home from the doctor's office, more information was provided about my accident. It seemed that the household was in a state of turmoil because my father had abandoned our family of eight children and moved to Boston, Massachusetts where he also had another family of two children. Because he worked in various capacities for the Seaboard Railroad, he traveled frequently.

After my birth, he was frustrated with the crowded conditions and was often heard asking my mother, "Mattie, what you gonna do with this "hundered" head of chi'ren?"

Apparently, I was the straw that broke the camel's back. I was one too many to deal with. With his desertion and lack of financial support, my older siblings had to assume more chores and responsibilities when mom, who had not worked, had to become the wage earner. Perhaps accidental or unintentional, my injury resulted from their inner frustrations. Not only was I hit in the eye, the right side of my face was pressed against a kerosene heater and severely burned during another rage of anger. Being the last child, twenty years younger than the oldest sibling, no one wanted to baby-sit, so I was shuffled around and told to "stay put in the corner" and in later years "to read a book." Obviously, I was a burden to everyone.

As I listened, I felt that my birth had been the cause of their unhappiness. Though these incidents happened years earlier, and I had no memory of them or of the pain that must have accompanied the blow to my eye and the burns to my face and neck, I now decided that I would be quiet around them. I began to seclude into my special corner. The characters in my books became my friends.

I cried all the way to school the first day that I wore those thick awkward glasses. I was constantly warned to keep them on so that nothing could happen to my right eye. Great fear of blindness was instilled in me.

"Don't take off your glasses at school. Make sure that you keep them on during recess, especially if you're playing softball. Duck or turn your head if a ball is thrown your way," everyone reiterated.

"Mildred"

"Do you want to go to the school for the blind?" warned Mildred, another sister who was attending college at Florida Normal in St. Augustine, Florida where the state school for the deaf and blind is located. "I see the students walking with their white canes when I leave campus and go into town."

I got a daily dose of how to protect my sight and was frequently reminded of the consequences of total blindness. I was so scared.

To make matters worse, the public school students had a ball teasing me. Now they had something else to taunt me about other than my uniform and shoes. I was called four-eyes daily. A neighbor, Jerona Bethel, waited for me in front of Liberty City Elementary as I walked home one day and provoked an argument. A crowd quickly gathered and before you know it I was being hit in the head and kicked in the butt after falling to the ground. As my body coiled into the fetal position, I covered my face with my hands to protect my eyes.

After that day, I began talking to my guardian angels so that I could tune out the hostile voices and constant insults as I hurriedly walked pass the buildings and stores on 71st Street and 18th Avenue across from the school. I prayed that I would never have to go to public school.

Holy Redeemer was only an elementary and intermediate school. I would have to transfer to Notre Dame Academy, an all girls' Catholic school by the ninth grade if I wanted to stay with my friends; but that would not be the case. Liz got married and moved to Cleveland, Ohio and mom transferred me to Dorsey Junior High School. I could have just died. Being among my tormentors daily was horrible. They teased, taunted and bullied me unmercifully as they did other students who had noticeable differences.

To add insult to injury, I had to wear my sister Pearl's hand-me-down, homemade clothing. Clothes were never important to me before. We all wore the same color coordinated garment to Catholic school. In public school, you were popular if you wore the latest fashions or were stylish. I was neither.

As time passed, I began to lose control of the muscles in my left eye; it began to drift to the side. Ironically, my next door neighbor Oppia Jean Smith, whose father was a devout deacon who often used biblical phrases in his conversations, noticed it first and referred to my eyes as the "wandering Jews." Other classmates soon noticed my meandering eye; pointed their fingers, laughed without mercy and called me "cross eyed."

To strengthen the muscles in that eye, the doctor suggested that I wear a patch over my right eye after school and on weekends. As I walked with it on, I noticed that I developed a blind man's gait, lifting my feet higher than usual as levels and patterns of flooring changed. However, as time progressed, the condition worsened and my balance was also affected. I started brushing against walls and running into protruding tree limbs and other objects. I was frightened; my depth perception was severely impaired. I started disguising my eyes by wearing tinted glasses and shades constantly. I was emotionally devastated.

Though I was an academically smart student, I purposely didn't excel. I did not want the recognition; I avoided any activities that would place me in the front of the class. I seldom asked questions aloud or volunteered answers. I didn't want to be the object of further derision.

I secluded even more as I found comfort and escape in books. My imagination was full of interesting places and exciting things to do. I pretended to have many friends all over the world. Finally, through a publication, I found a way to actually correspond by replying to a request for pen pals. I exchanged many letters with my pretend friends for about a year. However, I never wrote about the condition of my eyes; to them, I was perfect.

I stop writing to think about my early childhood experiences and on how they had influenced my view of the world and my daily interactions. Feeling that the timing of my birth created a problem for my siblings is the reason for my subconscious desire for acceptance. Outwardly, I secluded but inwardly I wanted to be loved and positively recognized. I wanted to be a valued member of my family. I wanted to be a contributing member of a group. But most importantly, I wanted to be invited into the rank and file by my works and deeds.

The fear of losing the sight in my right eye also caused a major shift in how I would interact with my peers. There were fights in the neighborhood. Therefore, I avoided all incidents that might lead to arguments. I became a passive spectator and observer, constantly thinking but not sharing my thoughts.

I pull out my dictionary and look up the word passive. Yes, I see the connection. A passive person is one who is submissive and suffers without resistance; one who does not act but is acted upon. Since that is the image that I presented, I must now project a more assertive personality. I must be more proactive and dynamic.

I stop reading and look at my watch. It's late but I'm too excited about how I'm progressing to stop. While my memory of events is clear, I'll concentrate on my adolescent years to help me understand what experiences shaped how I relate to men. Poised to record my thoughts, I pick up my pen.

HINDSIGHT

Unlike most teenagers, I wasn't permitted to court, thus date in high school. Six years earlier, my sister Pearl had become pregnant in the twelfth grade so mom was very strict when I enrolled at Miami Northwestern Senior High in the tenth grade. Mom never let me attend any parties, school dances or basketball games. I was only allowed to go to musical programs and football games because I played clarinet in the concert and marching bands. Mom didn't permit me to walk home with the other kids after the football games. She was always there to pick me up in her 1964 blue Chevrolet Impala. Some band members, Cheryl Austin, Joanne Fisher and Barbara Smith who were in the clarinet section, would see the car and then laugh as the bus turned the corner onto the school's parking lot. Her car was always parked in its usual spot. Even when the band accompanied the football team out of town to Tampa, Florida to play Middleton and Blake High Schools, mom's car was there regardless of the time the band returned. She was determined to protect my chastity until graduation.

My only chance to socialize was when I attended church. As a teenager I joined New Mount Moriah Baptist Church on 14th Avenue and 67th Street, and was baptized by Reverend Shipp. I immediately became involved in all of its youth programs. I particularly liked going to the Baptist Training Union activities on Sunday evenings. I later joined the choir and traveled with the group to competitions throughout the county. I seldom missed any big tent revival or vacation bible school session during the summer at Peaceful Zion Baptist Church with the Reverend Preston.

The only time that mom let me out of her sight was for the Junior-Senior Prom. She reluctantly let Chico, a senior football player, escort me. When I realized that it was her intent to go as a chaperon, I cried and begged her to reconsider. My sisters came to the rescue and convinced her that she was much too strict. After much debate, I was allowed on my first and only date in high school. We double dated with my neighbor Carolyn Wilcox and her companion Hank, another football player.

I was so excited about being with the team's star quarterback. I felt every eye on me as we walked into the hotel's ballroom. I saw the gestured hands go from mouth to ear as those with itching ears whispered, "How did she get him?"

If I could stop and tell them how we met I'd say, "I was walking home one hot summer's day from babysitting Pearl's two children, Deborah and Rodney. I was wearing a pair of Bermuda shorts. I heard a hissing sound and turned around to see Chico waving. He was on the field that ran parallel to the railroad tracks behind Dorsey Junior High School on 17th Avenue and 71st Street."

"Hey! You with the big legs! Where have you been all of my life? Don't you want to be my girlfriend?"

"No!" I stated emphatically. "I was in Mr. Austin's first period Algebra class with you but you never noticed me because you were so busy talking to Pamela Harper. I sat behind her. I've heard your tired lines before so don't try them on me." I quickly turned and walked away as fast as I could.

In the fall, when school opened, I was going down the staircase from Spanish class when I heard a familiar hissing sound. It was Chico.

"Hey! You with the big legs! Can I walk you to class?"

"No!"

The next day he was leaning against the wall with his hand over his heart. He said as if he was ailing, "My heart aches for you."

"You're sick," I uttered.

"I know and you're my remedy." I smiled knowing that he was referring to the title of a popular song.

Each day for a month, he appeared on the stairs and I ignored him. However, one day he saw me walking home after band practice and insisted that I talk to him.

"I can't date or even be seen talking to boys. Go away before you get me in trouble," I said.

"That's all right I'll just walk along with the crowd. When we get to the corner one block from your house, I'll turn around."

I smiled approvingly.

"You're so different from the other girls and I want to get to know you," he said as he returned the smile. Soon we began secretly talking on the telephone and exchanging notes as we passed in the hallways.

So tonight is my public debut and the prom is my cotillion. I looked around at the staring faces and smiled as we walked across the dance floor to our table.

After the prom, we went to the Bonfire Restaurant on 79th Street Causeway. It was packed with students. I was so excited and happy that I forgot about the time. Like Cinderella, mother had given me a 1:00 a.m. deadline. The prom ended at midnight.

On the way home, Hank detoured and drove toward Miami Beach. Suddenly he turned the car from the highway, parked along the shore and turned off the lights. The guys got out of the car, opened the trunk and returned with blankets. Hank put the key back into the ignition then helped Chico spread the covers on the ground. Carolyn and I curiously looked at each other.

Then Chico said, "Ya'll get out of the car. It's time to have some real fun now."

We refused. They laughed.

Chico jokingly said, "Well ya'll can fuck, fight or hitchhike."

I laughed at the expression but I knew that the guys were serious. I started crying. If I didn't get home on time, mom would never allow me out of her sight again.

"Please Chico; take me home," I pleaded.

"You wastin' time talkin'," he said without mercy.

The guys turned their backs and leaned against the car and said simultaneously, "Let us know when ya'll ready to git down."

Carolyn said, "Mary, the key is in the ignition. Let's roll up the windows and lock the doors."

"Great idea," I said.

As the guys heard the sound of the doors being locked, they quickly reached for the door handles. Oh, were they frustrated; they had not anticipated this move.

To get some fresh air, we slightly rolled down the windows on the passenger side and listened as the guys tried to talk us into opening the doors.

Suddenly we saw the swirling lights of the Miami Beach police and heard the patrolman yell, "Leave the area and go home immediately."

We opened the doors and the guys obeyed the officers as they escorted us back over the causeway. No one said a word in the car as we rode home. We were aware of the segregations laws and of the consequences for Blacks who did not have workers' passes being caught after hours on the famed Miami Beach.

It was now 2:00 a.m., an hour past my curfew. I was so scared. Whenever mom started fussing you could hear her voice for blocks. I didn't want to be embarrassed in front of my date and friends, especially on this special night. I feared being laughed at if they told the other kids at school about mom's relentless questioning.

When Hank drove up in front of my house, mom turned on the porch light immediately, opened the door and demanded an explanation.

"Didn't I tell you to be home by 1:00 a.m.?"

"Yes ma'am," I said with my head held down. I was never a liar so I told the truth. She was angry with Chico and did not allow him to take me out again.

In August, Chico went away to Florida A & M University on a football scholarship. When he returned for the Christmas break, mom allowed him to talk with me on the front porch within her view.

In April of my senior year, I called Chico and asked if he could come back to Miami to escort me to my senior prom. I didn't have a date. Most of the other boys considered me to be Chico's girl after he'd escorted me to last year's prom; but that didn't stop them from trying to score with me.

I remembered an incident that occurred near the end of last school year when the band went on a field trip. Rather than return to school after the event, a few members got together to go to Arthur Humes' house to have some fun. I was invited to go. Since this was the first time my mother was not going to be in the parking lot waiting for me, I followed the crowd because I didn't want to be called square. To my dismay, while slow dancing with Ernest Bethune, one of the drum majors, I was slowly guided into a bedroom. Realizing what his intentions were, I pleaded, "Please don't do this to me."

He laughed, "Everyone knows that Chico only deals with girls who give it up. So come on and give me some too," he insisted.

"No!" I began to scream; but he quickly placed his hand over my mouth to muffle my voice. After reassuring me that he was not going to force himself on me, he walked toward the door and just before he opened it, he unbuckled his belt and unzipped his pants. As he opened the door, he grinned and slowly zipped up his pants and buckled his belt as if he had just put on his clothes.

Everyone looked at me as I reentered the living room. Though nothing happened, I was devastated the next day as my name floated around school and in the band room as having had intercourse with him. I felt that my reputation had been forever ruined as guys would walk behind me in the hallway and snicker, "I want some too." But I was more scared that my mom might hear this gossip and "whup me to death."

Everybody knew Chico. He was even more popular in the community because he was one of the two quarterbacks for FAMU's football team and he had starred in the annual football game, "The Orange Blossom Classic" in December. The Miami Herald Sports column extolled his high school fame and quarterback statistics for that great cultural event.

I would have been very proud to be with him again for my senior prom but Chico wasn't financially able to come home. He came from a very poor family that received welfare. Chico's mom, Ms. Enith lived Overtown off of 20th street and 6th Avenue; but to attend Northwestern, Chico lived with his grandmother, Mrs. Molly Pearson in the James E. Scott Projects off of 22nd Avenue and 75th Street.

If it were not for the football scholarship, Chico would not have gone to college. In the tenth grade, he had gotten arrested for a pool hall brawl and was rescued then mentored by his football coaches. So to think that he could afford a roundtrip bus ticket was impractical. I went to the prom with a group of girls who did not have dates and had a terrific time.

A few weeks prior to my graduation, I was surprised by an unexpected visitor. Mom was going out on a date. She told me to lock the door and cautioned me to be vigilant. We were now living alone because my brother Bennie, who was in Chico's class of 1965 had been drafted. However, he scored so high on the military aptitude test that he was encouraged to enlist in the United States Air Force.

"My youngest brother Bennie"

I locked the door and returned to the sofa to continue watching television. Moments later, I heard voices outside. Having been informed that mom would use her key when she returned, I ignored the sounds. Suddenly, the door opened and mom entered with a very tall muscular man behind her.

"Mary, I want you to meet someone."

"Yes ma'am," I said politely as I stood to be introduced.

"This is your father, Ben."

Like a robot, I extended my hand to acknowledge him. Since I'd never seen a picture of my dad before, I stared at his face to make a physical connection with that of his two brothers, Uncles Isaac and Henderson who I knew.

"How do you do, sir?" I said.

"Mattie, look at my baby. She looks just like you as a teenager," he said in a flattering voice as he shook my hand. He attempted to embrace me but I resisted.

Mom seemed unimpressed and quickly asked him to leave so that she could continue with her plans. As the door locked again, I stood there for a moment and listened to their conversation.

"Mattie, I've come back for good. We're still married and the house is still in my name so I'll be moving back in tomorrow."

Mom turned to Uncle Isaac who had driven my father to the house and said, "Hell no! Isaac you took him to the train station fifteen years ago now you can take him back again tonight." With that said she quickly got into her car and drove off, leaving them looking baffled in front of the house.

Through the window I stared at the six feet five, three hundred pound silhouette as it lowered itself into my uncle's car. I felt no emotional connection with him as I slowly returned to the sofa to continue watching my program.

In June, shortly after my graduation, I was delighted to have received a letter of acceptance from Dillard University with a partial scholarship to attend their nursing program. I'd decided to become a registered nurse, like my big sister Liz and I chose Dillard because some of my Catholic friends were going to attend Xavier in Louisiana and I wanted to be near them. Secretly, I had a crush on Ronald Thomas and wanted to be near him. He was smart and polite; I deeply admired him.

I'd modeled my life after the pattern that Liz designed for me. She reared and groomed me to be very similar to her in attitude and values. I went with her everywhere as she taught me how to follow in her footsteps.

She associated with the sons and daughters of prominent people in our community like the Braynon's, who were lawyers, doctors, and teachers; and the Dorsey's, who were millionaire land owners, of which a local school and a public park are named. Liz attended high school with the kids of these noted families and after returning home from college as professionals, they were elite members of Miami's "Black Bourgeoisie."

Liz was far advanced for the times. Determined to be a socialite and a career woman, she often traveled to various ports of call with members of this group. I accompanied them to care for their kids. You see, Liz was much younger than her friends. She had graduated from Booker T. Washington High School with honors at the age of sixteen and enrolled in FAMU's School of Nursing in the fall of that year. When Liz graduated, she was still too young at heart to marry and have kids.

Liz bought only the best even when she bargain shopped. "Bebe," an endearing nickname that only she called me, "never buy cheap things, especially clothes. Always look for quality even if the garment is inexpensive. Check the inseams and the thread count. Look at the label and see what percentage of what fabrics are in the garment," she instructed.

She always gave me practical demonstrations as we selected garments from the racks at Richard's or Burdine's Department Stores. She explained everything as we shopped, traveled or visited her friends. Her goal was to expose me to the better things in life. Liz was very concerned about social protocol and class status.

"Bebe, always greet adults like this, Good Evening Mr. or Mrs. Whomever. Always be respectful and say "please" when asking for something and "thank you" when you receive something," she reinforced daily.

She was always teaching me something new and unusual. "Bebe, today I want you to listen to some of these albums by the great musical composers or read one of the classics or study about one of the philosophers. We'll discuss them later."

Liz was known for her elegant dinners and Sunday afternoon tea parties. I'd read Amy Vanderbilt and Emily Post from cover to cover so I knew just how to set the table for each occasion. Even the proper way to address the invitations was learned. When she hosted such an affair, I was instructed to observe everybody's behavior. After each event, I had to properly wash, polish and wrap the silverware.

"Bebe," she said, "silver will tarnish if it gets too much air, so wrap it well."

Dusk: Psychogenesis

Physical fitness, good nutrition and skin care were as essential to her as breathing. "Bebe, do not go to bed without cleansing and moisturizing your face and neck. Never frown excessively. It causes premature wrinkles. Take your vitamins and exercise daily to keep your hips and abdominal muscles well toned."

Establishing a family name was very important to her. We were not prominent nor middle class, but Liz insisted that we act as if we were and I was most receptive to her commands. It was very important for me to carry on the tradition which she had envisioned for our family. Through her I embraced the concept of the American Dream. To achieve this goal, I had to attend college and Dillard University was my choice.

The summer was uneventful so I eagerly awaited the beginning of the fall term. I could hardly wait to go to New Orleans. I'd heard that it was a beautiful city. As summer was ending, I could think of nothing else until early one morning when I received a long distanced telephone call from the Dean of the School of Nursing at Florida A. & M. University.

"Hello, may I please speak with Mary."

"This is Mary," I answered. "With whom am I speaking?"

"This is Dean Burgess at FAMU. You've been accepted into our School of Nursing but you've not returned any of our requests for additional information. Do you plan to attend in the fall?"

"No ma'am. I plan to go to Dillard University."

"Why have you chosen Dillard?"

"Because they've offered me a partial scholarship and I need the money."

"Well, I'm looking at your test scores and I'm calling to inform you that we're offering you a full academic scholarship specifically if you major in nursing, but if you change your major, you will have to forfeit the scholarship," she explained.

"I understand."

I was so excited because mother had been unemployed since I was in the tenth grade. The Florida East Coast Railroad, for which she worked cleaning the interior of trains when they returned to the yard, had gone on strike. During that time, we received public assistance.

In my senior year, mom was employed by the public school system as a custodial worker. Her hours were long and the pay was at minimum wage, which didn't help our situation. However, since the eighth grade, I'd been receiving a monthly Social Security disability check from my dad which would help to defray some college expenses, but I still needed additional financial assistance.

Liz had married and moved away to Cleveland, Ohio and Mildred, another sister, was now a school teacher at Phyllis Wheatley Elementary. They would assist me but the greatest financial responsibility was on Mom. So I knew that I would gratefully accept the scholarship.

Then Dean Burgess asked, "How is Elizabeth doing?"

I was surprised. How did she know about Liz? I then remembered that I'd named Liz and Mildred on my application as family members who had attended the university.

"Liz is fine," I replied.

"The nursing faculty was very proud of her. We still remember her brilliance. Elizabeth's state board of nursing exam score was the highest of any university student in the state of Florida the year she graduated. After reviewing your test scores, I was proud to submit your name as a scholarship recipient. I wanted to call you personally to entice you to our nursing program."

"I am happy that you called. I will come to FAMU in the fall."

The Seaboard Railway train ride to Tallahassee, Fl. was exciting. At each stop, new and returning students boarded. We laughed, talked and sang all the way there. Chico, who had returned to college early for football practice, promised to meet me at the train station to help with my trunk. When we arrived, I looked for him and waited, but he never came. I saw several male students assisting the returning female students with their luggage for a reasonable fee; so rather than continue to wait for Chico, I utilized their services.

After I settled into the dormitory, I took a tour of the campus for the first time. Later, I saw Chico strolling along talking loudly with a group of football players. He looked tacky with one pant leg rolled up above his knee and the other one down.

I signaled him over and asked, "Why didn't you meet me at the train station?"

"Shit, you here ain't you! I had things to do."

I was shocked at his attitude and foul language because he had always acted so politely around me with the exception of that prom night. Was this a different character? I wondered but said nothing to avoid a negative scene.

I soon discovered that Chico had another girlfriend on campus. I was disappointed because that summer he'd talked about the good times we were going to have when I got there; but it didn't work out that way. Chico openly dated whomever he pleased. He was especially partial to Andrea from New York. She was tall and very slim; wore a long straight hairpiece that flowed down the center of her back; and walked with a sexy sway.

Instead of being angry, I looked at his dating as an opportunity for me to date. College was my new beginning. I wanted everything about the next four years to be exciting. However, to have memorable college experiences, I would have to become more interactive. I was very friendly and quite humorous and knew that I would be liked if I could just stop being so self-conscious about my eyes.

I was still disguising them and wanted to stop wearing my masks of many colors. I called Liz and told her how I felt. During Thanksgiving recess, she again arranged for me to see Dr. Olga Ferrer, a renowned ophthalmologist whose office was on ritzy Bay Shore Drive. A second surgery was scheduled during Christmas recess to have the muscles in both eyes strengthened. A mild procedure had been performed on my left eye when I was in high school. This surgery was successful and my eyes were aligned again.

I was so excited about life and all of its possibilities. All of my dreams would now come true. Through group identification and participation, I began to broaden my horizon. Cultural and political activities kept my mind energized as I focused on learning of our historical roots. I was going to make a difference. My generation would be the first to benefit from the 1964 Civil Rights Legislation.

As I continued to matriculate, I realized that I didn't really want to be a registered nurse like Liz, nor a teacher like Mildred. What then would I do? If I changed from nursing I would have to forfeit my scholarship, but I'd become so intrigued with Speech and Language Pathology through my roommate Carolyn Taylor, from Deerfield Beach and her friends, Blanche and Helen. I had never heard of the profession before college but was fascinated because of what it represented. Since I'd been teased about my "proper speech" as a child, I now wanted to help others to overcome their impediments and dialect.

At the beginning of my sophomore year, I went to the financial aid office and explained my monetary situation. Because of my excellent grades I was given a job on campus and a stipend for tuition that I did not have to repay. I worked on the reception desk in McGuinn and Diamond Halls, the freshman dormitories, typing the mail lists, paging students, answering the phones and filing papers for Mrs. Teele, the dormitory counselor. This was a great job because I got to meet so many people, especially guys when they came to the desk and asked me to page their dates. Later, when I saw them on campus with other girls, they'd signal for me to keep their secrets. I was emerging from my cocoon!

Because I wasn't seriously interested in Chico anymore, I let him do his thing; but he wasn't as polite. One night I was visited by a very nice guy whom I'd met in the Chemistry lab. I liked him a lot because he was polite and studious. Chico sat outside the dormitory on the porch and intimidated the guy, who was much smaller than Chico in stature.

"Mary's my girl and one day we're going to get married."

I couldn't believe my ears.

"What makes you think I'm going to marry you?"

"You are! Believe me," he laughed. "And nobody on this campus is going to date you but me. I've told all the guys in Gibbs and Nathan B. Young Halls and the football players that you are my girl."

His words were true. Most times when guys were interested and I told them my name and that I was from Miami, they immediately backed off.

Why was Chico becoming so controlling? He surely wasn't committed to me, so why did he do this? Why did those guys listen to his nonsense? What was he telling them? Why did they take him so seriously? Did they fear him? What was it that they knew about him that I didn't know? One thousand questions flooded my mind.

Later, as I became more socially active, Chico started criticizing my actions. When I pledged Delta Sigma Theta Sorority, he would walk behind me and taunt, "You outta my league now, Miss Uppity." When I'd make the Dean's Honor Roll, he would condescendingly call me "Miss Smarty." When we went to the movies in Lee Hall and I'd sit up straight in the seat, he'd make comments about my being too stiff and proper. I was 5'10" tall and very slender, only 135 pounds, to walk or sit in a slumped manner would be tacky and I would feel uncomfortable. I began to wonder why if all that I did, stood for and aspired to become annoyed Chico, why did he discourage other guys from dating me? It was obvious that he wanted me, but for what purpose?

I often pondered his motives. I'd go out with him to try and talk some sense into him or to get an explanation. He'd always pretend to be understanding and then promised to stop misbehaving. I called home and cried to my sisters. To my surprise, mother was happy. Chico had replaced her as my warden.

In his senior year at FAMU, Chico's actions changed for the better. He became polite and considerate. He defended his previous actions as immaturity. "Mary, I realize your positive qualities and I want to marry you. I know that you'd be a loyal wife and a good mother to my children. I just wanted to keep you from being used while I sowed my wild oats."

I was somewhat flattered and allowed myself to believe him. My three brothers had always tried to protect me too while they "fooled" around with everybody else's sisters. Chico seemed more mature and responsible and was eager to enter the professional world. He no longer teased me about my proper grammar, but asked for assistance so that he could be more effective in upcoming job interviews. I was somewhat impressed and glad to help him again academically as I had done on numerous occasions when he was failing a course.

That Christmas, he purchased a small diamond solitaire from Original Ruvins Jewelers and presented it to me. I didn't accept the ring. Deep down inside I knew that I wouldn't be happy with him even with the supposed change in his attitude.

In January, Chico began his internship in Jacksonville, Fl. The coaches arranged for him to live in the dormitory at Edward Waters College because he didn't have funds to pay for a private room. During that time he telephoned regularly. Each conversation was filled with promises of the good life and happiness. He was convincing and his words sounded sincere but my doubts remained. In the spring, when he returned to campus, I reluctantly accepted his engagement ring. It was the proper thing to do. He had completed his studies and would not have to return to campus until June for the graduation ceremony. For the first time in my life I was on my own and I enjoyed my freedom. I finally felt independent. I took off his ring and placed it in my jewelry box.

Chico immediately got a job with the public school system as a Physical Education teacher. Luckily, he was placed at Olinda Elementary, a newly constructed site that was beginning a pilot program called "The Triple T" for teachers who worked in the inner city. It was a special two years program. The faculty, all veteran teachers, had been especially chosen from various schools throughout the county. Chico was included because a physical education teacher had not been assigned to Olinda; therefore, he was able to enroll with them at the University of Miami for graduate studies. All fees were paid and the staff received a stipend.

"Mary and Chico at wedding with their mothers"

The new staff was encouraged to get to know each other better before the school year started. So the group socialized and "partied" quite often that summer as they matriculated at UM. Though I'd remained in Tallahassee for the summer session, Chico sent for me to attend some of the parties and special functions. I was very impressed because of the caliber of people with whom he now associated. They reminded me of Liz's classy friends.

Chico was happy to be a part of a professional group. His actions now appeared more positive and constructive.

"Mary I've made it. I'm the first one in my family to receive a college degree. Just think! I can be a positive role model for the kids in the inner city Overtown."

I smiled. Chico's older brother, Wellington had gone to college first but had not yet completed his studies. Chico constantly talked about his plans for us and a family.

"You will make a perfect mother for our ten kids."

I stopped smiling. "Is he serious?" I thought. "I have other plans."

Dusk: Psychogenesis

That summer, Liz returned from Ohio and was formally introduced to Chico. She was impressed with him and his associates and encouraged me to give him a chance, but I continued to discuss my doubts and concerns about his character.

"Liz, I'm scared of him. He seems so rude and angry at times. His parents cuss and fight all the time and he has a real hatred for his dad. I won't be able to adjust to their environment."

She said, "Chico loves you so he won't hurt you Bebe. He's a young professional now who is going places girl. You can help him socially. He needs your skills. You'd better grab him. You're supposed to have prospects by the time you finish college even if you don't marry right away."

"You waited ten years after graduating from college before you married. Like you, I want to travel first. I'm not ready for kids and the domestic scene right now," I sighed.

"The competition for good men has stiffened and it's good to marry a man who loves you more than you love him," she assured me.

I'd always listened to Liz because I respected her judgment. Her lifestyle and success were proofs of her great wisdom. So I reconsidered Chico's proposal. I wanted to be happy also. Just maybe I could accomplish my goals with him.

After a whirlwind summer, I was elated to receive notice that I had been selected as one of four students to be sent to Miami for internship. This would be the first time that anyone in Speech Pathology would be sent there from FAMU. Dade County was the largest school district in the state of Florida and there were only six Black American Speech Therapists on staff at that time. This was going to be a pleasant challenge. Dorothy Bell, Patricia Cunningham and Cecelia Lawrence were also selected and the faculty counted on us to make good first impressions.

My internship began October 1st. Chico came for me every morning on his way to work and drove me to the designated school for each day. I rode the public bus home. My directing teacher, Mr. William Schroeder, a graduate of Notre Dame University, worked in five schools, one of which was Miami Jackson Senior High school where Chico was the assistant football coach afterschool. I never mentioned my relationship with Chico to anyone at the school because I wanted to establish my own identity.

It was in late October, after listening to Liz's positive comments rather than to my inner feelings that I reluctantly, and with great reservations, consented to marry Chico. He, however, was most insistent that when we married, he'd make me the happiest woman on earth. He'd promised that

I'd not regret being his wife for one day. I continued to be more excited about the possibility of receiving a grant for graduate studies to Ohio State University than I was about marriage.

However, Liz said, "Bebe, it will be easier to obtain your M.S. later in life than it will be for you to obtain a MRS. Girl, a good man is hard to find."

Chico had positively impressed Liz that he really loved me. He shared his dream of fame and fortune with her. Though he was very disappointed about not being drafted to play professional football after having received so many letters from the pro scouts in his senior year at FAMU; he was now trying to make a reputation as the greatest high school coach in the county. That goal seemed to dominate his actions. He talked of nothing else.

Though Liz was impressed by Chico's behavior and rhetoric, I knew that we were incompatible. Money, fame and the good life were not going to change that. Chico and I were from opposite sides of the track in our attitudes, values and priorities.

During my internship, he escorted me out at night and made life interesting. For the first time, Chico had money to take me to nice restaurants and movies. At the end of each date, he would say, "I can't wait for you to set a wedding date."

"What's the rush, Chico? Let's concentrate on completing graduate school first," I reiterated constantly.

"Baby I just love you so much, I can't wait that long," he pleasantly pleaded. "What if I get drafted and have to go to Viet Nam? You know some of our friends have already gone there. Remember John Dillard?"

"Yes!"

"He is dead. He was sent over right after basic training. He died after being there less than six months. I no longer have my student deferment. Think about that. We need to be together now."

I paused to think of my neighbor and other fallen classmates, but I refused to set a date. I didn't want anything, especially an unplanned pregnancy to defer my dreams. I wanted to travel and explore the world. I wanted to host elegant parties like Liz had. I liked the fun of planning an affair and the excitement that followed. But most importantly, I wanted to go to graduate school. I aspired to become a university professor, lecturer and writer.

Since Chico was in graduate school I felt that he would understand my desire to continue my studies also. However, he would still try to convince me that nothing would interfere with my plans, not even marriage.

As my internship progressed, Chico and I became more intimately involved than we'd ever been. I let my lust overrule my logic and soon began planning for a December wedding. Liz hired a social directress, Mrs. Ford, who was also a teacher at Floral Heights Elementary, to coordinate the event. Of course, Liz would be my matron of honor.

After mailing the invitations, I realized that my period would begin during the week of my marriage. I didn't want to spoil my honeymoon so I called Dr. Bridges' office and scheduled an appointment. After the examination, I was given birth control pills, Ovulum 21, that would alter my cycle. I began taking them as scheduled. I didn't tell anyone, especially Chico because he constantly talked about my getting pregnant immediately after the wedding.

With everything set, I returned to campus on December 17th to receive official notification that I had met all requirements for my degree and had earned the distinction of Magna Cum Laude. I was overwhelmed because I had also been honored in "Who's Who in American Colleges and Universities."

The head of FAMU's Speech Department, Dr. Boulware, was charged with selecting students from FAMU to attend Ohio State and Northwestern Universities on full academic scholarship. He summoned me to his office and said, "Mary, I'm happy to inform you that you've been chosen as one of next year's recipients."

"Thank you, sir. I am so happy."

When I returned to the dormitory, I called all of my friends and family to tell them the good news.

I returned to Miami a week later and was married on December 27. However, my honeymoon was a big disappointment. Though Chico had been asked many times during the planning of the wedding if he had made travel arrangements and hotel reservations, he had not. When pressed for a hint of where we would be going, he always said it was going to be a surprise.

After the reception, which was held in the banquet hall of Bonded Rental Agency, we drove away to what I thought would be to the airport or to the port of Miami. Instead Chico drove across the causeway to Miami Beach. I asked, "What hotel are we staying in?"

He said, "I don't know yet." My heart skipped a beat. He drove up to the first motel on Collins Avenue and 163rd Street and went inside. I looked at him in disbelief as he talked to the clerk at the registration desk; when he returned to the car he said, "They don't have any rooms available because it's the holiday season." I was devastated.

As we drove along US A1A as far up as Palm Beach County, the scene of his walking into a motel and returning to the car shaking his head from side to side was repeated. There were no vacancies. I cried profusely then said, "Take me home." I realized that I had made a big mistake and decided to have the marriage annulled.

On the quiet drive back to Miami, he stopped at the Atlantic Towers Hotel, and luckily for him, there was one room available for two nights. Tired and dismayed, we checked in; but instead of making sweet love, I cried myself to sleep as he pleaded for forgiveness.

When the two days were over, I went back home. Luckily, no one questioned my actions because the apartment building next to Carol City Senior High School where we would be living was still under construction and would not be ready for occupancy until March. We'd planned to rent a room from Maxine Ollis, a teacher at Olinda Elementary, until then.

I was livid and unable to forgive him for his behavior. Embarrassed, I told absolutely no one about Chico's gross thoughtlessness.

On January 5, when school reopened after the winter break, I got dressed and went downtown to the school board administration building to apply for a substitute teaching position. While I was seated in the office filling out my application, I overheard someone speak my name.

"Do you have an application on file for Mary Beasley?"

"Just one moment, I'll check."

I stood to see who it was and was surprised to see Mrs. Florence Canes from the office of Special Education. She had come to observe me during my internship and was highly impressed.

"Mrs. Canes, I'm over here completing my application now. Do you want to speak with me?"

"Yes! What a coincidence your being here right now in this office. We have an opening in the Speech department that I'd like for you to fill. A therapist was in a car accident over the holiday and won't be able to return. I immediately thought of you. If you take the job there's a good possibility that you may be hired full time in the fall."

"Thank you very much; I'd love to take the position. This is great timing," I said. However, I was not hoping for a full time position because I planned to be in Ohio in the fall; but I needed the added experience and exposure.

"Can you start Wednesday, January 7th?"

"Sure, I can."

"Well, meet me in my office tomorrow morning at 8:30 a.m. so we can process your papers. Thank you and welcome aboard."

Dusk: Psychogenesis

I rushed home and told my mom, sisters and friends. I was so happy. I was now a professional. I had arrived. The world was mine. I was ready to start living the good life, the American Dream.

At the tender age of twenty, I'd graduated from college, gotten married, separated and started my professional career all within a two weeks time period. Life was proceeding at an accelerated pace. I was excited about pursuing my dreams.

On Wednesday, January 7th I met Mrs. Canes downtown and was introduced to June Sinko, the chairperson of the Speech Pathologists. June drove me to all of the four schools that I would service. Westview Middle, Westview Elementary, Miami Park Elementary and Broadmoor Elementary Schools were my stops. On Thursday, I was proudly on my own, but my joy was only for a moment. Unlike the warm greetings that I had experienced the day before with June, I was now basically ignored. Like a sudden bolt of lightning, I was hit with harsh overt racism for the very first time. All of the schools in which I had been placed had all white faculties and student bodies. The only people of color were on the custodial staff.

This was a very emotional time for the teachers because the school system was going through court ordered desegregation. To achieve integration, the faculties at each school would have to conform to an 80/20 ratio of white to black teachers. Therefore, more of the white teachers were affected and they were hostile about having to go into black schools or into depressed neighborhoods. After having received their transfer notices, they openly expressed their anger with bitter and unapologetic remarks. They commented in front of me as if I was not present.

As I listened and observed their mannerisms, I reflected on seeing movies that depicted slaves quietly serving their masters and guests at the dinner table. Discussions of plans to lynch or squash rebellion among the insurgent slaves were openly voiced without regard to the feelings of the slaves who were serving. The slaves did not demonstrate any emotions about the horrific methods mentioned. It was as if they were deaf.

As I quietly sat in the faculty lounge, not one of them thought to ask who was "the spook that sat by the door" nor did anyone muffle their comments after glancing at me. To them I was insignificant, irrelevant or invisible. I felt terribly impotent because like the slaves, I said nothing.

I heard a comment that summarized all of their hostile attitudes and caused me to rethink race relations. It was, "I'll quit before I go and teach those innately savage children." Several teachers actually resigned.

In February, 1970, the schools were closed for a week to implement the staff transfers. After listening to their venom for a month, I anxiously awaited the arrival of the Black teachers to the schools in which I worked. However, by then my attitude about integration had completely changed. I felt that it would take another century, if not longer, for those ingrained, deep seated negative attitudes and stereotypes about Black people to be altered.

I also realized that I was not as strong as the freedom fighters and the demonstrators who marched during the Civil Rights Movement and I was ashamed of myself. Though I wanted equal rights, greater opportunities, higher pay, access to public places and protection under the law that the marchers had been brutally beaten and died for, I now preferred to live respectfully but separately. I wanted to embrace the richness of my history and culture without having to constantly prove that I was worthy of respect, life, liberty and the pursuit of happiness by any race. I felt like a hypocrite.

So much was happening that I didn't realize that my emotional state was also beginning to change. I began crying uncontrollably and unexpectedly. I complained of headaches and dizziness. I was gaining weight. I soon realized that these were side effects of the birth control pills. I went back to Dr. Bridges who prescribed a different formula but the side effects continued.

Also in February, Chico pleaded with me to reconsider the marriage. He promised to make up for his stupidity and lack of consideration. We moved in with Maxine until the apartment was ready.

Together again, I could not keep my secret from him. He was very upset when my period came on month after month. "Maybe you need to be checked to find out if you can get pregnant. I know ain't nothing wrong with me," he chided arrogantly.

"I've been taking the birth control pill. I didn't want to take a chance since I'm going to graduate school in the fall. I mailed the application last month and I'm expecting confirmation any day," I confessed.

"Do you think I'd try to get you pregnant on purpose?"

"Yes I do! But if you aren't then it shouldn't matter that I'm taking the pill as a precaution." He just laughed.

When the school year ended, Chico surprised me with a five days, four nights trip to Nassau, Bahamas to make up for the botched honeymoon.

By August, I was more listless and knew that I couldn't go away to school until I determined the cause. I telephoned Naomi Sampson,

Mildred's friend and asked about Dr. Aden, her gynecologist. I'd often heard her speak highly of him. I called.

My appointment was scheduled for the next week but a sharp pain on my lower right side began to throb; suddenly it intensified. I called Dr. Aden's office again and informed the receptionist that it was an emergency. Pearl drove me to his office.

"Pearl"

Dr. Aden's examination revealed that I was indeed pregnant. He cautiously stated, "I suspect that the baby is ectopic. That means that it's in the fallopian tube. I can feel a lump. You'll have to be rushed to the hospital immediately to undergo emergency surgery." I panicked.

Though I was twenty one years old, I looked considerably younger so Dr. Aden was very cautious thinking that he needed parental consent. The legal age in Florida was twenty-one at that time. I showed him my driver's license and a payroll stub and proudly stated, "I am a gainfully employed married woman, Dr. Aden."

"Great, I'll have my secretary call the hospital to secure a bed. Go there immediately. I'll see you in the operating room."

Pearl, a Licensed Practical Nurse, called Liz.

"Dr. Aden says that Mary has an ectopic pregnancy and has to have emergency surgery."

"Who's this doctor? Why didn't she go to see Dr. Bridges?" she inquired.

Liz, a public health nurse was skeptical of private white doctors. She'd seen numerous cases of PID, pelvic inflammatory disease, which she termed "pussy in distress," end in unnecessary hysterectomies when antibiotics could have been used to treat or cure the condition.

"What hospital are you taking her to?" she frantically asked.

"I'm taking her to Mercy Hospital on Bay Shore Drive!" Pearl responded.

"Good, Mercy is a Catholic hospital and because of the Catholic's stand on abortion, everything will be done at that facility to save her baby's life and prevent the doctor from performing an unnecessary hysterectomy," she assured Pearl. I'll meet you there." She hung up the phone and rushed over to the hospital to meet us.

I wanted my sisters to scrub and go into surgery with me. Of course they couldn't but just knowing that they were there calmed my nerves and made me feel safer. I left everything else to God as the anesthesiologist inserted the IV tube. I started counting backwards... 100, 99, 98.....

Severe gas pains awakened me. I looked around and realized that I was in the maternity ward with several women who had just delivered healthy babies. They were happy but I was thinking that I had lost my baby. I hadn't wanted to get pregnant but since I had, I didn't want to lose the baby, especially my first child. Now I wondered if I would ever be able to conceive again. What had happened to my body? What had they done to me in surgery?

As I lie there, the nurse rolled in another patient who was crying hysterically. She had lost her baby in childbirth. I cried along with her.

The next day, when Dr. Aden visited me, I was relieved to see a smile on his face. "You're a blessed young lady. After we opened you, we could see that the baby was intact within the uterus. I suspected that the baby was in the fallopian tube after I didn't feel "it" where I expected your uterus to be positioned because your uterus is retroflexed."

"What does that mean?"

"It is tilted at the top and somewhat displaced," he responded.

Dusk: Psychogenesis

I was still thinking that I had lost my baby when Dr. Aden said, "Your baby is safe but you'll have to be careful. We had to remove your right ovary and fallopian tube."

"Was my fallopian tube blocked or damaged?"

"No it wasn't and your left ovary and tube are fine."

"Then why did you remove them?" I inquired.

"You developed an ovarian cyst. We suspect that you had a hormonal imbalance and secreted an excessive amount of estrogen. That's why you probably had difficulty adjusting to the birth control pills. You are never to take oral contraceptives again. You have to protect your left ovary and fallopian tube if you want to have more children."

"Will I be able to get pregnant again?"

"You should. Many women have only one functioning ovary. Your body has gone through lots of trauma and you will have to be very careful if you want to sustain this pregnancy."

I looked over at the woman who had lost her baby. I now wanted this child more than anything. Going to graduate school was no longer important.

"What are my chances of carrying this baby to term," I asked.

"About fifty percent; but we have a pill that you can take that will reduce your chances of miscarrying. I've written the prescription. You'll start taking it today. Get some rest now and I'll see you tomorrow."

As he turned to walk out of the door he said, "Oh, I gave you a nice bikini cut in your pubic hairline. When it heals you won't be able to see the scar. You're such a young girl."

The words "this baby" kept reverberating in my mind. Everything had happened so fast I hadn't grasped the reality that I was going to become a mother. I felt blessed indeed that God had preserved the life within me.

For the next seven months, I endured the pain, discomfort, dietary restrictions and the prohibition of sexual intercourse. On April 18th, I named God's gift to me Renee. For the next six weeks, I nourished and nurtured my baby, while reading every page in Dr. Spock's Guide. I wanted to be the perfect mother.

As I gleefully scheduled my post natal examination, the fear of getting pregnant struggled against my desire to become intimate again. We had been totally restricted from having intercourse for months and for some reason it didn't seem to bother Chico. I'd often wondered if he had been with other women during my pregnancy. Naturally, he assured me that he hadn't. However, he'd stopped being affectionate and appeared indifferent. Now that we were a family, I was ready to rekindle our fragile relationship.

After returning from the doctor and having received the green light for lovemaking, I prepared for the night by wearing sexy lingerie, spraying on sweet smelling perfume, and lighting scented candles.

Perhaps I hadn't realized how late he usually came home, but tonight it seemed like forever. When he arrived, I was very disappointed because he wasn't interested and he seemed unimpressed with my enticing attire. It was not a special night for him and I was crushed emotionally.

I asked, "What's wrong? It's been seven months."

He said, "I'm too tired. I had a long day; maybe tomorrow night." With that said he turned over and went to sleep.

He didn't care nor did he want to discuss what was wrong. He seldom touched me sexually after childbirth. His gestures were so infrequent and unexpected that I could not predict his intents. When he did make advances I wouldn't always have my diaphragm, my newest secret method of birth control, inserted. As I dashed into the bathroom to put it on, thus inhibiting the spontaneous flow of his sexual energy, he complained that "it was a job screwing me."

After months of loneliness, I became fidgety again. Yes, it could have been postpartum depression but I knew that these were the symptoms of a woman not being satisfied, mentally, emotionally or physically. I felt guilty because, though I was caring and respectful, I was never truly in love with him and now his rejection of me hurt.

I encouraged Chico to talk about it but that led to verbal battles. He always denied having another woman and claimed that he was always too tired from work. He was coaching offensive players, scouting other teams, or studying with the group of teachers at the university's library.

One night I joked about the group's study habits by reminding him of their closely guarded secret.

"I should tell your secret about having bought the answers to the GRE test," I blurted out.

"You wouldn't dare do that 'cause if you did I'd kick your ass." The look on his face was intense. I was frightened.

"Well you shouldn't have taken me with you that night. I thought it was going to be just another faculty card party until just after midnight when some of you handed this stranger $50 each then hurriedly huddled together in the back room to study the information that was handed to you. Remember? That was the morning of the test. I was surprised that you made it to the testing site on time or that you didn't fall to sleep during the test."

He just stared at me. I wondered what he was thinking, but I continued to talk.

"The only reason I keep quiet is because too many of you are involved and it would surely be a scandal if the Educational Testing Service could actually prove that ya'll scored so high on your third and final test because you cheated. They aren't stupid. If you had any sense you would have just barely passed; but no, you wanted a score so high that you couldn't possibly fail knowing how the test is scored. Now you are so terrified that someone will tell because of the class action law suit against the group. That would mean no master's degrees, no promotions and the possibility of having your teaching certificates revoked."

My attempt to flex my muscles only quieted him temporarily. When he was sure that I wasn't going to tell and the ETS reached a compromise to allow the scores of those in question to stand for that testing cycle, but to delete them from their data bank so that they could not be referenced for post graduate work, Chico resumed his nightly arguments. As he came in the door from work, he'd immediately start fussing about the slightest thing.

One night he yelled, "Mary, I've noticed that hair pin on the floor in that corner for three weeks now and you haven't picked it up yet," he snapped.

"Why don't you pick it up? It's obvious that I didn't see it," I replied.

He complained daily about my housekeeping but he didn't lift a finger to help me. I stopped asking him to assist and hired a helper for one day a week. He complained about that and called me lazy. I didn't verbally respond to any of his trumped up charges and he found fault with that.

"So you can't speak, huh muthuh fuckuh," he'd curse. He'd sleep in the other bedroom for a week or more as punishment stating, "You don't deserve any dick tonight; you lazy bitch!"

The rude behavior and cursing that I'd observed in college was now incorporated in his daily expressions and his weekly diatribe. I didn't want the verbal abuse to escalate into physical abuse since I always avoided fights to protect my eyes from further damage. Marrying him was a big mistake. I pondered my choices and decided that a divorce was the only solution. I packed my bags, gathered Renee's clothing and moved back in with my mother.

I called Mr. Klein, a lawyer I'd met in a parent conference at Miami Lakes Elementary School. He was the father of one of my students. I shamefully told him the history of my marriage then listened to his advice.

"Wait a while because your income will not be sufficient to adequately support you and your daughter. The home you recently purchased will require both incomes. I suggest marital counseling if your husband is amenable."

Later that night, I called Chico and suggested that we seek professional counseling. He laughed. "I don't have any problems. You got the problems so you go see the shrink. I'm not signing for a divorce and I'm not leaving my house. You can stay at your mom's until you decide to come back. Take your time though," he said in a very sinister tone.

Adjusting to being back with mom was difficult now that I was a parent. Renee was very active and keeping up with her was difficult in the crowded household. Mom adoringly kept all of the grandchildren as often as possible. It kept her from being lonely.

One morning Renee, now a year old, pulled a boiling kettle of water off of the stove and severely burned her arm. Her skin peeled like a banana as the hot water poured from the spout. Mom demanded that I return to my house where it was safer for Renee. She really wanted me back with Chico. After such a big wedding, she was concerned about the neighbors' gossip. They had itching ears and she didn't want to explain.

I reluctantly returned home hoping that Chico would leave. He continued to sleep in the back bedroom and I slept in the front. Though we didn't have sexual contact, the verbal fights and arguments increased. As we passed in doorways, he would almost knock me down by forcefully and deliberately hitting me with his broad shoulders, pushing me out of his way.

Later Chico realized that I was serious about a divorce so he pretended to want to make love. "All you need is a good screw. I'm going to fuck you this weekend," he chuckled.

"What I need is a caring husband," I retorted.

I didn't want to take a chance now that I knew that Chico would attempt to get me pregnant again. I hurriedly called the doctor for an appointment to have an IUD inserted as a precaution; but that too was a big mistake. The controversial Dalkon Shield, which was later banned from the market, had been prescribed. Perhaps I should have gotten a lucky rabbit's foot or bulbs of garlic and worn them around my neck because a

Dusk: Psychogenesis

month later, after the IUD was removed, I got pregnant with my second child. Before I announced my condition, Chico left. He moved in with his cousin Archie Williams, also a teacher. I was relieved that he was gone.

I worked the entire school year from September to June in this detached state of mind without taking a maternity leave. I was physically and emotionally exhausted as I attempted to perform my duties. Barbara Burrows, a first grade teacher at Palm Lakes Elementary School and the PTA president at Miami Jackson Senior High where Chico now taught fulltime, would constantly talk to me about taking charge of my life. It was as if she knew something that I wasn't aware of and she wanted me to seriously consider my options. She was quite a liberated woman.

In May, during my eighth month, Chico returned to the house but slept in the back bedroom. I didn't want him there, but I needed him because I was approaching my due date.

Juanita was born two days after school closed on June 17. It was on Father's Day. Chico was at the hospital in body only. He didn't show any affection for the precious gift that I'd just delivered. My Hispanic roommate received dozens of flowers in decorative vases. Chico didn't think to bring me one rose in his hand.

I tried to mask my bruised feelings by showering Juanita with love and affection because I had not nurtured her in the womb as I had done Renee. I began to bond with her immediately when the nurses brought her for breastfeeding. As she sucked and stared at me with her big eyes, I realized just how dependent she was on me. I had to be strong. I vowed to always be there for her.

In fact Chico didn't visit or come back to the hospital until I was discharged three days later. He had several good excuses to justify his absence. Returning home with Juanita, my female intuition was highly activated as I entered the door. An energy that I was unfamiliar with aroused my senses. I immediately asked, "Chico has someone been here?" I was sure that another woman had entered my bedroom. My albums were displaced. Chico never played them because he didn't like my taste in music.

He laughed then said, "You're crazy."

Months later, after I returned to work, I felt like I would be stuck with Chico and wondered if I'd ever save enough money to retain Mr. Klein's services. I secretly opened a savings account at Atlantic Bank and calculated how much money I had to deposit each month to accumulate his fee. It would take me nearly a year and a half to save a thousand dollars because of the increased childcare expenses. I was going to have to make personal sacrifices.

I detached from Chico emotionally. He bored me mentally. Even though he had earned his master's degree from the University of Miami and had been promoted to assistant principal at Miami Jackson Senior High after only four years of teaching, he still acted and spoke like an inner city thug.

I didn't want Chico to ever make love to me; I mean to ever screw me anymore, as he so crudely put it. I realized that abstinence was easy when your husband didn't want or desire you and your feelings toward him were now mutual. I was turned off sexually when the verbal abuse escalated. Who could perform after being called dirty names, cursed at or belittled? When he did touch me, I wouldn't lubricate because I was not aroused so his forceful entry always tore me. I felt like Ms. Celie in the movie the "Color Purple." Chico was just there on top of me "doing his business."

Loneliness and frustration must have shone brightly in my face. One day at work Ruby, a school caseworker, asked me why I looked so sad. I told her that I was in a very unhappy, sexually unfulfilling marriage. She'd often joked with me about her sexual rendezvous and latest escapades when we were alone. Today I asked, "What's so thrilling about sex?"

She looked as if she wanted to cry for me. Then she amusingly said, "My man grooves me. He doesn't stop caressing and kissing me until my juices start flowing and I tremble all over. I can't fake it with him. He knows my needs and he aims to please."

"What's this "flow" and what are those "juices" you're talking about? I can't relate to anything you're saying. Chico is kind of a bim, bam, thank you ma'am type since we got married. Before then we only had quickies because of time or lack of privacy."

"Obviously you haven't had an orgasm. The flow is indescribable. You've got to experience it to understand. You need to have an affair. Like Millie Jackson sings, "You need a part time all the way lover." Men don't screw you worth a good shit after you marry them. Only girlfriends and mistresses get satisfaction. There is a bible verse that reads, "Stolen wine is sweet." That's why people cheat. It's the excitement, the challenge, the adventure and most importantly the secrecy that's the thrill."

"I really want to have an affair but I'm afraid that I might get pregnant. That damned birth control pill has messed up my reproductive system and my sex life. I cry myself to sleep every night dreaming of having a romantic affair."

Dusk: Psychogenesis

"You should just have one. Men do and think nothing of it. You can take a lot of shit if you have something to look forward to, even if it's just once or twice a month. Life's too short for bullshit."

I sighed.

Secretly I was wishing, hoping, and dreaming of Raymond. I'd recently met him in a class at Miami Dade Community College. He was a Viet Nam Veteran taking advantage of his GI educational benefits. I was taking a course to renew my teaching certificate.

Every night when class ended, I would gather my books, pull out my key, brace myself then run through the parking lot to my car. One night, just as I was going to charge, he placed his hand on my shoulder and said, "Do you know that you are attracting danger to yourself? If you are that scared, I'll just walk you to your car every night."

I took a deep breath and said, "Thank you."

Over the semester we talked and joked. I didn't see a ring on his finger and hoped that he wasn't married. However, he never gave me any indication that he was being anything but protective and polite. But I was so fascinated with him because he was so handsome, physically fit and open minded. In class I learned a lot about his character as he shared his thoughts. The class was a human relation, social psychology course. In the text, **"I'm Ok, You're Ok"** were lessons in transactional analysis which provided ample opportunities for spirited discussions. I didn't want the semester to end. Raymond had become the reason for my going to class.

Late at night, as I secretly read the sexually explicit magazine "**True Confessions**" which I first discovered at Pearl's house in her stack of old newspapers and books, I visualized myself as the object of Ray's advances and the recipient of the steamy sexual scenes that sent chills up and down my spine. It was then that I first began to masturbate and realized the ecstasy of an orgasm.

But in reality, I was becoming a nervous wreck and Chico was becoming more hostile. I worked hard day and night and would often fall to sleep with my work clothes on after I tended to the children. While slumped in the reclining chair in front of the television or as I rested on the bed, Chico would rudely awaken me by pushing me onto the floor from the chair or by rolling me over onto the hard floor from the bed when he returned home. He would then stand over me to ensure that I completed all chores to his satisfaction no matter how late it was at night.

He would joke, "Girl, you wouldn't have made it as a slave."

His actions were deliberate and malicious. I knew that he had problems that were greater than I ever imagined. He actually enjoyed tormenting me. It was as if he thrived on creating chaos and havoc.

The shoves, pushes and falls would cause my bones and muscles to ache for days. I often walked with a limp until the soreness subsided. Realizing that this would be a recurring bullying tactic, as soon as I heard his car pull up into the driveway, I would lock myself in the girls' bedroom and bar the door with the headboard so that I could sleep through the night without being harassed. Though Chico knocked on the door and talked nonsense, I ignored him and would not come out until he left the house for work the next morning.

However, I would sometimes have to stay in the room until noon on the weekends because he slept late. I kept a supply of snacks and drinks in the closet to eat and actually utilized the girls' training potty as a lavatory. As I waited for Chico to leave, I reflected on my life and on the terrible consequences of the choices I had made. With my dreams deferred and my aspirations extinguished, I would cry uncontrollably.

Chico noticed how much more detached I had become. One night he came home unexpectedly with a sinister look on his face, pushed me down onto the carpet in the family room and forced himself on me. His brutal entry felt like the obstetrician performing an episiotomy. Chico was so big and I was so dry. I screamed as my flesh tore.

Pulling up his pants he said, "All you need is another baby bitch. You think you're grown now, huh. I found your bank book. What you gon' do with that money?" he chided.

"Get a divorce, you bastard!" I cursed back.

"Well start saving all over again, I took the money out and closed the account. You ain't going nowhere soon."

Though I had just been viciously violated, I felt sorry for him. For the first time, I clearly saw that he was the product of a miserable childhood. I believed that he was acting out the outrage and disrespect that he internally felt for his mother but couldn't openly express.

In explaining why he wanted to keep me from dating other guys in college he often stated that I was different from his mother and he wanted to protect me from being exploited since I had been so sheltered. I thought that was a compliment after he shared the emotional pain he experienced after witnessing her many illicit sexual affairs as a child; the embarrassment he felt knowing that all four of his siblings had different fathers; and hating his father for being an abusive alcoholic.

Was he transferring his dislike and aggression for her unto me? Whatever the reasons, I had to save enough money to pay Mr. Klein's retainer. I had to get out of this marriage before one of us killed the other.

The next week, as I planned my budget, I cried profusely because I sensed that I had conceived again and would have to include another child into the calculations. Nine more months of total abstinence, I thought, what a relief. I couldn't stand the thought of Chico touching me again. I started bonding with my baby as I continued to tabulate the numbers.

Lonnie was born in late August, so I was unable to return to work in September. Money was scarce. Chico provided the necessities for the children but vowed to give me nothing personally unless I allowed him to totally control my checkbook. He wanted me to exhaust my savings on personal needs but I knew how to survive. I'd learned by observing my mother and sisters. Now I wished that I had their inner strength.

While on maternity leave, Chico was seldom home. Though I didn't have any proof, I knew in my heart that there was another woman in his life; but it didn't matter what he did as long as he found something to do to stay away from the house and from me. I could only bear life with him for a few hours on weekends; otherwise, I'd have to take a tranquilizer. I was trying to stop using Valium, which had been prescribed, but the temporary peace of mind it provided was so desired.

I was anxious to return to work so that I could start saving money again. I had almost completely depleted my freedom fund. With three very young children, all under four years old, going to work would be a relief. The stress was constant and it was beginning to show. I looked haggardly and tired.

My prayer was answered when Mom, who had recently retired and was bored staying at home called.

"Mary, let me come to your house every morning to baby-sit Lonnie until June. I know it's difficult getting three kids ready every morning."

"Great! When can you start? I need your help now."

"I know it's hard on you financially so I won't charge you. Just keep the girls in daycare so that they can get some schooling."

I immediately called the schools' district office and informed the Speech chairperson that I was available. She was pleased because there was a critical shortage of speech pathologists nationwide and a replacement for me had not been hired.

Working was so much easier on me with mom home. She lovingly cared for Lonnie and cheerfully greeted the girls as they arrived from daycare. I'd arranged for the childcare center to transport them home. For the first time in my career, I was able to relax and go out after work with co-workers for happy hour. I felt vibrant and hopeful again. Mom's intervention had saved my sanity.

However, my marital relationship continued to deteriorate. Chico and I were separated though we lived in the same house. We seldom crossed paths. He left the home early and returned late. One Sunday morning as he was ritualistically preparing to go to church, which he seldom missed, I broke the silence by asking, "Chico, what is wrong with you?"

"Nothing! You got the problem," he said haughtily.

"I'm serious! What's going on?" I begged for understanding.

"If you really want to know," he snapped his fingers, "You just don't satisfy me."

"What do you mean?" I asked.

"You too damned straight laced! You ain't wit' it," he laughed.

"With what?" I asked as a puzzled expression contorted my face.

Then I became furious because he wasn't taking the conversation seriously.

"This is a new day. Times have changed. People do things differently. You ain't keeping up baby, that's all," he grinned as he massaged his penis.

"Where are you coming from?" I yelled.

He grinned then said, "You don't go down on me."

It took me a second to grasp where this conversation was going. My eyes widened as I remembered when we were in college, he'd often point out guys or girls who were known to indulge in oral sex and would snicker. There was a social stigma associated with such acts and if you did indulge in the behavior you definitely didn't speak of it publicly. Chico had never even suggested that he was ever interested in such acts with me until that very moment.

"What? When did that start and with whom mother fucker?" I yelled. angrily. He screamed with laughter.

"Listen to you. It's, "wit' who, muthuh fuckuh! Nigguhs don't pronounce the letter R-ruh or the "t-h" when they curse. You just too damn prim and proper and try to act so high and mighty all the time," he retorted.

"So that means you got another woman out there doing all of that for you. So, are you reciprocating?" I shouted.

"Recipro...who? You crazy bitch! I ain't eatin' nobody's stuff," he said defensively.

"You sho'?" I laughed as I was tickled by using black dialect. I was good at that also when I chose to speak it.

Whap! Whap! Whap! Up side my head was his violent response. Like a defeated boxer, I fell down to the floor and stayed there for the full count. With my head aching and my eyes closed, I saw sparkles of light flashing before me. Until that moment, Chico had pushed, shoved, argued and even sexually forced himself on me, but never had he hit me with his fist.

As he stepped across me on the floor, walked to the door and opened it, he uttered, "You should go to church and pray for deliverance. You're in this marriage for better or worse and if you don't git wit' it, it's going to git worse."

As he drove away, I could hear the blast of gospel music coming from the car's radio. I thought, "What a hypocrite."

Later as I thought about Chico's comments, I realized that I lived in a time warp. Mother, the eleventh of twelve children born at the turn of the century in 1909 to parents that were conceived right after emancipation, was in her early forties when I was born and there is a twenty years gap between me and my oldest sibling, who was born during the Great Depression. Though I am a Baby Boomer, I couldn't help but be influenced by the social mores, morals and values of their time. Four of my siblings, who also doubled as my guardians, were the approximate ages of my friends' parents. My father, who had been a Church of Christ elder, reared them. Their conservative beliefs and practices were passed on to me. It would be hard to change, especially if I was not in love, and I didn't love Chico at all. I didn't even like him now.

I was just too square for Chico and I knew that I would always be that way. From that day, I avoided talking to him unless it was absolutely necessary and I stopped responding to his crude remarks. It was safer that way. I couldn't win an argument with him verbally or physically. He was very closed minded and was becoming very physically abusive. I had to protect my eyes.

I didn't tell my family about the incidents; but one Saturday morning my brother Aaron, unannounced, stopped by the house and heard Chico complaining. Thinking that the threatening tone of his voice would escalate into a fight, he intervened. They began to argue. Aaron had to be held back from hitting Chico by Roger Finnie, our next door neighbor. Roger, a professional football player for the New York Jets was home during the off season. Roger, Aaron and my other brother James were good friends. Our families were very close. We'd grown up in the same neighborhood in Liberty City.

"My oldest brother Aaron"

"My brother James"

In college Roger would see me walking alone on campus and safely escort me to the dormitory. Like my brothers, he was very protective. In his senior year he was drafted by the New York Jets and moved away. I did not have any form of communication with him for three years until discovering shortly after closing, that we had purchased homes next door to each other in a newly integrated neighborhood in Carol City. It was good to see him again. I felt safe around him.

Roger knew about the arguments and often knocked on the door to intervene when he heard the raucous. This morning Roger reminded Aaron, a semi-professional boxer who had sparred with former heavy weight champion Floyd Patterson in Miami Beaches' famed 5th Street Gym that, "Man you'll be held accountable if Chico is hurt. As a boxer, your hands are considered legal weapons."

To avoid further conflicts, I remained silent and stopped inviting friends and family over for any occasion other than birthday parties for the children. During this time of isolation, Melton Jones, a high school classmate and fellow band member had converted to Islam. Like clockwork he came by every week with his newspaper, ***"The Final Call,"*** his bean pies and his whiting fish. Because he was known to Chico, I welcomed his company without fear and listened to his message. I did not believe in his doctrine but his visits inspired me to read the Bible again. The Psalms, Proverbs and the Book of Ecclesiastes were my favorites. In them I found wisdom, encouragement and hope.

Without telling my mother, I secretly began communicating with my father. He had been trying to develop a relationship with me since I returned from college, but I always avoided him and refused to call him "daddy" when in his presence. I called him "Big Ben" since my brother Bennie was named after him.

I needed to develop a positive relationship with him if I was to ever get out of this horrible marriage and have a second chance at love and happiness. As we talked, I cherished his perspective and advice and looked forward to his weekly phone calls. More than ever, I wanted a man to love me. He soon filled that void with unconditional love and respect.

I continued to live a very isolated and austere life by not purchasing any new clothes or doing anything extra for myself. I continued to sacrifice because I had a mission to accomplish and nothing was going to keep me in this marriage much longer; my freedom fund was slowly but surely growing again.

Having my father as a mentor helped me to emotionally detach from Chico. My silence was a challenge for him as he would stare at me and make faces in an attempt to provoke me to anger. I could feel that he was plotting some evil scheme in his twisted mind. Though he seemed uninterested in me sexually, I didn't take any chances. I made sure that I was prepared for any encounter by inserting a diaphragm filled with spermicidal cream every night. While lying in bed, I felt like a lamb nervously waiting to be sheared.

One evening Chico came home unexpectedly. He was mad about something so he started an argument. I ignored him which made him angrier. He yelled while unfastening his pants, "All you need is another baby. You gettin' to be too independent. I'm gonna keep your ass barefoot and pregnant."

As he walked toward me, adrenaline rushed through my veins as my body prepared for the "fight or flight" mode. However, he quickly pounced on me before I could grab something to hit him with or escape his clutches.

I screamed, "If you don't want me as your wife then pay for the damn divorce, but don't do this to me again just to keep me down."

I begged and pleaded but he didn't care. I lost my balance but struggled to keep my legs closed as he wrestled me down to the floor and viciously raped me. I screamed as my flesh tore. Because there was no cushioning on the hard tiled kitchen floor, I felt the strength and force of each of his violent thrusts. I couldn't move. I wanted to die.

Weeks later, I cried buckets of tears when I missed my next period. Though I'd left the Catholic Church, I still believed in its position on life, but now I wanted an abortion. They were legal. Roe V. Wade had recently passed. I must have dialed the number to an abortion clinic five times a day, but I just couldn't bring myself to go through with it. I convinced myself again that this time was the last time. I began to bond with my baby, another human being to share my love.

About two months into my pregnancy, I was awakened by the sensation of wetness. I got out of bed, went into the bathroom and turned on the light. I was hemorrhaging. It was about 2:00 a.m. Chico was not home yet as usual. I called Pearl who lived nearby but before she could get to me, Chico came home and rushed me to Mount Sinai Hospital's Emergency Room on Miami Beach.

I was there a very long time as they examined me inside and out. They took so many vials of blood from my veins that I thought that they were vampires. After hours of waiting, the emergency room staff doctor came out to talk with me.

"We are not quite sure what the problem is, but this is definitely going to be a "high risk" pregnancy. You'll have to be examined weekly and carefully monitored until delivery."

As he drove home, Chico grumbled, "Why are you going to Mount Sinai in the first place? Isn't Dr. Aden's office closer?"

"Idella, my sister-in-law, works at the hospital. She told me about their great maternity clinic and helped me fill out the application."

I didn't let the staff know that I was a professional with health insurance by using my maiden name and my mom's address. Even with insurance the copayment and deductible for the private doctor was too expensive. At Mount Sinai, the fee was minimal which allowed me to save money with this pregnancy. This time I was determined not to deplete my savings. That was my freedom money.

Even though I was threatening to miscarry, I continued to work two days a week against the doctor's orders. Seeing me looking very tired and walking very slowly down the corridor, Mrs. Doretha Mingo, the principal at Palm Springs Elementary and my sorority sister warned me of the consequences of disobedience. I looked at her and sadly said, "I can't afford to keep the children in nursery school and aftercare if I don't work a few days a week. They will surely exhaust my energy if I keep them home with me all day."

I continued to sacrifice physically and financially over and over again.

Every Monday, I kept my scheduled appointment for a sonogram in the hospital's nuclear medicine department. I'd finally been diagnosed as having complete placental privia. The fetus had implanted in my cervix. As he grew, yes it was a boy, my cervix opened more and more which caused me to hemorrhage continuously.

"How had this happened?" I inquired of the doctors.

"We are not sure but there's the possibility that the sperm did not have adequate mobility to help transport the fertilized egg to a higher position in the uterus," they replied.

"Does my having a retroflexed uterus contribute to the condition?"

"No, that's not the problem. There is a possibility that during conception, your husband's sperm count was low. Had he been drinking alcoholic beverages or was he on any type of medication?"

"I don't know. I'll have to ask him." Naturally, Chico denied everything when confronted. After several more weeks, the doctors said, "You will not be able to sustain this pregnancy. You're becoming anemic and your baby is developmentally retarded. It hasn't grown since the twentieth week."

I cried. Vincente, whom I'd already named, was now kicking and turning.

I screamed, "Oh God, why are you punishing me like this?"

"We want to induce labor since you are too far along for a regular abortion. Do we have your consent to proceed?"

"No!" I refused. "I've heard about how painful the saline abortions are at this stage of development. Vincente is alive and doesn't deserve to be killed in that manner. If the baby is imperfect, I'll miscarry. I don't want the guilt of an abortion to haunt me eternally," I lamented.

After a few more weeks of anemia, weakness and depression, I began to miscarry. I didn't tell Chico of my condition as he dressed for work that morning. I just let him leave as usual knowing that he wouldn't return until after midnight. I just suffered through the contractions in silence. Finally, I called the clinic and my mom.

As she and Idella drove me to the hospital, they consoled and assured me that they would wait. I wasn't a private patient so I couldn't stay overnight especially since I hadn't gone full term. The mood in the car was very morose.

With the other three children, I'd been given scopolamine; a drug used in labor and delivery to block the memory of the pain; but I saw this delivery. I was awake and fully aware and I'll never forget the contorted look on Vincente's face. There was no slap on his butt for the breath of life to enter into his lungs. I watched him suffocate as they wrapped him for disposal. I then remembered the emotional pain and agony of the woman who had lost her baby in childbirth while I was hospitalized with Renee. I too now cried uncontrollably in the recovery room.

A week passed before Chico noticed that I wasn't pregnant. He then accused me of deliberately having an abortion. I didn't care what he thought. I didn't want him to ever touch me again. Mentally I became celibate. Like a good Catholic nun, I took a vow of abstinence before God. I no longer thought of Chico as my husband. I wanted him to disappear or die.

Weak yet determined, I returned to work the next week. There was no time to rest. I had to continue making regular deposits into my freedom fund savings account.

Ten weeks later, on the morning of August 14, I awakened with severe cramps in my abdomen. I took Tylenol to ease the pain but they didn't go away. The cramps would ease and then strike again moments later. As the cramps increased in frequency and intensity, I realized that it was my delivery date. Vincente was scheduled to have been born on this day.

Subconsciously, my body was in labor. I mentally relived the moment of seeing Vincente and blessed his spirit. I knew that his soul was alive somewhere out there. As I laid him to rest in my mind, the physical pain subsided.

Several months later, I decided to get the house exterminated.

"Please remove all food and medicine from the premises," instructed the Orkin man.

I began clearing the cabinets. I checked the kitchen shelves and drawers and found an empty prescription bottle. It was Chico's. It was dated approximately three weeks prior to the date that I conceived Vincente. I read the name of the antibiotic and called Pearl.

"Hey Pearl, what can you tell me about this drug Keflex that Chico was taking?"

"Hold on until I get my Physician's Desk Reference. I'll read the information to you." I waited anxiously.

"Ok, I'm back."

"I'm listening."

"It's in a group of very powerful antibiotics that can cause a drop in the male sperm count and decrease sperm mobility."

"Now I understand why I had a difficult pregnancy with Vincente. Thanks Pearl, I'll talk to you later."

Knowing that I had suffered needlessly and that a life, though not planned, had been lost helped me to conclude that I could no longer stay in the house, as I had been advised by my mother and Mr. Klein. As I searched the classified section of the newspaper for rental accommodations, Chico provided the perfect catalyst for me to do what I should have done years ago, throw him out of the house and change the locks.

It was on Renee's 7th birthday. She was in the first grade and had gone to school as usual. I dropped Juanita, age four at the Golden Glades Daycare Center and Lonnie, age two at Martha's home for baby-sitting. Renee would walk to the sitter after school along with other children in the neighborhood.

That day Chico picked up Juanita from the daycare then drove to Martha's and picked up Renee and Lonnie and took them to his mother's house to have a party with his family.

I was surprised when the daycare receptionist told me that Juanita had been released to her father. I quickly drove to the sitter, who informed me that Chico had come earlier and taken the other two. Why had he done this without informing me? He'd never ever picked them up for any reason in the past.

I was worried sick about Lonnie who suffered from asthma. Chico wasn't as careful about what foods he fed him and when Lonnie became ill, I had to take time off from work to care for him. I waited anxiously for Chico to call and explain his behavior.

Around 8:00 p.m. they cheerfully walked in the door. Chico threw a Publix bakery box on the table and disrespectfully said, "We saved you a few crumbs. We had a birthday party at my mom's."

I peeked into the box and saw a very small slice of cake. "Did you give Lonnie any ice cream or cake? You know that he's allergic to wheat and dairy products."

Chico started cursing and laughing. He wanted to start a fight.

"Get out," I screamed as I ran to the closet, grabbed some of his clothing and began throwing them outside on the ground.

"Nothing and nobody is going to negatively interfere with the positive relationship that I have with my children. They are not pawns in this crazy marital game that we're playing."

Chico knew that I was mad, in fact more mad than he had ever seen me. We began to argue. He swung at me; I ducked and ran into the kitchen for a butcher's knife.

"No more licks to my head nigger, I screamed. I'm going to kill your black ass this night. I'm tired of you disrespecting me."

"Oh shit, you really are mad or are you just a crazy bitch?" he laughed.

"Both! And you'll be a dead mother fucker tonight."

I ran straight toward him. Chico saw me coming and got out of my way. He quickly ran into the bathroom and locked the door. I stabbed the door repeatedly as if it were his body. Then I cussed and screamed until I was exhausted.

"I'll plead temporary insanity, but if that doesn't work, I'll gladly serve time in jail as long as your ass is dead."

Thinking that I had calmed down, he came out of the restroom and got into his car. I quickly ran to the bedroom and grabbed another armful of his clothing and threw them out the door onto the ground. He got out of the car and gathered his belongings. As soon as he picked up one batch, I threw out another. When I finished I slammed the door and looked out of the front window.

He cranked the engine and turned on the headlights and saw me looking. He put the gear in park, opened the door and stepped out of the car with one leg standing on the ground and the other inside of the car. He called me a few more vulgar names and raised his middle finger and pointed it towards me and yelled, "I'll never ever come back to this house bitch."

Then in an angry voice he happily told me the reasons why he married me in the first place. His words stung like wasps.

"I didn't ever love you bitch. You ugly cross eyed muthuh fuckuh! I just married you to keep from going to Vietnam. I knew that you were only good for having babies and reading books. You can't do nothing else worth a good shit anyway. I gave you an opportunity to be with a star. Now you don't deserve me. I ain't never gonna come to get the kids off your black ass either. I won't ever be your babysitter. I won't ever give you a chance to get out and have some fun and I ain't never gonna give you no extra money. I'm gonna destroy your reputation and no man is gonna want you when I finish talking about your ugly ass. I'm gonna tell everybody that you're crazy as hell too. Kiss my black ass bitch."

He lowered himself into the car, backed out of the driveway and speedily drove off.

I replayed his words over and over again. His rant was premeditated and rehearsed. I was exhausted, hurt, saddened by his remarks, yet relieved that he was gone.

I didn't know where Chico went and I didn't care. I took the next day off from work and called the law firm for an appointment. I went to the bank for a withdrawal then hurriedly drove to see my attorney. The lack of money was not going to stop me this time. I had seven hundred dollars in my purse. A thousand was needed to retain the firm for their services. As I waited in the office, I quietly sang an old Lou Rawls song, "I'd rather drink muddy water and sleep in a hollow log" than remain in this marriage.

After discussing the urgency of the situation with Mr. Klein, he said, "I can see that you are really desperate to get out of this very negative situation. I'll start the procedure as quickly as possible. Don't worry about where he's living. His papers will be served at his work location by the end of the week. Our office will collect the rest of the retainer after the divorce is finalized. Call me or Carol, my secretary at anytime. We understand what you are going through and we're here to help."

I was overwhelmed. I went home and started rejoicing. I could smell freedom in the air. I was as happy as a lark until I received a phone call about 2:00 a.m. a few weeks later.

The caller did not identify herself but said, "Keep an eye out for a large manila envelope that will come in the mail. The information in it will help you with your divorce."

Who knew so soon that I had filed for a divorce? Was it someone at his job who saw him been served? I wondered.

Sure enough the parcel came. It was filled with copies of love letters and greeting cards from Chico's college-aged girlfriend. The letters were dated back as far as three years. Who had taken the time to do this and why? I felt that one of the many secretaries in Chico's office must have sent them since the envelopes were addressed to Miami Jackson High School.

Shortly after Chico was served, he began bragging about having left me and started assassinating my character. He made sure that the remarks got back to me. Several of his male friends came by the house pretending that they always wanted to date me. I refused, knowing that Chico had sent them. I vowed to never date anyone who knew him.

All of the gossip and unsolicited information hurt me emotionally. I shouldn't have listened, but I wanted to know the truth and many people were now eager to spill their guts.

I discovered that Chico had begun a romantic relationship with Rita Duren, a high school senior and had maintained their involvement throughout her college years. After graduation, she was hired to teach at Booker T. Washington Middle School where my neighbor, Stacy Jones, was principal. Even Chico's brother, Wellington, knew about her. He taught music at Booker T. and was the school's band director.

Knowing the timeline, I could reference when Chico became more verbally abusive and critical of all of my actions. With her home, they began to openly display their affection in public places; the gossip circulated unabated. It seemed that I was the only one left in the dark. Neighbors and coworkers had smiled in my face while relentlessly gossiping behind my back.

Chico and Rita, among other women, had been lovers before my wedding day and throughout my marriage. I finally understood the deception and his lack of sexual interest in me.

I felt like such a fool to have stayed in the marriage so long. When I found out about these women, I couldn't eat so I lost twenty pounds in three weeks. At 115 pounds and 5'10 inches tall, I looked anorexic. My hormones were truly imbalanced now. I could hardly talk or think straight. As I mumbled and rambled on and on, some believed that I was having a nervous breakdown or going insane and should be committed to a hospital's psychiatric unit. I wasn't crazy; I was emotionally devastated and very angry at myself. I cried and I prayed.

As I waited several months for my day in court, I intermittently lost the ability to speak above a whisper as my body reacted to the extreme levels of stress that I was under. The principal at my base school, Miami Lakes

Elementary, an advocate of the Equal Rights Amendment and a member of the recently established National Organization of Women, observed my behavior and came to my rescue.

"Mary, I want you to call this number and talk with someone who understands your needs."

I began to cry.

She continued, "You are falling apart emotionally and getting further behind in your testing and delivery of services."

"I'll be patient and a little lenient. You'll get it together soon." She held my hand in support and smiled.

"Thanks, Ms. Nash."

To further help me through this difficult time were my biological sisters: Liz, Pearl, Mildred and Eurie; several very caring friends, and my sorority sisters.

Pearl, an LPN and Liz, an RN rotated as private duty nurses. They never left me alone or idle. They made me get up and go to work every day. I had a terrible absentee record. Mildred kept the kids on weekends and allowed my niece, Willette, to sleep over often to baby-sit during the week. Eurie, who lives in Cleveland, called frequently with words of wisdom and scripture readings.

Arselia was the wife of Jacob Caldwell the head basketball coach at Miami Jackson High. "Cee" as she was affectionately called, is a registered nurse who worked at the Veterans Medical Center. She observed and cared for many soldiers who had returned from Vietnam suffering from post traumatic stress syndrome. Professionally, she helped me to understand that my feelings of anger and guilt were similar to those of injured soldiers who had returned from battle. Seeing that I was losing weight rapidly, she referred me to a doctor of internal medicine and monitored my health status weekly.

Dr. Luvernice Croskey, the maid of honor in my wedding and godmother to my daughter Renee, is a certified licensed clinical social worker. Using her clinical skills, she guided me through my ramblings until I was able to coherently talk about the awful experiences in great detail.

Gwen Bryant, a second grade teacher at Miami Lakes Elementary, was with me at work. On weekends, she took me shopping to Casual Corner, redressing me from head to toe while lovingly reinforcing the fact that I was better off without Chico. She occasionally bought groceries for the children.

Dusk: Psychogenesis

Karen Bullard, a teacher at Crestview Elementary, taught each of my three children in kindergarten and first grades. She lovingly mentored my daughters and monitored my son's behavior throughout their enrollment in spite of a misunderstanding that we had when I falsely accused her of gossiping. She remained a trustworthy friend.

Fredericker Rolle Rhodriquez, a teacher at North Glade Elementary School and my daughter Juanita's godmother is also a close family friend. With her wit and candor, she left no stones unturned. She was compassionate yet very frank, never allowing me to indulge in self pity. Her insight and anecdotal tales helped me to draw parallels between my life and the lives of many other abused women, who not only survived, but succeeded.

Joan Pullum Duckworth, a teacher at Norland Elementary school is a gifted and talented master organizer. She arranged for me to meet with her attorney, Jesse McCrary, to begin the process of having the child support payments deducted from Chico's check. Her expertise helped in restructuring my household financially.

Marsha Sims, a Speech Pathologist, was a budding entrepreneur. Through her I realized that I could use my musical skills to earn additional income. Earlier, I'd purchased a piano; so I created a flyer to circulate and was pleased to receive several calls. For the next four years I taught music lessons for a nominal fee.

Cecilia Lawrence, who was on my pledge line, let me know that I could call her at any time. She'd always been very frank and honest with me. She always told it like it was; not like I wanted it to be. Mona Bethel Jackson, my big sister while pledging, also extended her unconditional support when it seemed that everyone was against me. Parthenia Days, a Speech Pathologist, made me realize how nonproductive it was for me to continue to use the physical appearance of my eye as an excuse. She said in a humorous manner, "Girl, I'd take off those glasses and put a flower in my hair and go about my business." Then there was Ruth Harris, also a Speech Pathologist and the wife of a minister, who often recited the serenity prayer. She would call in the middle of the night to console my bruised soul.

Finally, there was Mrs. Raymond Adderly. I saw Ray, a salesman at Modernage Furniture Store shortly after my separation. He confided that he was protective of me during the time that we were enrolled in class at Miami Dade Community College because he knew Chico and of his many escapades. He realized that I needed reinforcement at this crucial time and invited me over to his house to meet his wife. He said of her, "When I was away in the military, she held my family together during the most difficult time. If she did it, so can you."

I only met Mrs. Adderly once, but in her face, I saw the strength of character that I needed to sustain me, and in her voice I heard the confidence that came from a woman who was truly loved and respected. Collectively, all of these strong sisters taught me how to fight for my life.

When my day in court came, my lawyer used the information that I received in the parcel brilliantly. I was awarded my home as lump sum alimony as it was immediately quit claim deeded over to me. Mr. Klein wasted no time having it officially recorded at the courthouse.

Though I hadn't resumed going to church regularly after the divorce, I continued to read my Bible and pray. I needed the strength that only God could provide. I was doing well emotionally until one day I read an article in the Miami Herald about a certain pill that had been given to women who had difficult pregnancies.

This pill, diethylstilbestrol, was used to prevent miscarriage. I had taken that pill along with Provera during my pregnancy with Renee. Both pills had been recalled years earlier but the evidence of their devastating effects were just being reported. I continued to read. These pills not only caused cancer in the daughters of women who had taken them, but the women too were now predisposed to breast cancer. I screamed, "My God, why have you forsaken me."

Now I was angry about having switched from Dr. Bridges to Dr. Aden. Surely, Dr. Aden must have known about the consequences of the medication before he prescribed it since the literature and journal articles were reporting its findings years prior to my pregnancy. Why didn't he warn me? Would I have taken the pills if I'd been adequately informed? I wasn't sure because of the emotional state that I was in at the time. Was I a part of a genocide conspiracy? I thought of the Tuskegee incident and of the deception and experimentation on the Black men in the syphilis project. "Why has this happened to me?" I cried.

I made it my mission to read everything that I could find on the subject. I needed to know how to reduce our chances of developing this dreaded disorder. There wasn't any solace in the medical literature. Our only hope was in God and in good nutritional practices. We stopped eating beef immediately because the farmers continued to feed DES to their cattle. We also stopped eating pork. Herbs and vitamins became daily dietary supplements.

Dusk: Psychogenesis

The thought "God is my answer" just kept reverberating through my mind. I started studying the Bible and faithfully praying for a miracle. I didn't worry about myself and I didn't care what people thought about me anymore, especially my neighbors, who were in full gossip mode.

Joan Floyd, a teacher, was the most disturbing of the group. She would call regularly after work pretending to understand my plight then offer advice on how to proceed with my life sexually.

"You should come down to my house on Sunday mornings. A group of guys gather with Leroy," her husband, "to go play basketball. I'll try to hook you up with some of them."

However, no sooner than she hung up the phone would she call her friends, mostly teachers, and purposefully exaggerate or distort most of what I shared.

One evening she called and asked me to walk down to her house. When I arrived, she handed me a small booklet entitled "Forum." It was a publication of Penthouse magazine.

"Take this home and read it. Look through the pages and see if there are any sex toys you want to order."

With that said she opened the night stand next to her bed and pulled out a toy, turned on the motor and described in great detail the sensation that I would experience while using it. Then she asked, "Do you want to borrow it?"

"No thank you," I responded. I left her house thinking, "If desired, I could stimulate myself just fine." The thought of using her personal toy was disgusting.

Aida, a neighbor's teenage daughter later cautioned me to be careful even when talking to her mother, Florene, also a teacher. "Mrs. Floyd and my mom discuss your conversations every night. It is not right. They should be helping you," she warned sympathetically.

Eddie Mae Narcisse, a math teacher whom I had been close to, accused me of enticing the husbands on the block by wearing short pants outside; of going through her mail, though I was just returning a letter that had been mistakenly placed in my box; of seeking sympathy and, of course, going crazy. She and her cohort Samella, an elementary school principal, even accused me of trying to steal Samella's husband Marvin Gaines, who worked with me as a Teacher on Special Assignment at the district office, after he stopped by the house to demonstrate how to change a flat tire.

The only neighbors that I felt comfortable around were Mary Jones, Lillian Kindle, Elizabeth Finnie and Josephine Jordan. However, Mary later presumed that I had knowledge of some underhanded dealings of Chico's and falsely accused me of being jealous of his interactions with her. I was devastated when I heard echoes of her gossipy remarks in the teachers' lounge at Norland Middle School where we taught.

I had become their sideshow. Having an emotional need to explain my situation and defend my actions, I soon realized that my naive justifications were fueling the flames for continued gossip. There wasn't anyone on the block to trust except Richard Welsh, Florene's husband and Lester, who promised to "keep an eye on us." I decided to cease communicating with the women. I didn't want them to accuse me of seducing their husbands. I secluded into the impenetrable walls of my fortress and began to read self help books and the Bible.

Less than a year after the divorce, my life improved as I continued to work out the logistics of being a single parent. One morning while happily walking down the breezeway of Norland Elementary School, dust and sand particles flew into my right eye because I wasn't wearing my protective lenses. The sensation of blindness was emotionally traumatizing. It seemed like the top half of my left eye was closed, like a window shade that had been pulled half way down, and little black dots floated recklessly within my view.

I panicked as my stride turned into a blind man's gait. My depth perception was severely impaired as I lifted my legs and feet awkwardly to cross over the grooves in the sidewalk while quickly reaching to the wall for support.

After navigating my way to the teacher's lounge to rinse the dust particles out of my eyes, I telephoned Dr. Olga Ferrer, the ophthalmologist who had previously performed surgery on my eyes. She advised me to leave work immediately and drive to her office.

After the examination, she reported, "Mary, this is serious. You'll have to have surgery as soon as possible."

"What's wrong?"

"Your left retina is detaching. It's been like that for some time. I can tell by the debris that's floating around in the back of your eye. It looks like dried blood particles; but there's fresh blood also. That means something is seriously wrong."

She looked at my medical chart then asked, "Mary were you in an accident or did you sustain a severe blow to your head?"

I knew right away how the incident must have occurred, but was too ashamed to tell Dr. Olga the truth.

Dusk: Psychogenesis

I recalled the evening when Chico and I left Sam Collins' house. For years he had diligently prepared our tax returns. Chico was angry because I refused to sign the return if he purposefully inflated the figures just to get a greater refund. Sam had become frustrated with Chico's dishonesty and stated that he would no longer prepare our taxes. When we returned home, as soon as I walked through the door, Chico twisted my arm and quickly placed my head in a gridlock under his arm, like wrestlers do, and punched me repeatedly in the forehead. The severity of the blows with the pre-existing scar tissue, must have detached my retina.

However, surgery had to be delayed. Dr. Olga wasn't a provider on my new HMO insurance plan nor was she a macular-retinal specialist. I had to wait weeks to be referred to another ophthalmologist by my primary care physician. Now I regretted not choosing the PPO option just to save money.

I became so stressed as I waited anxiously to see Dr. Reese, who later agreed with Dr. Olga's diagnosis. He immediately arranged to have me evaluated at Bascom Palmer Eye Institute. A battery of tests was needed prior to surgery.

A week later, as I was making arrangements for someone to assist with the children's care, John Kelley, a former professional football player for the Washington Redskins, knocked on my door. I talked with him through the front window.

"You don't know me but I was at FAMU with Chico his freshman year. Now I am an insurance agent with New York Life and Chico has written a policy for $500,000 for you and the children. He asked me to deliver it."

"I am sorry but I don't talk to anyone who is referred by him."

"He knew that you would not talk to any of his local friends. So he located me after hearing that I was back in town and pleaded with me to come over. He knows that I can be trusted. He wants to come home. He wants another chance."

The following week, Chico knocked on the door. In his hand was a schedule for family counseling that he had arranged with his minister, Rev. Thedford Johnson of St. John's Baptist Church in Historic Overtown. He pleaded with me to talk to him. I listened behind the protective steel bars on the window.

"Mary I really miss the children. I want us to go to these counseling sessions."

"I don't want to get involved with you again. My retina is detached and it is your fault. I don't trust you and I've heard really awful comments about your character since the divorce."

"You can't believe everything that you hear."

"That's true but I heard your cruel words and I can't erase them from my mind. So go away!"

"I was stupid and didn't mean what I said. I just wanted you to regret throwing my clothes outside. I was embarrassed because the neighbors were peeking out of their windows."

"I'm the one who has had to live among them with their vicious gossip," I retorted. There was silence.

"I promise that I won't hit you again. Just go with me to these sessions. Remember, it was your suggestion that we go to therapy. I've changed. You'll see."

"I only want us to be respectful if possible so that we can share time with the kids. I don't want a relationship," I reiterated.

"Kelley told me that you were going to have surgery. Let me stay with the kids to help out. Then you can decide about the counseling."

What did I have to lose I thought. I needed help and I didn't want to impose on my family during my recovery.

"I'll go with you to counseling after I recuperate if it will help us to be cordial, but I won't remarry you."

"Thanks, Mary you won't regret it."

Chico kept his apartment, but moved back into the house so that he could care for the kids daily. The next week I entered the hospital.

The night before the surgery, a team of doctors examined me. I was so frightened especially after being informed that I would not be given total anesthesia. No way could I go through this semiconscious. I was so nervous that Dr. Reese ordered my eyes bandaged during the night to force me to rest them, but I cried profusely through the gauze pads.

As they prepared me for surgery the next morning by washing my face with Betadine, a harsh antibacterial solution, shaving my eyebrows and clipping my eyelashes, I prayed. As they rolled me into the operating room, my pulse rate accelerated and could not be stabilized so Dr. Reese decided that it would be best to put me totally to sleep. I visualized my kids as the medication began to take effect. 100.... 99..... 98....

Bandaged and in excruciating pain, I awakened feeling like someone had hit me in the head with a hammer. I had to take powerful doses of Tylenol with codeine every four hours. During the period of time that the medication was at its peak effectiveness, I thought about my conversations with my dad, "Big Ben."

He was most grateful that I had forgiven him for his abandonment and was happy that I allowed him to become a part of my life. He expressed how as a young man, he was foolish and if he had to relive his life, he would never ever leave his family again. I thought, "Could Chico have possibly come to the same understanding?"

Based on my dad's confession, I decided to give Chico another chance; first by going to the counseling sessions that he had arranged and secondly, if I perceived a genuine change in his behavior, I would live with him again for the children's benefit, but I knew that I would never ever remarry him. I hoped that he, like me, coming from a broken home now wanted a true reconciliation and an intact family unit. I prayed for the best but decided to keep up my guard.

During my recovery, which took a little over a month, Chico purchased a wedding ring from Mayor's Jewelers and proposed. He constantly played the song, "Second Time Around" to entice me. Again, I refused to remarry him. However, I wore the diamond but not the outer ring which would signify that we had legally reunited. We lived together for a year. He bought flowers regularly and took me out socially. Chico also insisted that I regularly attend church with him; something that he seldom cared about.

Now I didn't want to go because Herb Day also attended St. John's Baptist Church. Though our relationship had been very private, Herb had confided in one of his fraternity brothers about it; he later revealed our secret to Chico.

In church, Chico would insist on sitting in the balcony so that he could look down and see Herb through the mirror that was behind the pulpit. One Sunday I saw him poking his tongue out at Herb as Herb glanced up into the mirror to see me. Chico was jealous and wanted me to know that he was aware of Herb.

Sexually, Chico wanted to prove that he was better at making love than any of the suitors that I may have had. However, the subject of oral sex never came up again because Chico knew that I would ask him to demonstrate before I reciprocated in any way with him; he was not ever going to admit to me that he actually did indulge in the behavior.

Now I didn't care; someone else had already demonstrated the beauty of the experience. While Chico huffed and puffed, I pretended that he was the lover that had so gently demonstrated the art of love making. I closed my eyes and remembered.

One night at dinner Chico surprised me by saying, "Mary, I want you to sell this house and move into a new home with me in South Miami. I don't feel good about living here anymore because we don't share ownership."

"Chico and Mary at the Alpha's Dance"

Dusk: Psychogenesis

"The judge felt that it would not be fair if he left your name on the deed until the kids reached eighteen, especially since I had proof that I made the initial down payment and also paid for the construction of the additional family room."

"I know, but it still wasn't fair."

For the next month he tried to persuade me to move. We rode to South Miami to see the newly constructed Lennar Homes, but I didn't allow the décor or amenities to sway me. When I continued to object to his increasing demands, his frustration over my stubbornness provoked him to anger; thus revealing his true motives for returning.

"Mary, I want my share of the equity. I deserve some money for my investment."

"Your investment was minimal," I reminded him.

Now he was furious. Suddenly and without warning he shouted, "You're so negative. I'm going to whip your ass once more before I leave and I ain't ever coming back again. You're too grown since you've had some other nigguhs pokin' you! You still can't fuck worth a shit."

To protect myself, I ran to the kitchen to get a knife but wasn't fast enough. He followed and with his fist tightly clinched, aimed straight for my head. The impact of the punch was so great that I was lifted up off of my feet. As I fell to the floor, sparks of light flashed before my closed lids.

Chico hurriedly left the house, slamming the door with all of his might. As I lay in a semiconscious state, I could hear him cussing as he cranked his car.

I realized that he returned only because he wanted compensation for his share in the property; and to get out of paying child support and enormous attorneys' fees. I wasn't surprised by his comments because I knew that he was capable of the most cruel and vicious remarks. I was hurt because I knew that this was the absolute end of my fantasy. My children would not ever live in an intact family unit and the broken home cycle would continue for another generation.

The next morning after taking the kids to school, I went to Lindsey Lumber to purchase new locks for the doors but when I returned home two hours later, Chico had come back to the house and removed his clothing and most of the new furniture that he had purchased. On the kitchen table was the $500,000 insurance policy. Chico had burned the edges of the papers after writing in bold print, "cancelled."

Again, he had maliciously planned and carefully timed his actions. Weeks earlier, he'd rented an apartment in the Lake Shore area in preparation for his move. A week later he was sporting his new girlfriend, Ferrecita and her kids, all around town. He had dumped Rita shortly after our divorce.

Knowing that Chico was vindictive, I should have anticipated his next move, but I didn't. Two weeks after he'd left, I came home to find that he had turned off the electricity, the water and the gas. Because of the deposits required to change them into my name, I'd kept them in his name. I was so embarrassed when I had to tote several buckets of water from the neighbor's faucet to bathe and flush the toilet.

A month later, I went to Liz's house to tell her what happened. In the past she always seemed to logically explain Chico's bizarre behavior. Tonight she was not supportive of him and said that I should never reunite with him. I wondered what had happened that caused Liz to adamantly reverse her opinion of him. I soon found out. The next week, Pearl shared the details.

"After Liz resigned her position at the Veteran's Hospital to become a public health nurse, she was assigned to several schools. Chico, though an assistant principal, had been reported by a student as a possible contact for a sexually transmitted disease and Liz had to investigate. Sworn to confidentiality by law, she had threatened to expose him if he ever infected you. His tactic was to make you feel unwanted and undesirable, thus not engaging in intercourse other than to get you pregnant. That's why he often slept in the back room."

When I discovered that Liz had known for years about Chico's infidelity, I blamed my miserable life on her because she had persuaded me to marry him. I stopped speaking to her for a year.

When I reasoned that her threats had protected me from acquiring an STD, I soon forgave her, but vowed to never be pressured or influenced by anyone else. I would live life on my terms.

Later that year, I had to be readmitted to Hollywood Memorial Hospital for a CAT scan as my vision worsened and I suffered from a perpetual headache. Knowing that Chico had hit me again, the radiologist was instructed to look for "hair line" fractures in the orbital socket of my left eye. My eyelids were beginning to droop over my pupil as the globe began to recess further into the socket. I had to have surgery again; this time to repair my eyelids.

Dusk: Psychogenesis

    Feeling remorseful that he had unknowingly participated in Chico's deception, John Kelley vowed to protect me and the kids. I discerned his sincerity and allowed him into our lives. On the day that my surgery was scheduled, he drove me to the hospital and promised to care for me while I recuperated.

    As I lie on the operating table, I felt the nurse insert the IV tube into the back of my right hand. It didn't matter now that I was not going to be anesthetized completely. I was already numb emotionally. The Demerol burned as it began to travel up my arm. As I counted backwards from 100, I swore that I'd never speak to Chico again…. 99….98…

BLIND FAITH

Having physically survived the horrors of our reconciliation, I decided to enroll in graduate school so that I could earn a higher salary. Initially, Chico's financial support was meager and infrequent. My days were long as I also taught pre-GED classes at the adult education center four nights a week. Every Saturday, for two years, I was in graduate school from 9:00 a.m. to 5:00 p.m. working on my master's degree in exceptional student education. Sunday was the only day to shop, relax and prepare for the upcoming week. It was a rigorous cycle, but it helped me keep my mind positively and productively centered. Without my family's help I could not have achieved my educational and financial goals.

Upon graduation, I scaled back to teaching two nights so that I could get Juanita and Renee involved in the girl scouts. To my dismay, their school Crestview Elementary, which I had recently been assigned as the Speech Pathologist, did not have a troop. So I called the local council to inquire of the nearest group. Would you believe it; they talked me into becoming a scout leader.

I attended many meetings to qualify. As soon as I received my certification, I went to the principal, Mr. Moye and asked for permission to meet in the school's cafeteria. He was delighted to have a staff member in this role. I circulated flyers and he made announcements and before Halloween I had a Brownie troop of over twenty five students. I was ecstatic! I now needed a support group of parent volunteers. Merdene, a neighbor, became my right arm.

Our troop was a success. We had an ambitious agenda. We not only participated in traditional activities like camping and selling cookies, our troop went to the ballet to see "***Swan Lake***" and to a backstage production of the opera ***Turandot*** hosted by the cast. We had a party for every holiday. On Christmas, we had them to dress in their best as we walked from door to door caroling.

I felt vindicated. Though I continued to hear malicious gossip about my divorce, the parents of my troop adored me for my sincerity and dedication to their daughters. They trusted me to help in the mentoring and development of their children. I began to smile again.

Dusk: Psychogenesis

Then one day, about five years after my divorce, in December, I received two notices in the mail to appear in court the same week. One was for family court and the other was a summons to fulfill my civic responsibility by serving as a juror at the Metropolitan Justice Building. I didn't know then, but this would be another life changing event that would lead to the destruction of my good name and works among the parents I valued, the girls in my troop and with professional colleagues.

As I read the summons, I thought of ways to be excused from this civic duty. I felt certain that I would be dismissed after I presented my order to appear in Family Court to the bailiff.

"Denied," replied the judge to my request. "However, you may be excused on Thursday, if you're not serving on a case, but you must return to Criminal Court immediately following your civil proceedings."

Given this charge I sat down and prepared to spend the week reading several good books while observing the criminal justice system at work.

I was wearing a dark green and red plaid winter skirt, with a light green turtleneck blouse. A matching scarf draped from my shoulders. My feet were shod with knee high leather boots and my head was covered with a long curly wig. And yes, dark, very darkly tinted eyeglasses framed my face. My body was totally covered. I didn't want to be recognized by anyone. My cocoon of warm clothing was a perfect disguise.

The waiting room for the prospective jurors was very large. It was equipped with many activities for entertainment such as backgammon and checkers boards, reading materials and vending machines. The chairs and tables were so arranged that jurors could easily gather and communicate while waiting to be called. Very little time was lost. Groups quickly gathered and laughter could be heard sporadically. Some, like me, chose to sit alone and read.

After hours of sitting, being interrupted only to listen for my number, I looked around to find a group or an individual to talk with. My attention was directed towards a very studious looking, well-groomed guy wearing aviator shaped eyeglasses. He was very quiet and appeared detached from everyone in the room. Seated next to him was a woman, who also seemed stoic. I thought them to be college students studying for exams. Then I noted that one of their books was a Bible. I began to wonder about their interests, because at that time I'd stopped attending regular church services and was in search of a practical doctrine that would guide me to live the abundant life in the "here and now."

I rejected the concept of long suffering and poverty on earth, just to die and go to heaven to receive my proper reward. I wanted to be loved, happy and prosperous in this life.

The young man and his friend were reading from a yellow booklet entitled *"YOU ARE NOT A NIGGER: The World's Best Kept Secret"* by Moses Israel. I was so fascinated by the title that I aggressively walked towards them and said, "Hi, I'm Mary. Where did you purchase that book?"

The young man just handed it to me and said, "My name is Ricky. Why don't you read my copy first?"

"Ok, I'll return it before the end of the day."

"Don't rush. You may keep it."

"Thank you." I returned to my seat and began to read.

That night, after I put the children to bed I reread the one-hundred page booklet. The Black history within its pages fascinated me. I'd become an avid reader of African- American History since my sister Mildred, who was in college during the Civil Rights Movement in the 1960's, brought friends home on weekends who discussed racial and political affairs. When riots occurred as a result of student demonstrations, protests and sit-ins, the campus closed and the students were sent home until the tension eased. Mildred would bring home foreign students from the Caribbean and Panama who did not want to leave the country for such a short period of time. I'd sit quietly and listen to their versions of the events as they also related them to civil strife and neo-colonialism in their countries. I developed a tremendous sense of ethnic pride and awareness.

Years later, when I attended college, I sat with pride at the McCrory's luncheon counter and ordered a meal. I reflected on the events by acting as if I'd been a part of the sit-ins. I welcomed every occasion to attend a play or lecture concerning Black History on campus. The most memorable event was Stokley Carmichael's Black Power presentation in Lee Hall auditorium. After listening, I was highly motivated to learn more about my roots.

When I finished reading the yellow booklet, I was ecstatic. The information, which I perceived to be a plausible explanation of our plight in America, changed my perspective. Within its pages I found the answers to most of my questions about African American peoples' lost lineage: Jesus was a dark-skinned man and so were the prophets. The major events in the Bible occurred in or near our native land of Africa. I thought, "We are special. Religion is now ethnically relevant."

Dusk: Psychogenesis

The next day, I asked my new-found acquaintances more and more questions. When it was time for the lunch break, I asked, "May I eat lunch with you today?" thinking that they were going to eat at a restaurant close to the courthouse.

Ricky said, "We're having lunch at the Temple of Yahweh on 62nd Street."

Until that very moment I had not associated the historical information in the yellow book with that infamous group. I'd heard rumors of the alleged beheading of a former member. Not wanting to offend Ricky, I said, "62nd Street is too far away for us to get back to the courthouse on time. I don't like to be late. I'll take a rain check."

When they left, I went to the cafeteria in the justice building to get a sandwich. Later, observing that they did return on time, I mustered up the courage to go with them the next day when invited.

Arriving at the temple, I was impressed with the number of businessmen from the community dining there. The food was delicious and the people were extremely friendly. The environment was aesthetically appealing and very clean.

Finally, I relaxed but I wasn't planning to return anytime soon. I didn't want to openly associate with the group because I thought that they were too racist. I didn't want to equate Black pride with White hatred. That would be the same as the Klu Klux Klan's and the Aryan Nation's beliefs and practices.

The next morning I reported to the criminal courthouse, signed in and was excused to go downtown to civil court. There were several issues to be resolved; a dispute over who could claim the children for tax purposes; delinquent child support payments; and Chico's refusal to pay Mr. Klein's legal fees. My new attorney, Jesse McCrary had petitioned the court to arrange for each financial transaction to go through their system for accountability purposes. Chico had petitioned the court to require that I return the diamond ring that he had given me during our reconciliation. I was allowed to keep it and that angered him. I suppose he wanted to sell it for cash or give it to someone else. Just seeing Chico again was terribly upsetting. I was visibly distraught while driving back to jury duty.

Upon entering the waiting room, I obviously looked dismayed. Ricky asked, "What's wrong, Mary?"

"I need a good accountant. I just discovered that my ex-husband also claimed the children for income tax purposes last year and my divorce decree didn't specifically state who could claim them, so I'll have to keep good records to prove that I contributed over fifty-one percent towards their care to be able to claim them each year."

To my surprise, this studious looking young man was a certified financial planner and tax accountant. "Here's my business card. Give me a call in January when you receive your W-2 statement. In the mean time, keep all of your receipts."

"I usually do. Thanks Ricky."

The rest of the week was uneventful. As I drove home, I looked forward to Christmas vacation. I needed the rest.

Early in January, I observed a Black couple, being shown a home that was for sale across the street from my house. My neighborhood, though a predominately white community, was a newly integrated development in the suburban North Dade area. The last street of the development had a higher ratio of black families causing most of the white owners to sell. Ricky, the studious juror was the realtor. After showing the house, he looked over and spotted me on my lawn. As we waved he began to walk over to chat.

"Could I come by sometime and discuss more of our biblical history with you?"

I remembered being impressed with his knowledge of the Bible and said, "Yes, I'd like that."

After nearly a year of once a week home sessions, which I likened to those I received from the Jehovah's Witnesses, I was becoming well versed in the scriptures and had learned many passages that referred to our biblical history and cultural roots.

The following December, the Temple hosted a community fellowship. Ricky invited me. I didn't promise but said, "I'll think about going."

Realizing my apprehension, Ricky suggested, "Why don't you attend a Wednesday night class prior to the fellowship? That may ease your tension." I didn't respond. Home study sessions were fine with me because I liked the spirited discussions; but I didn't want to openly associate with any non-traditional doctrines that were considered sects or cults.

"Oh! I understand. You're scared. I double dare you to go."

"I'm not scared. You'll see." He'd tricked me into a response.

The following Wednesday, before I left the house, I rechecked the electrical appliances, the doors and windows. For the very first time since I divorced six years ago, I left the children unattended. Not expecting to be gone for more than two hours, I prayed that they would remain safe and asleep until I returned.

I dressed in a gold and green plaid wool skirt with a tan long-sleeved blouse. My hair was permed and pulled back into a bun. My face was framed with brown tinted eyeglasses. I looked like the typical school marm. I nervously recited the 23rd Psalm: "The Lord is my shepherd ... I will fear no evil."

As my two-toned green Pontiac Grand Prix turned into the temple's parking lot, the cars in front suddenly stopped and the occupants got out, turned toward the east and raised their hands.

I looked around and saw that even those persons who were walking stood still at that moment. I patiently waited after realizing that they were praying. I parked the car and walked slowly to the entrance.

Inside the temple's lobby, security procedures were explained. A woman in a colorful African garment searched my body and my handbag then asked, "In which area of the city do you live?"

"North Dade!"

"We'll seat you with others who live in that area so that you'll feel comfortable."

"Thank you but I was invited by a friend, and I'd like to sit with him. His name is Ricky."

"What is his Hebrew name?"

"What do you mean?"

Before she could answer Ricky appeared dressed in a colorful robe with a turban on his head. He looked official and serious. I was speechless. I'd only seen him wearing Armani business suits and Bally shoes before. Tonight he wore plastic sandals from K-Mart and a homemade motley colored long tunic.

"Shalom, Mary."

I just nodded my head.

He whispered in my ear, "You'll be seated with my wife. She's expecting you."

As I followed the usher, I observed the most beautiful array of colorful African cultural attire being fashionably worn by some of the most beautiful Black women on earth. They were without makeup and yet their skin glowed radiantly. They were adorned with sequins, gold and silver trimmings and sparkling jewelry. I quickly reflected on the posters of African Kings and Queens displayed around the schools during Black Heritage Month. For a moment, in this place, I was on the Nile River surrounded by my sisters Sheba, Cleopatra and Nefertiti. My fears were subsiding.

A tall man wearing a robe and a turban stood at the lectern expounding on the historical relevance of the scriptures from a Black perspective. I was absorbed in the text when suddenly the crowd began to scream, chant and clap uncontrollably. The band started playing and the double doors in the lobby swung open. A group of men wearing long dark robes with shiny swords around their waists fearlessly looked around the room as they slowly walked down the aisle.

What was this spectacle? People were screaming and reaching toward the aisle to touch someone. They were blowing kisses and thrusting babies forward to be touched. Should I use this distraction to escape their madness? No, I became more curious.

Finally, my eyes spotted a very fair skinned man wearing a lavish gray robe in the midst of the guards. He was different from the others. Carrying a brightly polished staff, he walked erect and majestically. Was this the author of the yellow book, Moses Israel? I wondered.

When he reached the podium, everyone stood, the band changed its melody and the crowd began chanting to a drone like cadence. "Yah—weh -- Yahweh" echoed throughout the building in a dull monotonous manner over and over again. This continued for nearly fifteen minutes.

My legs were tiring so I decided to sit. Suddenly, the mystery man leaned forward and spoke loudly into the microphone, "Praise Yahweh."

The chanting stopped instantly. Great! I was eager to hear more of the history lessons.

Then he said, "There are people who go to football games and stand up cheering for their team as players run down the field with a pig-skin ball all night, but these same people have a hard time standing up praising the name of our great, good and terrible Black God YAHWEH for a few minutes."

Everyone, including the lecturer looked in my direction. I reluctantly stood again, respecting their protocol. The chanting resumed for it seemed another fifteen minutes.

Again, I tired and sat down, but before I could rest my feet, I again heard him say, "Praise Yahweh." Again there was complete silence!

"You know there are those who go to concerts to hear comedians such as Redd Foxx, Richard Pryor and Wild Man Steve tell lies all night and they stand up and cheer these comedians untiringly."

I was now sure that he was talking directly to me. On cue the band struck up its monotonous beat with renewed energy and the crowd resumed its chant. I was ready to go home. I was very disappointed that the mystery man at the podium did not resume the history lessons that night.

When I returned home, having survived this initial experience, I decided not to press my luck. I would not go there again. Mentally, I tried to erase the mystery man's face, particularly his eyes from my mind. Like mine, they appeared asymmetrical. It looked as if one lacked muscle tone because it wandered as the other focused on the audience. The color of his eyes was most unusual. First they appeared gray, then grayish-green and finally grayish-blue. Who is he? I thought.

Ricky came by the next day. "What's your first impression of the temple?"

"Weird," I laughed. "Was the man wearing the gray robe the author of the yellow history book?"

"No."

"Then who is he?" I persisted in my questioning. "Why are you being so evasive Ricky?"

Ricky just stared at me. Then he folded his arms and looked up as if he was trying to find just the right words to satisfy my curiosity.

Finally he said, "Moses Israel has journeyed to Israel for a few weeks. I'll let you know when he returns. OK!"

"OK for now but I have plenty of questions to ask about his book."

The following Wednesday evening I felt ill. My sinuses were inflamed and my eyes were red. The silicone band that surrounds my left retina was throbbing. This was the perfect excuse for not returning to the temple tonight if Ricky called; but my thoughts were focused on the temple. Would I dare go back?

Just as I was about to lie down, I wondered about the mysterious man. Yes, I would go back! I don't remember how long it took me to get dressed but I was out of the door in a flash. I had on a pair of dark grey slacks, a light gray silk blouse and a black blazer. My pocket was filled with Kleenex. And yes, I had on a pair of smoked tinted, light gray eyeglasses. I had a pair to match each of my colorful outfits.

I arrived moments late. The outer doors had been locked to prevent entry while the mystery man made his grand appearance. I waited patiently. When allowed, I quickly went to the North Dade section and sat with Deborah, Ricky's wife.

After the prolonged chanting ended, the mystery man began to teach. I intuitively felt that he was the author of the yellow book though he spoke of the author in the third person.

He began, "As students you are encouraged to research the name of God in the dictionary, Bible reference books and encyclopedias. The name Yahweh is found in numerous literary works. Why have most African Americans not known this most powerful name? Why were the names, languages, traditions and religious practices of African people suppressed during slavery?"

Many questions concerning the biblical identity of Blacks were asked rhetorically and each answer provided was very plausible and believable. The crowd reacted emotionally. I took notes.

He continued to lecture. "During the African slave trade, all African-American-Caribbean peoples were "cut off" from their parts and knew not who they were as a unified people as evidenced by our constantly searching for national, cultural and historical identity. Every few years we decide to rename ourselves. We've gone from Colored, Negro, Black, Afro-American to African-American. What will we be next year? It's obvious that my people are lost."

"But for you who are here tonight, your search is over. Think how wonderful it is to discover within the pages of the greatest book on earth a magnificent and glorious past which you can proudly claim. All nations know our true identity but conspire to keep it secret by directing our attention to the New Testament where they had given our forefathers a "master-servant mentality" during slavery in this country. What a diabolical scheme!"

The congregation stood and applauded. I realized that I was becoming emotionally involved in this message. In academic settings, I'm usually detached and logical. What was happening to me?

The speaker's lesson focused on the Old Testament. He quoted scripture after scripture that supposedly verified the ineffable name of "our" God in the Hebrew language.

"Wherever the words LORD GOD appear in large and small capital letters, the original Hebrew read "YAHWEH." This is the most sacred, highly praised and well hidden name in the universe. Those who invoke this holy name could summon the forces within the cosmos immediately. The name is not ineffable to us, God's chosen people. Our conspirators never wanted us to know it because of the powers it contains. This name is the greatest secret weapon that all nations wanted to keep from the former slaves and their descendents, thus keeping their children and children's' children in darkness. But I am here to shed light on the matter."

Dusk: Psychogenesis

The crowd began to chant, roar and dance in the aisles endlessly; I sat in amazement trying to figure out how I had not come across this information before. I surely had read enough religious books. The name of God was not new to me because it had been presented by the Jehovah Witnesses.

I remembered questioning them about it. I'd asked, "Why don't you call yourselves Yahweh Witnesses?"

"Because we don't speak the Hebrew language, we speak English and in English God's name is Jehovah."

"What about multilingual members of your group who live in countries that do not speak English? What do they call themselves?"

I challenged them with my questions, but now I realized that I had not logically processed their teachings nor had I associated with any name of God. Something strange was happening to me here.

After the history lesson, the speaker announced, "Those persons in the audience who have attended classes for a month or more and have received your Hebrew names, I want you to come forward and shake my hand."

A long line formed down the middle aisle.

Deborah explained, "This phase of class is very similar to the traditional churches' call for membership. But unlike the churches, you don't have to be escorted to the back by the secretary to fill out an application or schedule a baptismal date."

"Why not?"

"All of our African American people are genetically Hebrew Israelites by birth; therefore, biologically we are members. When you accept your original biblical name, it signifies that you are consciously aware of your true identity."

"What names? Where are they located?"

"The names that we now have are considered our slave names. Our true names are found in the books of Chronicles in the genealogy of Israel. Our last name is Israel."

"All of our last names are Israel?"

"Yes, collectively all African Americans and blacks of the Caribbean who are descendants of slaves transported from the West Coast of Africa in the 1500's are Israel. We are the tribe of Judah." She quickly turned to the scriptures in Genesis 15:13 to support her statement.

"And he said unto Abram; know of a surety that thy seed shall be a stranger in a land that is not theirs, and shall serve them; and they shall afflict them four hundred years." Then she turned to Deuteronomy 28:15

which listed all of the curses of disobedience. I quickly read the verses and immediately related them to our slavery experience in America.

"Seeing is like believing; isn't it Mary?"

"Well it seems so. My name is Mary Alice. Mary is a Hebrew name." I then remembered the name of a Jewish student I'd taught and quickly decided that it would be an appropriate substitution for my middle name. I voice, "I'm Mary Ilana."

Before I knew it I was up walking briskly down the center aisle. The lecturer had already begun his return to the podium when one of the guards told him of my approach. He turned around and opened his arms, hugged me on one side of my body and then switched sides to hug me again.

"Welcome home my daughter. What is your name?"

"My name is Mary Ilana and I now know that my last name is Israel."

This was all so very strange for me. My body appeared weightless as I returned to my seat. Internally, my body was buzzing and I vibrated all over. My ears were also humming. What was this feeling? Was it the Holy Ghost? Strange! Unexplainable, even weird can't describe it. Whatever it was; it was overwhelming.

After returning home, I wondered if I had officially joined this group. If so, what was going to be expected of me? Suddenly I felt very uncomfortable. I didn't like the uncertainty, but I was curious. I wanted to learn more.

Months later, after having attended a few more classes, and against my better judgment, I told Merdene, my parent assistant for the Brownie troop that I was going to the temple. Thinking that she would be opened minded to the concept of our biblical history, I shared my experiences with her. We laughed as she joked about the rumors of foul play that circulated about the group.

I thought nothing of the conversation until there was a dispute over the money collected for selling Girl Scout cookies. There were strict rules for who would have access to the funds and who would deposit them into the bank. As the troop leader, I delegated those responsibilities to two trustworthy parents; but somehow, when the account was unable to be reconciled, I was accused of giving the funds to the temple. To keep the peace, I relinquished my position.

In the fall, when school opened, Merdene became the troop leader and began hosting the scout meetings at her home which was adjacent to the house across the street. I watched as the girls gathered on the sidewalk and gleefully greeted each other as they waited for the meeting to start. As the school year progressed, they completely stopped waving and speaking. Instead, they pointed at me, screamed frantically, and then quickly ran away as if they were in mortal danger. They were reacting to the gossip they'd overheard from their parents. Their actions deeply saddened me. Obviously, all of my good deeds meant nothing; having attended bible study classes at the temple nullified everything.

THE FIRST DAY: ON THE SEA

I awaken at 10:00 a.m. look at my watch and realize that I have overslept and missed my breakfast seating. I immediately call for room service and while waiting for it to arrive, decide to watch TV.

How ironic, "Father of the Bride" is the featured film. My teenage dreams about a festive wedding, a sensual honeymoon and a joyous family with the love of my life had been shattered. Being married to Chico was a nightmare. I audibly renew my vow to never remarry while affirming that no one would ever hold me in bondage or physically abuse me again.

"Knock, knock"
"Who's there?"
"Room service!"

I open the door to receive my meal and generously tip the waiter. As I sit to eat, I reflected on the early days at the temple. Initially I was so excited about learning African American History from a biblical perspective, but what intrigued me most was trying to discern Moses Israel's role; to understand his purpose; and to see how his mission would affect the lives of our people. As my thoughts return to the present, I quickly reach for my pen and notepad and begin to write.

THE TEACHER

After attending a few more bible classes at the temple, I was still curious about Moses Israel, the author. I anxiously awaited his return from Israel as Ricky had mentioned. The current lecturer constantly referred to himself as Yahshua. I decided to reread lesson #1 in the yellow book for clues to their identities and purposes.

"*First, it stated, it is important for you to remember that the bible is past, present and future at the same time. The bible is written literally, figuratively, prose and poetically, symbolically, metaphor, and simile. Unless you are a religious scientist, you have no idea when to read the bible as prose and poetry or whether to read it figuratively or literally or when to read it as a prophecy or how to understand the symbols such as found throughout Revelations. Thus you need a teacher from God. Don't leave it up to someone else to read it for you, get your bible and follow these scriptures for yourself. Read them! Study them and ask questions for yourself.*" (YNAN pg.6)

I had always been an avid reader of African-American History; so as a Speech and Language pathologist, I found it natural to analyze the above statements which would help me to understand the Bible as our hidden story.

I realized that a student of this philosophy would also have to have an excellent command of the English language to decipher the mystically coded verses within the Bible. This intrigued me more because I could relate to the Bible professionally. Reading English literature was a favorite leisurely activity. I thought that if I could just talk with Moses Israel personally I could get some tips on our linguistic history from a biblical perspective. I'd always aspired to become a writer of historically relevant books and articles, so my enthusiasm was mounting. I thought that I could live the experience while learning of my "true" biblical identity. My literary works would have a realistic yet personal flavor like Alex Haley's "Roots."

I continued to read more.

"*Now the next thing that I want you to get straight in your mind is that I am not a false Christian. I cannot lie to you and say that*

God called me to preach. I would like for you to turn to I Corinthians 12:2."

"And God hath set some in the church, first apostles, secondarily prophets, thirdly teachers, after that miracles, then gifts of healing, helps, governments, diversities of tongues. My gift is the third one mentioned in verse 28. I am a teacher of God, bringing you the whole truth of God. I am bringing you that which is perfect, the perfect truth. (YNAN, pg.8)

I wondered if Moses Israel the author, and Yahshua the lecturer, was the same person. I continued to listen very intently as he expounded on this topic and bible verse: "Take heed and beware of the leaven of the Pharisees and of the Sadducees. And they reasoned among themselves. Then they understood that he bade them not beware of the leaven of bread, but of the doctrine of the Pharisees and of the Sadducees."

"All of you have been deceived through every form and bit of information that has ever been provided through television, radio or textbooks. The devil has deceived not part of the world with his doctrines and philosophies, but the whole world. Because African-American-Caribbean people have bought into this belief system, it is now necessary for us to deprogram our thinking by not listening to those erroneous philosophies any longer. Black people need a teacher from God who can guide them into all truth and understanding. ***I am God's anointed teacher.*** All other teachers, particularly uneducated Christian ministers who were trained by the slave masters, are as "dumb dogs."

The congregation laughed hysterically when the teacher mocked Black ministers' preaching style after quoting this scripture.

"His watchmen are blind, they are all ignorant, and they are all dumb dogs. They are shepherds that cannot understand." (Isa. 56:10-11)

"Because the temple consists of members from various denominational backgrounds which taught different versions of the slave master's philosophy, it's best to cease listening to any interpretations of the scriptures except mine. To do otherwise would cause more confusion. If you were satisfied with what you had been taught, you wouldn't be here. So all of you are to become as "little children" and trust me to guide you in the "way that we should go," he stressed.

"If you value these lessons and high teachings from God then you will make every effort to attend classes regularly. Those of you who miss class obviously think that you don't need the lesson so you should not be taught the message by any other member. If a person not in attendance asks you about a lesson they missed, you should just say "the lesson was awesome! You should have been in class!" Never are you to teach or explain or provide information. Class tapes will be available for the absentees to purchase during the High Holy days," he humorously interjected.

"Remember, the Bible, called the book of wisdom; the dictionary, the book of understanding; the Interpreters Dictionary of the Bible and *my publications* are the only books sanctioned by the temple. Those students who want to read other literary works for clarification and understanding will find themselves being led astray," he cautioned.

Some students began to label those who openly discussed their personal points of view as "philosophers and self-appointed teachers" who were seeking recognition.

When the teacher called students, most of whom had been his pupils from the onset of his lectures in Miami in the early 1980's, to come before the congregation to share their thoughts concerning the night's lesson, I realized that my understanding significantly differed from their views. I grew from their discussions and attributed the differences in viewpoints to our varied religious and educational backgrounds.

As I continued to study alone, I wondered how such interest and enthusiasm for researching and studying could be perceived as negative or how could having an open discussion about the bible be misconstrued as being anything other than having a "holy conversation." I continued to keep my thoughts and opinions to myself. For me, the edict to ban the reading of other books was a moot issue. Reading was my passion.

However, I was almost certain by now that Moses Israel and Yahshua were one. Many clues to their identity had been given as I listened and read, but I needed more information before drawing a conclusion.

THE PROFESSIONAL CLASS

The lecture began: "All of the one hundred and forty-four thousand men mentioned in the book of Revelations are from the twelve tribes of Israel. Twelve thousand are of the tribe of Judah. We are Judah, the chosen of God and the chief rulers. Judah is the tribe from which The Messiah was descended. The tribes of Judah and Benjamin were captured and enslaved over four hundred years ago and carried to the Caribbean Islands and then to America," the teacher informed the congregation.

"Who are we?" he asked enthusiastically.

"Judah!" The congregation shouted.

"It is the responsibility of all members of the temple to search for these men, known as the godheads. These gifted men can be easily identified by their unusual demeanor, positive characteristics and moral actions. They are the brightest, most talented and skillful among us. When they hear the words of our testimony their genes and chromosomes will be activated. Thus agitating their souls and bringing former things to their remembrance."

"Praise Yahweh!" echoed throughout the building."

"Everything is mathematically calculated to effect this transition in their minds. Eventually these men will return to the fold "where Yahweh has chosen to place His name," and prepare to take their places as righteous rulers with me Shiloh, the gatherer of the people. These prophesies will soon be fulfilled."

My ears perked up. The teacher now referred to himself as Shiloh. I continued to listen.

"Genetically, these men are descendants of kings and prophets: David, the mighty warrior; Solomon, renowned for his wisdom, and Moses, the great deliverer; the blood of mighty men flow through their veins. Our great patriarchs, Abraham, Isaac and Jacob, talked with God personally. ***Now, a type of Moses is among you today teaching the laws, statutes, judgments and commandments of God from the Old Testament.***"

These statements now confirmed my thoughts. Moses Israel was primarily a teacher, not a prophet or a deliverer; and he was definitely not the resurrected Jesus.

The First Day: On the Sea

Seeing so many well educated, professional men and women at the temple was encouraging and provided additional motivation for me to continue my studies. They worked diligently and gave freely of their time and resources. They enunciated well and appeared well versed on various subjects, especially Black History.

This "talented tenth" held positions of importance at the temple and in the community. This cadre consisted of architects, lawyers, politicians, doctors, teachers, tradesmen, bankers, social workers and former clergymen who worked together for a common cause, to uplift the status of African American people. For me, this was most impressive.

My son, Lonnie then seven years of age, needed the mentoring and guidance of very positive male role models. Chico's visits were few and far in-between. He was never there to assist me when Lonnie, who suffered for asthma, was hospitalized. He was keeping his promise to never ever help me care for the children even in an emergency. I could understand how he might remain cruel and bitter towards me, but how could he ignore his children?

I remembered an old adage that my mom often repeated. "When a man stops sleeping with you, he stops loving you and your children even if the kids are his. When he starts sleeping with another woman, he loves her kids, even if the children are not his kids. They love who they sleep with at the time," she stated with authority and from experience.

It didn't take much for me to believe that now. Chico was seen entertaining other women with their kids all around town. Lonnie, almost three when we divorced, had very little memory of him.

Subconsciously, I wanted to break the abusive cycle that Chico's father had passed on to him. I didn't care if Chico ever visited Lonnie. I prayed daily that he would mysteriously disappear from the face of the earth and considered the child support checks the same as death benefits from social security.

Startled by the sound of the applause, I refocused and continued to listen to the lecture.

"Every passage in the bible is our hidden history. Why has this not been known to us, a people who read the bible daily and pray for deliverance constantly? This magnificent book, which has been translated into numerous languages and is the undisputed best seller of all times, is so heavily coded with esoteric knowledge that only the initiated could ever attempt to decipher it."

"The secret societies are the only ones privy to this sacred information. The members of the fraternal orders know our identity but guard the knowledge of our genealogy and divine purpose with their lives. If the initiated have vowed to keep us in total darkness then how are we to know when we are truly in the midst of a sage brave enough to reveal these mysteries to the masses of our people?"

He stepped away from the microphone and walked from one side of the podium to the next staring out at the crowd. Finally he said, "Well, search no more. You are honored to be in the presence of *a master teacher* who has come to decode the parables in the bible. *In **my book** titled*: "**You Are Not a Nigger,**" *I wrote* that in the beginning, race was not an issue because the original peoples were all black skinned. The tribe of Judah was captured and sold into slavery for over four hundred years. Today that represents African Americans and Caribbean peoples. The scriptures could only be referring to us, because unlike the Jews, we were the only ones truly cut off so that we would not even remember our names, language, history and God."

My ears perked up as I heard him use the pronouns "my and I." Now I was absolutely sure that Moses Israel, aka Yahshua and Shiloh, was the teacher and the author. I decided to only refer to him in the future as Moses Israel. I could not relate to the other names and their implications. Nor could I imagine that I was in the presence of the long awaited "Messiah." I continued to listen and take notes.

"What is Judah's purpose? It is to be the chief rulers of the world forever. We are Judah! All we have to do is remember who we are and begin following the laws, statutes, judgments and commandments that are written in the Old Testament. Doesn't that seem easier than marching and demonstrating before "Pharaoh Reagan's" government or by voting for temporary legislative changes?"

I was so fascinated with his presentation. He was a masterful teacher. His use of figurative language and analogies were intriguing. He was humorous and often down to earth in his use of slang and colloquialisms. He was also a great entertainer. I could sit for hours and listen to him and not once look at my watch to see if it were time to go. I continued to listen to his lecture.

"The intellectual class has been attracted to this movement first. But we all know that the race is not given to the swift but to those who endure to the end. How do we develop endurance and how are we going to accomplish our goals?"

He paused, looked around then stated emphatically, "Through Study! The pride generated from the knowledge and sincere belief that we are somebody special, the chosen people of God will sustain us."

Chants of "Praise Yahweh" echoed throughout the building for several minutes.

His words shaped my behavior and that of those who came later. We believed and acted accordingly. We studied from the book of Ezra about the great businessmen of Israel; about King David, the great warrior, and of Solomon, the master builder as portrayed in the books of Samuel, Kings and Chronicles. We imagined that we were them and hearkened to the voice that cried out in the wilderness for unity and progress. We were determined to be the vanguard that would help identify and restore Israel and Judah to their glory and splendor.

A list of approved books was distributed. The temple's printing press quickly duplicated copies and sold them after class. The fact that they were copyrighted didn't seem to matter. We researched journals, anthropological findings and genetic testing data which proved that people of African ancestry were the original people. We read books like ***"The Secrets of Lost Races," "From Babylon to Timbuktu," and "Chariots of the Gods."***

Scripturally we were the first, kings and rulers, who through time had become the last in social and economic status. This condition could be seen globally. In every area of life we were portrayed as the borrowers, not as the lenders; the tail of civilization rather than the head; and the last hired and the first fired.

I continued to study alone. But with so much knowledge, I was no longer ashamed of openly attending classes; however, I didn't dare broadcast my continued association with the temple to anyone but my immediate family, who understood my love for academic pursuits and knowledge. Some things were better left unspoken.

THE LINE

It was on Christmas day at my very first Sabbath worship service, that I observed the temple's selection process for marriage. It was most unusual. I likened it to the "Price is Right's" announcement to "come on down." Anyone who was eligible and desirous of a mate came down and stood in front of the congregation in a horizontal line. They walked up and down the row and looked each other over and briefly chatted. It was a humorous occasion. I'd never observed such a courting ritual before. Everyone appeared to be familiar with the practice and was happily laughing. I was amused but puzzled thinking, "Why would anyone marry a stranger after just a few moments of chatting?"

After the selections were made and the vows were taken, Moses Israel humored those women who were desirous of marriage but were left standing.

"Fear not; for thou shall not be ashamed: neither be thou confounded; for thou shall not be put to shame, for thy Maker is thy husband." I laughed along with them but I sensed a hidden message in his words.

However, as I continued to observe other practices were noted. Husbands and wives did not sit together. If you were to ask a mother who her children's father was, the response would always be "Yahweh is the father." If you asked the children their fathers' names, they would all respond "Abba," the Hebrew word for father. Also, if a sister were on her monthly period she would carry a pillow or towel to sit on wherever she went for seven days. Rather than touch you during this time, she would "blow you a kiss" which indicated that she was unclean. Therefore, you were not to touch her.

Having been divorced for nearly five years, I'd found myself consciously looking at the brothers too. I'd read all of the discouraging statistics on the black male-female ratio and the difficulty that single parents and professional women were experiencing in finding compatible mates.

As I reflected on the marital ceremony that night I also thought, "No newspaper announcement, no invitations, no relatives, no flowers, no reception, no gifts, no honeymoon suite. This haphazard lifestyle isn't for me."

I didn't want the headaches of the married life again, but I wanted and needed to feel like a woman. My marriage had destroyed those feelings and I wanted them restored.

I'd been lucky, for lack of a better term, to have met Herbert, an elementary school principal, shortly after my divorce. He was twenty years older and had recently divorced. Herb frequently mentored me on "life's lessons," occasionally shared my bed while giving me the freedom to remain emotionally detached as I transitioned from being a married woman to a single mom.

Later I clandestinely dated a white guy. Almost all of the Black guys I met knew of Chico and therefore prejudged me. Professionally I lived in a white world. The schools that I serviced were in predominantly white neighborhoods and I was always the only Black member on the multidisciplinary team of school psychologist, school social worker and educational placement specialist. Through them I learned to relax around a few men, white men. Therefore, when I was approached by Ron, I didn't see color; I saw my needs being met.

I was eating lunch at "**Granny Feelgood**," a health food restaurant in Miami Lakes. His approach was anything but subtle.

"Hello, my name is Ron. May I dine with you?"

After looking around noticing that the place was nearly filled to capacity I said, "Sure."

"I eat here often and I've noticed that you are always alone. Do you have a friend?"

"I have lots of friends," I responded as if I didn't know what he was specifically asking.

"I am sure, but do you have a companion? I notice that you are not wearing a wedding ring."

"No one special," I cautiously answered.

"I ask because I'm interested in getting to know you better. I've been intrigued by your demeanor for a few weeks."

I didn't respond.

"Let me tell you about myself."

"Please do," I said as I put down my fork and focused on him.

"I am single, a graduate of Florida State University with a degree in Engineering. In college I became fascinated with African American women. I attended classes with some of the best and the brightest. I liked their style, attitude and sense of humor. So if you are uncomfortable about our racial difference, let me assure you that you are not the first Black woman that I've approached then dated and you will not be the last if this doesn't go anywhere."

"I appreciate your straightforward approach. Obviously you are just looking for an affair with no commitment."

"No, I'm interested in great conversations and in sharing some great times. Marriage is not on my radar screen at the moment."

"Great! If you promise me that you will not change your mind about marriage then perhaps I'll consider going out with you."

He was amused by my response. As we ate, we continued to talk and later exchanged telephone numbers.

For nearly a year, he wined and dined me in classy places. I never knew that there were such fabulous locations for entertainment on Fort Lauderdale Beach, Miami Beach and in Coconut Grove. I had a great time with him and easily forgot about our racial difference when interacting.

I didn't have to worry about being seen with him because the crowd that I would be concerned about was at *Big Daddy's Lounge* on 119th Street, the *Satellite* on 7th Avenue or at the *Jet-A-Way* on 36th Street in the heart of the inner city. All I had to contend with were the curious stares from white women and the puzzled look from Black busboys as they cleared the tables. Ron and I had lots in common but I knew too much Black History to remain in an interracial relationship. In the back of my mind I desired a brother of pure Mandingo stock.

Two years later, a brother came to the temple who I found intriguing enough to consider a relationship with. Josiah was a talented musician who stated that he had studied at Julliard in New York City. He was very articulate, well read and mentally stimulating. As we grew closer, he decided to become a full time disciple at the Fort Lauderdale temple. That was a big turn off for me because I knew that disciples gave their earnings to the common fund and needed permission to leave the premises. That alone was a recipe for a failed relationship, which I didn't need.

Though he was legally single, I'd heard "through the temple's grapevine" that he had taken a wife or two. Therefore, when the call for the line was announced during the Feast of Tabernacles, he walked through the temple to find me. He stood next to the aisle where I was sitting and gestured for me to come down with him. I ignored him and kept looking forward. He slowly walked away after realizing that I was not going to accept his impromptu proposal. I now knew that polygamy was practiced at the temple but I was incapable of knowingly sharing a man. If I were to ever reconsider marriage, I wanted to be the first and only wife.

THE PASSOVER PLOT

I was thrilled to experience my first Passover celebration in March. Believing that the scriptures told our "hidden" story made this feast particularly significant. It was important that my children also share this momentous event. Pure white linen was to be worn for the occasion symbolizing our former prosperity. Rather than buy the temple's predesigned identical garments, to express our individuality and my creativity, I bought the fabric, selected the patterns, sewed the garments and marveled over the finished products.

Members of the temples from all over the country gathered in Miami. There was a great sense of national pride and unity. At sundown the doors were locked. The feast began. Elders came to the microphone to expound on the scriptures. At midnight Moses Israel, dressed in a richly adorned high priest's breastplate symbolizing the twelve tribes of Israel came out to conduct the ceremonial portion of the service. He expounded on the symbolic interpretation of the sacrificial lamb and Azazel, the scapegoat.

"It is time to reflect on our people's struggles. The Passover compares to our experience as slaves in America and to our current efforts to affect justice, freedom and equality. We celebrate this feast a week earlier than the traditional Jewish people as a significant sign to the world that we are the true Hebrews of the Bible. We are following the solar calendar, the great light versus the lunar calendar, the lesser light."

There was so much history taught that night and I absorbed it all. I bubbled with joy inside. The time seemed to pass so quickly. Before long it was sunrise. The doors were unlocked and the congregation went outside and marched around the building several times symbolizing our journey out of Egypt.

Returning home, we slept and refreshed ourselves then drove over to Liz's home to tell her of our wonderful experience. While talking with her, the children telephoned their father to proudly share their story.

"Mommy, daddy wants to talk to you," they interrupted. I put the receiver to my ear and said, "Hello."

"Bitch, what's this shit about spending the night at the temple? I'm coming right over to whip some sense into your ass."

Frightened, I hung up the phone immediately and hurried home. We quickly dressed, gathered our study aids and rushed back to the temple for the evening service. A crucial plan for survival was quickly being formatted within my mind's computer as I sped down the avenue. Could the shelter of the temple be a "present help in the time of trouble," a safe haven for a verbally and physically abused, emotionally battered woman? God help me I prayed.

Class began promptly at 8:00 p.m. I relaxed, sat back and listened attentively to the message.

"Behold, the people of the children of Israel are more and mightier than we: Come on, let us deal wisely with them. Therefore, they did set over them taskmasters to afflict them with their burdens. But the more they afflicted them, the more they multiplied and grew."

"The essence of this lesson is that today's government, called the modern Pharaoh, is conspiring to commit genocide on our people through abortions, forced birth control and sterilization of welfare recipients."

"Our men are being "cut off" through drugs, prison, war, concentration camps and black on black crime, the brutal results of slavery and oppression. I recommend that all of you read the book, "**100 YEARS OF LYNCHING.**" The shockingly graphic images of the horrible scenes will be indelibly impressed on your minds," he paused.

Scenes from the book were then flashed on the television monitors throughout the temple. Almost everyone reacted with shock and outrage. The congregation, now emotionally charged, vowed, just as the Jews do of the Holocaust, shouted, "Never Again."

Suddenly Moses Israel stepped away from the podium, stood erect, like a five star general, clicked his heels together and raised his hand to his forehead to salute the audience. "Attention!" he commanded.

Surprisingly to me, the congregation immediately stood and began reciting "The General Orders:"

"Rule # 1. I will take charge of my post and all temple property in view."

"Rule # 2. I will obey my commanding officer."

After repeating all ten orders of military protocol and duties, Moses Israel said, "Soldiers recite "The Warrior's Pledge."

"I will never surrender to my enemies."

"If captured and questioned, I will recite the Lord's Prayer....."

The First Day: On the Sea

After completing the pledge, a smaller battalion of soldiers quickly got into formation and began marching, as if in a parade, throughout the temple.

"Oh Jesus," I cried as I wondered if we were actually being prepared for war. Had I missed some classes, or were there some secret meetings scheduled? When had they memorized those orders and pledge? I questioned.

My immediate fears however were neither of the government nor of impending war. I still felt that I needed protection from my ex-husband. Chico was increasingly bitter and continued to threaten me verbally. He sought incidents to demonstrate his hatred. I had become a very frightened woman again.

After the week long Passover celebration ended, I became even more fearful of Chico's verbal threats. He continued to call and curse me daily. One morning I tape recorded his threats then called Arnold, a policeman who lived in my neighborhood. He came over immediately.

After listening to Chico's vile language, Arnold wrote up a formal complaint. Handing me the card with the case number, he said, "Mary, go to the justice building next week to press charges. This has got to stop. If you ever need me I'm right around the corner. Don't hesitate to call."

"Thanks, I really appreciate your assistance. Keep an eye on the house at night when you return home from your patrol."

"Sure will," he assured me.

The following Monday I faithfully went to the courthouse to file my complaint. I had to stand in line with many others. As each person reached the window they had to tell the clerk their story.

Everyone could hear what was being said. I wanted to leave rather than openly discuss such a sensitive matter.

"Next," the clerk called out dispassionately. We were just a number to her. I stepped up to the window and told my story in a soft low voice.

"You have to call the police at the time of the assault. Their proof will be the visible bruises and the fresh blood."

I took off my sunglasses and said irately, "Look at my eyes. I've had to have surgery because of his attacks. Aren't they proof enough?"

"There is no way of telling when or how that occurred," she said nonchalantly. I walked away feeling defeated, ashamed, hopeless and very helpless.

Later that week I discussed my fears and apprehension with Ricky. He listened then quoted this scripture, "This day will I begin to put the dread of thee and the fear of thee upon the nations that are under the whole heaven, who shall hear report of thee, and shall tremble, and be in anguish because of thee."

"I don't understand what that has to do with my situation. Please explain."

"Moses Israel taught us that the "name of God" in Hebrew is so powerful that all nations fear our knowing it. To invoke "Yahweh" in the time of trouble would summon the ethers and immediate protection would be provided. Your enemies will be destroyed or would retreat."

Later, I began to study the Old Testament's history of Israel and of its many battles. God intervened on their behalf repeatedly and they were always victorious if obedient. Before Israel had kings or rulers over them, they had a direct line to the Almighty through the prophets.

As I studied the Holy Name of God from a Kabahlah, a book of esoteric writings, I became more convinced that God was my only protection from Chico. The local authorities had proven that they could not nor would not protect me before another incident occurred.

Months later, Chico called to speak with the children just to question them about their "comings and goings."

"Put your mammy on the phone."

"Mammy, daddy wants to talk to you."

"Haven't I told you that you don't repeat vulgar words after your daddy? Mammy is vulgar, Mommy is polite," I reinforced without scolding them.

For the first time in a long time, I placed the receiver to my ear and forcefully said, "Yes!"

Chico cussed and fussed and called me some new dirty names that he'd added to his list of profane terms. I listened and waited for him to be silent. Then I confidently said, "I am not going to stop attending the temple no matter what you threaten to do to me. I now have the true and living God on my side and I no longer fear you. If you continue to harass me, I'm going to let the brothers at the temple know where you live and where you work. I'm warning you. Leave me alone." I hung up quickly.

For months after that, Chico didn't telephone. I felt that God was protecting me through the temple. The temple became my safe haven from Chico, but little did I know at the time that I would need all of that strength, faith and trust in the Almighty to battle the foes within the temple.

I stand to stretch my body and wiggle my fingers. I've been writing for two hours. This would be easier if I had a laptop, I thought. I am getting writer's cramps.

As I prepare to leave the room, I remember the faces of passengers who had approached me last night. They seemed so friendly and concerned about my sitting alone for so long. I quickly affirm, "I must become friendlier. I will talk to strangers today." I laugh as I open the door. I feel like a child, who having been told not to talk with strangers, knowingly plan to disobey. I reaffirm loudly, "I am not a child. I am an adult. I will talk to strangers. In fact, I will initiate a conversation today."

THE SECOND DAY: ON THE SEA

"Mary exercising in the ship's gym"

After a good night's rest, I awaken at 6:00 a.m. put on my jogging suit and go to the exercise room. The area is crowded and all of the equipment is in use. Not wanting to wait, I join a group of joggers and enjoy the exhilarating breeze and the breathtaking view as I run several laps around the track. Feeling refreshed, I return to my cabin and prepare for breakfast. I decide to eat with my assigned group, at the assigned time, at the assigned table this morning.

Surrounded at the table by seven white passengers and a couple from India, I relax. I'm good at just being myself when in the company of those whose judgment of me is unimportant, and I'm especially good at being around white people. I understand their game better. Their behavior around black people is predictable because they have one unified agenda: to continuously demonstrate their dominance and superiority.

"Good morning everyone."

"Good morning," they respond collectively, and then there is a prolonged silence. It rattles my bones. I know that I have been the topic of their conversation since I have not eaten with them since the first night. Obviously, having a lone African American at the table is restricting.

The husband seated in front of me turned to his wife and said, "We should have brought Sadie along with us. It seems like we can't get away from her wherever we go."

Not realizing that I was looking at him, he nodded his head towards me and blinked his eye. His wife's face turned as red as a beet with embarrassment knowing that I had heard the statement and perceived its negative meaning. She smiled and said out of guilt, "Sadie is our maid. We were considering bringing her along to help with the kids but ..."

I interrupt her. "There is no need to explain. I do understand."

As I eat my meal, I think about race relations. Will blacks and whites ever get along? I start mentally counting the petals on the floral centerpiece until I am distracted by the couple from India.

"What is your name?"

"Mary."

"What is your profession?"

"I am a writer."

They look around at each other curiously. Their eyes widen as their foreheads lift showing fold lines across their frontal lobes. I could just imagine what they were thinking. Again the silence is deafening. I quickly complete my meal so that I could retreat to my special spot to write. I want nothing to distract me from my goal.

"Excuse me, please," I say as I stand to leave.

"Enjoy your morning." I chuckle to myself as I walk away. Just think about what their reactions would have been if I'd told them that I was a Speech and Language Pathologist!

THE EXODUS

Fifty days after Passover, the Feast of Weeks was celebrated. This annual feast is also called the "Feast of Harvest," "Day of First Fruits," and "Pentecost." The celebration commemorates the giving of the law. Again members of the temple from all over the country attended. Excitement filled the air.

Moses Israel's theme for this seven day celebration was the biblical statute "Working for Yahweh." He began.

"Israel, being God's chosen people, are forbidden to work for any other people or nation."

Initially, everyone sat back and listened as if this were just another history lesson, past tense; but it soon became apparent that it was a law that was to be implemented right now, present tense.

"Elder Elijah, Elder Boaz, Elder Samuel come down and stand before the congregation and openly declare your intentions to obey this law." They slowly come forth.

"Would you quit your jobs to work fulltime for Yahweh?"

They stuttered while attempting to justify their responses, but did not answer the question directly.

They began to look anxious. Wasn't this just a test of their faith and commitment I thought? Wasn't this just a teaching technique used to get them to search their souls while meditating on the significance of the law? Surely they understood this method of instruction. They were the college educated, middle class professionals.

"Ah ha," Moses Israel continued. "It is also a commandment that other nations cannot teach our children. They are to learn from books written by trained teachers from within our nation. The false Jews are practicing our law and are the most literate people on earth. My people this is our inheritance. What are you going to do?" he said in an exhausting tone.

There was silence throughout the building.

"What's the problem? How many of you would enroll your children in a school governed by God's laws?"

Many raised their hands.

"What certified teachers among you would quit your jobs to teach in such an institution?"

Very few hands were raised.

The rhetorical questions continued on and on and on.

The feast lasted for six more long days and nights and Moses Israel expounded more and more on this law and called more and more persons to the microphone. The tension was great. Attendance began to decrease. The absence of high ranking elders did not go unmentioned. Moses Israel openly ridiculed them.

"God will soon reject these hypocrites for trying to serve two masters. You can't serve Yahweh and mammon at the same time."

The congregation looked frightened. It was obvious that no one wanted to be called a hypocrite. Why? I wondered.

The exodus of the middle class from the temple had begun. Other members who did not have tangible possessions such as homes or property; neither job security nor tenure came forth and assertively stated that they, without reservation, would immediately begin working fulltime as disciples. Because they would live on temple properties they were to be called "house."

Moses Israel lauded their commitment as being "on fire for Yahweh."

"These faithful few are shining examples of strength and courage for all Israel to follow. I liken the group of hypocrites to the young man whom Jesus told to sell all of his worldly possessions and come follow Him. It is written that "it is easier for a camel to go through the eye of a needle, than for a rich man to enter into the kingdom of God."

"House" stood, cheered and chanted, "Praise Yahweh!" He continued to speak.

"For those of you who have come before us and openly declared that you will obey God's statute, I give you this scripture: "And every one that hath forsaken houses, or brethren, or sisters, or father, or mother, or wife, or children, or lands, for my name's sake, shall receive a hundredfold, and shall inherit everlasting life. But many that are first shall be last and the last shall be first."

As "house" jumped and shouted enthusiastically in the aisles, he ominously read this scripture.

"Whatsoever thou shall bind on earth shall be bound in heaven. Then charged his disciples that they should tell no man that he was the Christ."

Wow! Was there a subliminal suggestion in that quote? Was he purposefully identifying himself scripturally as the Christ? I wished that they would be quiet and stop jumping up and down. I wanted to think.

This great exodus of the middle class was a pivotal point for me. I'd been studying for six months and had been impressed by the professional people who attended classes and I'd looked forward to having many more intellectually stimulating discussions with them on our history. I wanted to work with them to help restore our people to a higher status. Now few of them remained. Even Ricky, was now "persona non grata." He and a select group, called "the executive board" had left under the continuous verbal pressure to quit their jobs and work exclusively for the temple.

Later it was obvious to me that this exodus had not been the desired effect of the lessons. Moses Israel appeared emotionally "stirred" by their departure. For weeks after the feast, he continued to refer to them in his lessons.

"Those who left are hypocrites and vipers. They're like the Pharisees and Sadducees of Jesus' day who wanted to retain their earthly positions under Roman rule, but when the coming rulership which I prophesy is come, they'll then want to share in the glory and receive credit for helping to restore the kingdom of Judah. But oh, there will be crying and gnashing of teeth in that great day. The hypocrites don't want to fulfill the law of Yahweh now if it means jeopardizing their hard earned posts under Pontius Pilate, aka President Reagan. They are unwilling to submit to the laws of God and to my being God's personal representative, but I am God's anointed messenger whether the hypocrites accept me or not."

Why is he taking this so personally, I wondered?

A few weeks later, a newspaper article appeared in the Miami Herald indicating that a former member had revealed a violation of the electrical code at the temple's building. Only one meter was being monitored for billing by the utilities company while another meter, which had been installed by an electrical worker of the temple, was in existence. This alleged disclosure infuriated Moses Israel, who reiterated, "This negative behavior of revealing information to the enemy is typical of Uncle Toms and is intolerable. The Jews and the Cubans always "stick together" to promote their better interests. We must do the same."

I became a little confused with this message because I wasn't sure that the emphasis was on unity and progress or on the concealment of information from authorities.

He continued to teach. "The ability to keep secrets, not only from the powers of principalities, but from each other, is to become a virtue among us," Moses Israel confirmed.

"Yahweh has revealed to me who the hypocrites are who remain among us but I'm not ready to disclose their names. Until they are identified, don't trust anyone but me."

As more of the professional class left, more of the underprivileged came. Such a contrast, I thought. The new group started verbally insulting the few professionals who remained.

"The higher you have gone in "Lucifer's school system" the more unlikely you are to conform to the laws of God. Ego and intellect are the problems," he taught repeatedly.

Did these lessons reflect Moses Israel's resentment of the college educated who had abandoned the temple? How could that be when he also earned post graduate degrees from state universities? I continued to listen.

"The exodus of the professional class is living proof of this. The "I" mentality has to be eliminated. If you suffer from this malady because of your education, you need your minds exorcised. This intellectual foolishness has to be purged from your system. You need to humble yourself to those members whom you thought were beneath your status and become submissive and meek."

"Praise Yahweh," echoed throughout the building.

"Regarding those professionals who left the temple, all power and authority has been given unto me to bind them on earth. So unless I release them, they cannot enter into the kingdom of God on earth in which I will preside as Shiloh, the gatherer of the people."

It didn't take long for the transition to be completed. The newly configured leadership was being placed in posts of authority, and like Pharaoh, they ruled with rigor. They were unyielding and apathetic when giving orders.

They intimidated others by using degrading or condescending remarks, and their body language was very disrespectful. These hard taskmasters were so unlike the polite, smiling members who I had first met. Their hearts quickly hardened even more as they pursued the chief seats in the synagogue.

As I continued to listen and observe, I noted a difference in the interpretation of scripture that he'd taught before. Initially those professionals who returned to Yahweh at the temple were the first fruits of the harvest. Now, that this group had gone, they were considered the last in the kingdom; and the last to come, the poor rejected underclass, were now considered the first. They rejoiced exceedingly and continued to prove

The Second Day: On the Sea

to Moses Israel that they were smarter and wiser than their predecessors, the disloyal educated professional class.

Several members of the professional class who remained eventually quit their jobs. I remembered Areille, a teacher. After resigning from the public school system she immediately began teaching at the temple's school which was then housed within the east wing of the building. She was a diligent, honest, faithful believer in the Word.

Months later she became very distraught. After class she asked me for a lift home because she'd missed her ride. Though she still lived in her home and retained the title to her property, other members could cohabitate on the premises. Also her car had been repainted and the temple's logo was etched on the doors. The supervisors now drove her vehicle.

As I drove, she solemnly confided in me. "At the recruitment meeting for new disciples, Judith announced that all of our needs would be taken care of. Everything would be perfect. I now realize that I've made a mistake. You have to request everything in writing, even for something as simple as a toothbrush which may be denied without explanation. I even have to request permission to leave the premises if it's not my scheduled time, and that, also can be denied without explanation."

I listened without commenting. She continued.

"No groceries are provided for me to take home to store in my refrigerator. So if I miss dinner at the temple's cafeteria, I have to wait until the next day to eat because only one meal per day is served and there are no snacks provided.

"Monies are not provided for anything extra. I'm becoming very weak physically. I have to work long hours for seven days a week without a break. I'm so very frustrated," she sighed.

Shortly thereafter Areille disappeared. It was rumored that she had a nervous breakdown and that her parents, who lived up north, had come for her. Months later I saw Areille at the teacher's credit union. She'd returned to Miami to resume her teaching position. She was pleasant but her words were very few and guarded. She seemed to no longer trust anyone who was associated with the temple in any way.

I smiled and greeted her. "Shalom, Areille. It's so good to see you. Will you be coming to class Wednesday night?"

She said cautiously, "My faith in God remains strong, but I do not want to continue my studies at the temple. I've decided to worship God in a church that makes fewer physical demands on its members. During my convalescence, I discovered that the kingdom of God is within me."

I wanted her to explain the revelation, but the teller indicated that she was ready to serve me. As Areille walked away, I pondered her statement. I didn't fully understand what she meant even though I'd heard the scriptural reference before; but I was destined to learn as I blindly continued my very academic and pedantic journey through the temple.

Later that next year, Moses Israel announced, "It is time to prepare to go forth and gather our people across the nation. The time is near and destruction is at our very doors."

The disciples interpreted the urgency of this message as the end time. Moses Israel's slogan became "Next Year Jerusalem." Those followers who were marginally committed but had not yet quit their jobs proudly did so. They wanted to be a part of the great ruling class. As they passed each other, they smiled and quoted this scripture: "The race is not given to the swift but to those who endure to the end. Praise Yahweh! The end is near."

A light came on in my mind. I perceived that Moses Israel needed a group of people unattached to the work force to conduct this mission. If you were working on a regular job, your time would be limited. A nationwide bus tour would last three months, more time than most people had accrued as vacation leave.

Aha! I could see the scenario more clearly. There had been a long range, dual purpose in his teachings. I felt that his goal was to attract those persons whose mentalities were predisposed to being dependent as fulltime workers while retaining the professional class at the temple for financial purposes. I was sure of my conclusion because I never heard him actually command the professional class to quit their jobs. He only asked them if they would. He'd just taught the biblical statute with authority.

I was intrigued by his communication skills as I watched his plan unfold. I began studying his teaching style. Moses Israel's ability to control and agitate minds to produce desired actions fascinated me, but I did not quit my job neither sell my house nor give up my individuality. I'd struggled too long to gain my freedom from Chico and was determined to never place myself in a position that I couldn't easily leave. I became an ardent student, rather than a "disciple" of the temple.

With the same energy that I had studied the works of Skinner and Piaget, the great behavioral scientists who were model teachers for psychology and education majors, I now studied Moses Israel's techniques. I wanted to learn personality dynamics to help me rear my children more effectively. I'd set my long range goals and focused my attention on my objectives. As I studied more, the exodus of the professional class, and the elevation of the new ruling class within the temple, became less important. I continued to learn by observing their unusual behavior.

CRIMESTOPPERS

At each class Moses Israel taught a little more about our "biblical" history.

"The Torah or the first five books of the Bible contains the laws, statutes, judgments and commandments that Hebrews are to follow. There are six hundred thirteen perfect laws which relate to every aspect of our lives. If understood and practiced we will become more united and prosperous as a people. All nations of people, the Japanese and the Jews in particular, are following these laws and their prosperity and collectivism are visible signs that the principles work. But remember, these laws were given to our forefathers, for those of us alive this day," he stressed.

"The justice systems of the United States and of most nations are still based on the structure of laws and statutes given to Moses at Mount Sinai. An analogy of the three branches of the U.S. government can be easily recognized within the scriptures. However, because the true righteous rulers are not in power, the laws are flexible. They're bent whenever necessary to protect the rich and special interest groups. Therefore, the present system should be called the "Criminal Injustice System. The Bible teaches one law for all."

He paused and slowly paced back and forth on the podium.

"You are to carefully and diligently study the Torah. As a law is learned, you are to consciously incorporate it in every aspect of your lives immediately. This habitual practice will ensure that as time progresses, the laws will become indelibly etched in your inward parts. Our goal is to become righteous rulers."

"Praise Yahweh!" they chanted repeatedly.

I knew that rulership, in the context that he taught, should begin from within first. However, most of the disciples, as overheard in their conversations, had made rulership over others their first priority. I could hardly distinguish their actions from those of harsh, duty oriented employers.

But I dove into my studies with full force and enthusiasm. I wanted to learn the laws so that I could practice them daily. I considered them my personal prescription for health and success. I worked with many Jewish teachers, taught many Jewish students and interacted with many Jewish parents. I admired their sense of purpose and global unity. I wanted to model their behavior because though they were reviled, they were the most literate and successful people on earth.

Since I didn't attend Morning Prayer, I was often behind in my lessons because there were no study guides or checklists available to determine which laws had been discussed after prayer.

In the nightly class, Moses Israel explained that, "Some laws are not to be enforced until our people are in total power. Those laws could be identified in scriptures that read "in that day." However this law is to become effective immediately. Leviticus 5:1 reads: "If any one sin in that he is sworn to testify and has knowledge of the matter, either by seeing or hearing of it, but fails to report it, then he shall bear his iniquity and willfulness."

The explanation of this law put fear into the souls of many disciples. Moses Israel stated, "You are duty bound to report any suspicious actions. You do not have to be absolutely sure of the intent or the behavior observed. I will be the judge of that. All that you have to do is report it and your identity will be protected. You will remain anonymous. It's so simple. Just write down your observations or the bits of conversations that you overhear and slip the note underneath my office door. By obeying this law you would escape the penalty for disobedience and would also be protecting the nation from conspirators, spies and infiltrators."

I thought, "Was there going to be a diligent inquiry about the matters reported? Would the accused have a chance to confront their accuser? Or what about going to your brother or sister first to get the facts of the matter straight before misjudging their actions?" I didn't like the sound of this law, especially if it would be implemented as stated, "In this day," as opposed to "in that day."

Moses Israel continued. "The story of how the government and the FBI, under the leadership of J. Edgar Hoover, had used "wolves in sheep's clothing" to infiltrate the Black Panthers should never be forgotten. There is justification for this law to be put into effect immediately. Your only true friend is Yahweh and I am His anointed messenger. Only trust me."

This practice soon turned brother against father, sister against mother, family against family and disciples against followers, believers and supporters. Everyone became suspicious of everyone.

Though the temple's motto was "One God, One Mind, One Love, and One Action," it was in theory only. Unity was taught openly, but division apparently was secretly practiced. Would the temple stand? This house was surely becoming divided.

As I studied, a scripture which I'd never read before captured my attention. "If a ruler hearkens to lies, all his servants are wicked. The poor and the deceitful man meet together: the Lord lightens both their eyes." I began to have mixed feelings about continuing my studies at the temple.

One day while at work, I started debating within myself whether or not to continue attending classes when I looked at a sign posted over a secretary's computer. It read: "I really don't want to be here but I hang around just to see what happens next." That sign reflected my attitude. I laughed.

Later that night as I kept pondering my decision, the words on that sign dominated my thoughts. What did that expression have to do with the temple? I rationalized that though I was no longer as intrigued with the position that the temple was assuming, I was not quite sure that Armageddon wasn't going to happen overnight, or in a twinkling of an eye. Hal Lindsey and Herbert W. Armstrong were constantly predicting the signs of the end time on their weekly television programs. I wanted to play it safe for the kids' sake, so I decided to "hang around just to see what happened next."

As time progressed, I decided to assist the mothers who had to distribute literature nightly. I noticed how very tired they appeared, and their children did not look tidy or well groomed. I identified with their plight, having worked two jobs when my kids were in nursery, preschool and kindergarten. I volunteered my services after work to baby-sit hoping to change my image of being a "snob."

After adjusting to the routine and getting the babies settled, I would just walk around the area and pick up paper or straighten out the tables and chairs. At that time the temple was the main building operated by the group, so all of the printing, proofing, and packaging was done at this site. Scraps of paper were crumpled on the floors and tables.

One night as I tidied up, I picked up two pieces of paper that were neatly folded. I read the contents to determine if I should throw them away or save them. I was shocked at their contents. They were logs of dates, times, and names of people who were seen talking at their work posts. Excerpts of the conversations were written as were brief descriptions of the setting. Disciples were smiling in each other's faces while secretly recording information that would be used against them. What was the motive?

The Second Day: On the Sea

Would the informers be promoted to higher posts? I thought, "Where is the trust, the unity and the friendship?"

CAUTION! CAUTION! That ever present yellow sign began flashing before me; when would I heed the warning? What were my choices? If I severed my ties with the temple I faced Chico's re-invigorated wrath and harassment and the disciples' scorn; my neighbors would continue to gossip and my coworkers would still not embrace me. Since the legal system had proven that it would not protect me either, I decided to stay.

PASSING THE WORD

Initially, attending the temple did not conflict with my attitudes about wearing ethnic attire, long dresses with turbans or doing door - to - door field service such as the Jehovah's Witnesses. At that time, the temple's dress code was explained as a symbol of cultural awareness only and followers wore traditional African garments to class. Because the first members had been professional persons who contributed their tithes and offering, field service was not a requirement but a gesture of faith and commitment. So, my level of involvement did not dictate that I change my attitude, attire or any practices.

Those followers of the temple who later committed themselves as full time disciples were soon obligated to "pass the word" daily, but I continued to do my part by purchasing their personal care products, and giving a donation for the literature. I had no desire to walk the streets at night or to knock on doors.

After attending classes for nearly two years, Moses Israel announced, "It is time to harvest our people on a national scale. The temple will go on its first nationwide summer tour that will involve passing Yahweh's message in twenty-five major cities on the east coast of the United States. Those members who are followers, believers and supporters, are invited to participate if your schedules permit. You will not be obligated to spend the entire three months on tour. Any portion of time that you assist will be sufficient and Yahweh will reward your works."

I thought that this would be an excellent opportunity for me to go and see how expansive the movement was nationally. It would also be an opportunity for my children to travel across the country as I had done as a child on the trains.

However there was one requirement that escaped my attention in the excitement surrounding the announcement. All participants who traveled on the tour would be required to wear the long, all white cultural garments that would easily identify them as members of the temple as they knocked on doors to distribute literature. With this news, I purchased a few garments from the temple's boutique for us to wear on the trip.

The summer's itinerary included the twenty-five major cities on the east coast of the United States where the majority of African American people were reportedly concentrated. Explicit rules of conduct were discussed in the classes that led up to our departure.

"Your responsibility as sheep is to go out and "pass the word" while testifying that the Black people of America are the tribe of Judah that was captured and brought here over four hundred years ago, and that our true history, culture, land, language and God can be found in the Old Testament Bible," Moses Israel instructed.

"Wisdom cries without, in the city she utters her words saying, "How long you simple ones will you love simplicity? And the scorners delight in their scorning, and fools hate knowledge?" This scripture is the basis for your actions as you go out among our people. It is called traffic light wisdom. There are some people to approach. You are to "**go**" to them; and others to avoid, you are to "**stop**." Do not approach them. Be cautious and you will be able to discern the difference."

"Be strong while doing this noble work. You will encounter three types of personalities: the simple, the scorner and the fool. Discern and identify who they are by their words and actions. Only the simple ones are to be approached. They will be open and receptive to the message. Remember that all of the words of the testimony are mathematically formulated to attract the elect."

I reflected on a woman in Dallas, Texas who appeared to be open and receptive to the testimony that we are Hebrew Israelites. She listened respectfully as I cordially invited her to come to the convention center to see and hear Moses Israel on Saturday night. Suddenly she became enraged and quoted this scripture: "No man knows the hour that the messiah cometh." "Now you are telling me that he is going to be downtown tomorrow at 5:00 p.m. If you don't get off of my porch immediately, I'm going to get my broom and chase you away." As I turned and walked away, the caution light that I repeatedly ignored began to flash again.

As the word was passed in each city, the simple ones were invited to attend Moses Israel's lecture at the end of the week. His theme in each city was "The Good Shepherd."

He taught: "I am that one prophesied to come and preach good tidings that will set the captives free. I am the potentate's potentate that the masons and all of those in the secret orders are anxiously awaiting. The porter is symbolic of the doorkeeper who guards the lodge against eavesdroppers and the profane. I am the one who the fraternal orders had been worshipping secretly. Now I have arrived to reveal to them the esoteric meanings behind their well guarded teachings and I am ready to reward those masons who can adequately defend their knowledge when "called on the square" and questioned by me. Who is ready to return to the fold tonight?"

The crowd cheered as those accepting this testimony came forth to affiliate. At the end of the program, the group boarded the busses and proceeded to the next city. This daily charge to gather the simple ones continued for three months.

At the end of each day, the group assembled around Moses Israel to make comments about their experiences. I was very surprised to hear all of the positive responses. I listened but said nothing. I was tired. This was hard work for me. I got up at six in the morning, dressed, boarded the bus and was at the drop off point by 9:00 a.m. I walked all day knocking on doors, testifying and handing out literature. I had to knock on each door on the block, street after street after street. I didn't have anything to drink so I looked for the closest McDonald's, Burger King or Wendy's as a place to "refuel." Pick up time was always at 9:00 p.m. and the pickup point always seemed to be miles away.

After I returned from the field each night, I stood in long lines to report my earnings for that day. I didn't want to appear privileged. Though I had given Judith a donation earmarked for the tour before we left Miami, I worked very hard to attain the daily quota.

Those disciples who had not made their financial quotas were denied dinner. Instead they were told to "pray" all night long for tomorrow's success. Initially, I was not aware of this "no dinner - prayer" policy. I was so tired at the end of the day that I didn't care about who was not at dinner. Getting off of my feet and going to sleep was my concern. Anyway, I had brought an extra suitcase filled with packets of trail mix for me and the kids to eat; and I had my credit card in my wallet.

When I discovered what was going on, I shared my snacks with some disciples who were obviously hungry. They were easy to identify because they were losing weight quickly. On days when it was difficult for everyone on the team, the kids and I would share the extra money we collected with the disciples as they quickly counted their intake on the bus as we returned to the base.

Even though I was friendly and helpful, I found that most of the sisters were not appreciative of my generosity. Envy led them to gossip, which I attempted to ignore. They conjured up so many false tales of lustful encounters between me and every brother that I was observed talking to that I stopped having what I enjoyed most, spirited discussions. Why were their minds so bent on sex? Weren't we supposed to be doing a spiritual work?

I wondered more and more about the women's relationship with Moses Israel by observing their conspicuous behavior. Supervisors would circulate among the group and ask certain women if they were clean that night. This frequently happened when Judith flew back to Miami to take care of business. The sisters who were not menstruating soon disappeared. When I saw them later they had a different aura, or did I have an overactive imagination?

I tried to stay focused on my purpose for being with the group by concentrating on my children. They enjoyed the countryside. As a child, I had traveled this route many summers on the Florida East Coast Railroad's Silver Meteor. My mom worked for the railroad, so we always got free passes or reduced fares. My sister Pearl, my brother Bennie and I traveled every summer. Being familiar with the itinerary, I taught them geography and pointed out historic sites and discussed relevant state history. I was a "natural - born teacher" who saw a lesson in everything.

It became obvious later that I lived in a world separate from the others on the tour. They complained all of the time. I likened them to the children of Israel in the wilderness. They began to gossip, lie and steal from each other; beg for food in the streets and at the homes of strangers; and could be overheard at night plotting on how to use the information taught by Moses Israel to identify men and woman associated with secret fraternal orders such as Elks, Shriners, Masons and Eastern Stars to collect more funds.

As weeks passed, some disciples reported more highly exaggerated stories of how everyone they encountered was open and receptive to the teachings of Moses Israel. I thought that they were trying to impress him. Did we not "pass the word" and recite the testimony in the same neighborhoods? Did I not hear their cries of frustration as they boarded the bus at night? I realized how much pressure the disciples were under; they, like priests and nuns, had taken vows of poverty and had given up their personal freedoms. Now they were frustrated when they had to comply with all orders dictated.

The disciples were also impatient because they had misinterpreted Moses Israel's slogan, "Next Year Jerusalem" as an immediate calendar event. They thought that everything would be glorious and their reward was just around the corner. I empathized with them, but I knew then that unless I saw New Jerusalem actually descending, that I would not become a disciple. I valued my freedom.

With less than three weeks and five cities to go, I couldn't wait to return home to the privacy of my sanctuary. I yearned for "Home Sweet Home!"

However, when I returned to Miami, to what appeared to be an abandoned house, because my lawn had not been cared for, I had to contend with another round of gossip. Some neighbors decided to spread the word that I had given my house to the temple and run off with "that man." I began to wonder if they were happy or just pretended to be.

WEARING WHITE

In spite of the disciples' grumblings after realizing that there was more work to be done in the kingdom before the end of time, I'd returned from the summer tour feeling proud that I'd been part of an adventure which would later have historic prominence. I'd helped to plant the seeds that would eventually wake up our people who were still "walking in darkness." I'd likened myself to the civil rights marchers in the 1960's. It had been a most unusual experience, yet my pride and enthusiasm was at an all-time high. Armed with the scriptural knowledge of who we, the former slaves were as a biblical people, and what our ultimate destiny was gave me a sense of pride. I felt strong and walked with my head held high. I was more positive and assertive in my personal and professional life.

Life was full of hope and promise. Friends who noted a difference in my attitude attributed it to my finally recovering from the divorce but that was only partly true. It was the knowledge of self that inspired me. I couldn't wait to attend another class.

Moses Israel began his next class by saying, "It is now time for every one of us who believe in our great, good and terrible Black God to wear our righteous white robes at all times. We must identify with our God for there are lords and gods many. It will be a sign for the world to prepare for the second coming of the Son of God in the clouds."

After pausing to let his words settle in our minds, he said, "I am the anointed of God, chosen to set the captives free." He paused again and looked out at the congregation. There was silence. I wondered, "What is he going to say next to shock us." I'd been studying his body language and noted that whenever he paused and stared at the congregation for more than a few minutes, he revealed a little bit more about his identity.

He returned to the microphone and asked, "If a father's name is Smith, what will his son's name be?"

Everyone shouted, "Smith!"

"If a father's name is Johnson, what will his son's name be?"

"Johnson" was heard echoing throughout the building.

"Well if I say that I am the son of God, and that God is my father and God's name is Yahweh then what is my name?"

"Yahweh! Yahweh!" they screamed and shouted as if a great secret had been revealed.

I was thinking that's a perfect syllogism, good deductive reasoning. Did Moses Israel actually say that he was "THE" Son of God? No, he just planted the seed in the congregation's mind. Boy was he a great teacher, I thought.

Later, after the group settled down, Moses Israel defined "clouds" as being a mass of people adorned in white robes.

"The chosen people of God, the elect are to wear white robes as a sign for the entire world to see that the end of this present order of government is near. The world won't be destroyed; the current ruling class will have to acquiesce to me."

I understood the message but I wasn't ready to "go public," not here in Miami at least. It was fine on tour in New York, Memphis, Washington, D.C., Chicago, Detroit, Cleveland, Houston, Dallas, Birmingham, Arkansas and Atlanta. I wasn't known to anyone in those cities. I wouldn't be able to handle the pressure in my own home town. It would just stir up more gossip.

Many disciples began wearing all white garments immediately. It had become a symbol that they were more devout than those believers and followers who did not. Moses Israel began praising them for their strength and courage in making that choice.

His praise was a sign of approval which caused them to behave in a more self-righteous and arrogant manner toward those who did not conform to this biblical statute in a timely manner.

Moses Israel began to ridicule and tease members, particularly women, who continued to wear their hair permed or for wearing "dead clothing," which was shorter, European designed styles. These women were called "Eve," the mother of the wicked ones. I remembered how he had criticized the professional class for weeks until many of them left or conformed to his teachings. But I understood his tactics and thought that I wouldn't fall victim to the pressure.

I saw a pattern in his techniques to persuade his disciples to conform to biblical laws without him actually saying, "Do this or do that." He always made it appear that you chose to act because of your righteous desire to do the will of God.

Initially, I wasn't affected by their behavior or his rhetoric. I didn't think that the outer apparel was an indicator of the inner sincerity. Then he taught the scripture that alluded to believers of the word who were ashamed of the Son of God, that the Son of Man would also be ashamed to confess their names to the Father.

Well, that scripture was worth studying. I wanted to do everything right so that God would answer my prayers for healing. My heart rate increased as my mind became agitated. I put my brain into high gear and thought of a way to compromise. That was it! The Great Compromise! Yes, I'd wear white to the temple for classes to demonstrate my unity and I'd continue to wear my "dead clothes" everywhere else, especially to work.

Being a very good seamstress, I purchased fabric and made white garments for my family. I selected Vogue patterns and made the dress as designed. Then I made a matching longer skirt to wear underneath. Now, I was completely at peace. Not only did I have a fashionable cultural garment, but all I had to do was to remove the longer skirt and I had a beautiful shorter garment to wear for other occasions.

I smiled as I modeled my new wardrobe, but little did I realize then how the subliminal clues that were being planted deeply within my subconscious mind by Moses Israel would actively control my future behavior.

One night he taught: "After this I beheld, and, lo, a great multitude, which no man could number stood before the throne, and before the Lamb, clothed with white robes. These are they which came out of great tribulation, and have washed their robes, and made them white in the blood of the Lamb. For the Lamb which is in the midst of the throne shall feed them, and shall lead them unto living fountains of waters: and God shall wipe away all tears from their eyes."

He turned to Judith and said, "Affiliated temples across the country are to be notified that "headquarters," the Miami Temple, is accepting persons who want to transfer here to become fulltime workers. The harvest is ripe but the laborers have been few."

"Additional members are needed here to accomplish greater works. It is time to let the world know that "Judah" has awakened and is preparing for rulership. "The scepter shall not depart from Judah, or a lawgiver from between his feet, until Shiloh comes; and unto him shall the gathering of the people be."

"Did I gather our people this summer?" he asked proudly.

"Yes," responded the group cheerfully.

"Then who am I?" "Shiloh!" they screamed.

"And you are those spoken of in the book of Revelations as being clothed in white robes. This scripture is not to be interpreted symbolically but literally. So from this day on disciples are ordered to discard all of their colorful clothing. Only white robes are to be ever worn again. Everywhere we go we are to be dressed in white. The end is nigh."

"Praise Yahweh," they chanted repeatedly.

As I looked around, I sensed mixed emotions though nearly everyone stood and cheered. Since I was not a disciple I didn't feel compelled to comply with this statute. Therefore, I continued as planned until I overheard a conversation by two Black teachers in the faculty lounge at Myrtle Grove Elementary, one of the four schools that I serviced that year. They were negatively talking about the idea of being the chosen people.

"Honey I am so tired of those people from the temple knocking on my door trying to convince me that Black people are the true Jews. What difference does it make? We don't have any money or power."

"Yeah, my preacher told us that we are the children of Ham and that we are cursed because Ham looked at Noah's nakedness. There isn't anything we can do about our color and condition."

"That's right. They believe what that man is telling them. They need to leave people alone before they stir up trouble like the Black Panthers and the Black Muslims did. White people will never let us rule over them."

"I got better things to do than to listen to their foolishness."

"They're getting to be as worrisome as the Jehovah's Witnesses."

"Makes you not want to open your door on the weekends."

"Huh."

I just sat there and said nothing in defense, conveyed no light on their interpretation nor voiced my opinion. I felt like a hypocrite. How could I not even identify with the group? Was I ashamed? That scripture of being ashamed to confess the Son now resounded within my mind. Was I ashamed to be linked to the name of God and to the people who proclaimed that name?

I had to solve this conflict for myself. Remembering that for too long I'd been perceived as passive, the next day, as I went to another school, I wore a white garment to determine if I could withstand the scrutiny. If I could not then it would mean that this belief system that I was embracing was not for me. I knew that anything that you felt good about within your soul shouldn't cause you distress.

I walked boldly into Skyway Elementary School and as I passed groups of teachers and students I could feel their surprise, dismay, anger, hatred and disbelief. Body language and facial expressions often speak louder than words. It was tough for me to do this but I kept my head up and continued to speak kindly to all. As I went about my day, I began to feel good about my actions. I'd basically proven that I was not ashamed and that was good enough. I would not wear the white garments to work again. I had accomplished my goal and objective.

However, near the end of the day, the principal, Mrs. Wilson, reacted unfavorably. I could tell by her facial expression and body language that she disapproved. I said nothing as I passed her.

Later that week, I was called by an acquaintance who was a local elementary school principal.

"Mary, you were the hot topic of discussion at our administrator's meeting yesterday. Wilson stated that a member of the Yahweh cult wore white from head to toe at her school and frightened the children. Be careful of your actions because you are going to be monitored daily by covert means at all of your schools. The time that you arrive; the time that you leave one school and arrive at the other; and the time that you leave that school at the end of the day will be recorded. Whenever you speak with someone, one-on-one, that person will be questioned to determine if you were proselytizing or distributing literature. The public address system in the rooms where you conduct therapy will be randomly activated so that what you say to your students can be overheard and possibly recorded in the office. Don't ever tell anyone that I warned you."

"Thanks, I won't."

Later as the word spread throughout the school system that I had worn the white garment, several other teachers contacted me with similar warnings. I was convinced that I was indeed under surveillance and could clearly see how I was being observed and documented for possible dismissal if I violated any school board policies.

An incident later occurred at Wilson's school that forced me to take a stand. The head custodian, Mr. Cox was an aspiring minister. I'd known him for a number of years. We'd worked together at Norland Middle School. One day he approached me and said, "I've been taking classes at the community college and would appreciate it if you could help me with my diction and pronunciation."

"I'd be glad to help. I'll bring you some materials the next time I come to this school. Call me tonight and remind me to put them in my trunk. Here is my number."

"Thanks!"

The following week, he approached me. "Did you remember to bring the lessons?"

"Yes! Walk with me to the car." I opened the trunk and handed him the books and briefly flipped through the pages to emphasize the lessons that I'd highlighted."

"This is great. It's just what I needed."

"You're welcome. I'll come to hear you preach your first sermon."

We both laughed. I got in the car and drove off. He returned to the building with the books.

The next week, as I entered the building, he pulled me to the side and whispered.

"Wilson questioned me about what you gave me out of your car. Someone told her that they saw you selling products. She wanted to know if you were distributing temple literature. She seemed disappointed when I showed her the textbooks. Be careful, she's not pleased about you wearing white to school."

"Thanks for warning me."

I knew that I would have to confront her. I waited until noon, went into the main office and asked her secretary if she was available. Wilson overheard me and yelled, "Sure come on in." She was eating her lunch. As I approached her desk, I began to speak.

"Mrs. Wilson, You have not conducted a formal observation of my performance yet and I know that you were displeased with the Speech Pathologist who serviced your school in the past. Do you have any concerns about my program?"

"No, the teachers say that you regularly pick up your students on time and it seems that the kids are eager to go to therapy."

"I'm happy to hear that you are pleased with me professionally." She smiled then took a bite of her chicken. "Then why are you probing and questioning everyone that I talk to about the topic of my conversations? Do you think that I would discuss anything personal with your faculty or staff?"

She stopped chewing and looked at me as if she was surprised by my change in tone and attitude. I continued.

"When I see you, I see a principal, a mother, a woman, a daughter and someone's wife and friend. I'm sure that you behave differently in each role. Don't you think that I am capable of doing the same? I know how to separate my personal life from my professional life."

She gestured as if she wanted to interject, but I quickly turned to leave.

"If you ever have any complaints about my work, please let me know and I will quickly satisfy any requirement that is in need of improvement. Thank you. Have a great day." I felt great as I walked away.

I mentally reversed my fear of being fired and used the positive energy as an opportunity to demonstrate my proficiency. I didn't like being the center of attention, but I had to put back on my "white garments" to demonstrate that I had no fear. I could not turn back now even if I wanted too. I was no longer "undercover" as some of the believers and supporters were who never wore white to work or in public. Some of them were so careful that they changed into their "temple white" only after they were within the confines of the building.

I smiled as I wondered what Wilson would do if she knew that her sorority sister, Renee Allen, the educational placement specialist who she enthusiastically greeted as a member of the school's multidisciplinary team and who sat at the same conference table with me during exceptional student education staffings, also regularly attended classes at the temple. Renee, whose temple name was Torah Esther, was more involved than I was. She was a part of the inner circle that got to go behind the "heavily guarded" double doors. In fact she was studying to become a midwife and had actually aided in a few deliveries. Because she never wore "white" publicly, she was protected from the negative scrutiny and criticism that I was experiencing.

I respected her privacy and didn't reveal her secret to coworkers or the district staff. However, I soon began to resent her because she would share gossipy tidbits of information that I was not privy to about the temple or about Moses Israel to some of her friends, who then openly discussed it in the teachers' lounges in various schools.

Because Renee and I were initially very close and we serviced many of the same schools, most people thought that I was providing her with this "firsthand knowledge." In reality it was the opposite; but because Renee was "undercover," I had to deal with their scornful stares and ostracism because I'd personally revealed my association with the group by wearing white and would forever be identified as the "Yahweh teacher."

An incident occurred that was so negative that it created a stir at Rainbow Park Elementary where we both worked that the district office removed me from the school when in actuality it was Renee and Jackie Rawles, a special education teacher, who were the culprits. I stopped speaking to Renee as a result of that situation and for other incidents where I found her to be selfish and arrogant; but I continued to keep her secret because I also recognized that she didn't have the strength of character to withstand the criticism that I withstood daily. She continued to be welcomed with "open arms" by principals and staff who never once suspected her involvement or association with the temple.

However, during the next two years, Wilson was respectful and began to greet me with a smile as I passed her in the building. I returned the gesture but never let down my guard. I was surprised however when a staff member asked, "Would you like to purchase a ticket to go to the Ebony Fashion Fair?"

"Are you a member of Alpha Kappa Alpha Sorority?" I inquired. This group sponsored the annual event.

"No, Wilson is. I'm selling the tickets for her."

"Really! She's selling tickets on school property!" I suddenly had an idea that would surely create more gossip about me at the school.

"Yes, I'll buy three tickets. One of my daughters is attending modeling school at Barbizon in Coral Gables and the other one goes to Claudette Barrett's "Hot Gossip Modeling School" in Carol City. I'd like to take them to this event." I took out my checkbook and wrote in the amount and handed her the check.

"Thank you!" she said as if she was surprised.

The next week, Ann Gilbert a kindergarten teacher, beckoned me to her area and said, "It's all over the school that you have control over your own money so you must be one of the "elite" members of the temple." I smiled knowing that that would be their response.

I started wearing regular colorful clothing to work when their fears were allayed and school administrators, teachers, students and particularly parents began to respect me for my good work and professionalism. Some teachers, who were always curious about the temple's doctrine, now felt it easier to approach me. As they asked questions, I quickly changed the subject. I never ever discussed my personal or religious beliefs with anyone at work.

Periodically, I'd wear white clothing to give people something to talk about. They needed it, but all was well within me. I'd taken a stand for what I believed in which was my constitutional right, and that made me happy. I felt strong.

I continued to attend bible classes at the temple, but now I felt estranged from both groups. The disciples doubted my sincerity while coworkers questioned my sanity. I quickly learned how to be in the world yet not of their worlds.

BLACK ON WHITE

Class started promptly at 8:00 p.m. I was seated and ready to take notes. Moses Israel began to speak. "Still experiencing the negative effects of over four hundred years of slavery in America, it is easy for many African Americans to continue to believe that white people are practicing racism covertly in spite of the changes in the laws. The civil rights marches during the 1960s and the Arthur McDuffie murder which triggered the Miami riots in the 1980s are signs that our people cannot trust the present system of "injustice."

"The Constitution of the United States was composed when African Americans were enslaved therefore; the "we" in "we" the people" did not refer to Coloreds, Negroes, Blacks or Afro-Americans." Everyone chuckled because of the many adjectives used to refer to our people.

"At that time slaves were considered as property and therefore without any legal rights. The Three-Fifths Compromise was not for the slaves benefit either. The "WHOLE" in "whole free persons" let us know that only for taxation and representation purposes were slaves even considered as people, but not "whole or free." The Civil Rights Bill has expired, and we're about to lose all governmental imposed quotas that were suppose to rectify the inequities of the past. African Americans are still sharecroppers and tenants rather than landlords. We are not property owners."

The crowd stood nodding in agreement.

"You may be seated."

He continued to expound. "The Brown vs. The Board of Education Supreme Court decision did not solve the educational dilemma either. Our schools are still inadequately funded and staffed. We continue to receive inferior or used textbooks and out-dated equipment. The busing of our children to achieve desegregation and integration has torn the country apart."

"African Americans are now able to see "who is who" among white people without their being cloaked in long white robes with hoods covering their faces. Racial hatred is overt to those who can see."

"It is not just rhetoric when the Black community hears and responds to my voice in the wilderness of North America. What we hear is a brother's cry for justice and his desire to help solve the social, economic, spiritual, educational and political problems that plague our people. A disenfranchised people will continue to seek and strive for equal rights regardless of past setbacks and obvious failures. When one plan fails another is devised and implemented. I have come with an infallible plan of action."

As the congregation stood and cheered. I thought about his words. Did they mean that everyone who came to the temple only responded to his "white people are intrinsically unfair, unjust and cruel" theme? That couldn't have been the case. I felt that those among the group, who were already negatively oriented towards hate in general, were the ones who distorted the true motivation, drive, efforts and positive works of the faithful few who wanted to help elevate the minds and improve the conditions of our people.

Assisting our people first was our primary focus. So we responded to the information within the scriptures that helped validate our national and spiritual identities. As a people, we have always searched for our roots and what greater literary source could there be but the Holy Bible. That void was being filled at the temple.

Personally, I reflected on the scripture in the book of Genesis where Yahweh was going to destroy Sodom and Gomorrah. Abraham pleaded with God to not kill all of its inhabitants. God compromised. If Abraham could find just one righteous man, the whole city would be saved. Well, I knew one white person Bob Grasso, a speech pathologist, who is my friend. It is because of him that I could not group all whites together as insensitive and wicked. Without just and honest white people like him, the Underground Railroad would not have been a success. Bob was the one bright light in my life that kept me from hating. I valued his friendship.

However, those of us who persevered and held steadfast to the vision of unity and economic empowerment among our people were continually experiencing forms of prejudice, injustice, inequality disenfranchisement, educational and social class harassment from the very people we were diligently striving to help, Black people.

The self-hatred that existed within the temple was a reflection of what was going on in the minds of our people within the community at large. Friends and relatives denounced us, coworkers shunned us, supervisors misjudged us, neighbors talked about us, other religious groups ridiculed us, and some members within the temple considered us to be passive, thus weak.

I refocused and continued to listen to the lecture.

"Lucifer, the devil, was originally a black-skinned man as were all people in the beginning of civilization. Eve, the mother of all the wicked ones deceived Adam after having sexual intercourse with the serpent Lucifer. Cain resulted from that relationship. The biblical genealogy in the book of Genesis is proof because Cain is not listed as a son of God. So whose son was he?" He paused and scanned the crowd then said, "He was the son of Lucifer!"

"Cain's jealousy toward Abel resulted in Abel's murder. Cain's lethal motives were fueled by his desire to ensure his inheritance, as the first born, to rule the world. Upon Abel's death, God cast a mark, called leprosy, on Cain as a sign for the entire world to easily identify him. Cain left Eden and journeyed to the land of Nod where he found a wife and married. Their children are the white race today. Their race was given 6,000 years to rule. They are now living on borrowed time."

Cheering erupted!

"The year 2000, which will definitely be their end, is termed an "odyssey" because white people wouldn't be able to predict their future after then. African-Americans, represented biblically as Abel, however, will be preparing for righteous rulership as white people's dominion diminishes. All African-Americans who are joined onto his system are to be destroyed."

This lecture is why some members totally detached themselves from the world outside of the temple while others quit their jobs so that they could not be traced by their social security numbers. Others stopped registering their children's birth with the Bureau of Vital Statistics. But some mothers at the temple continued to receive welfare and public assistance. I thought that this was a contradiction in the doctrine of independence and self-sufficiency. Surely they couldn't officially use their Hebrew names when applying for aid.

To my dismay an HRS social worker appeared at my door early one morning asking for a woman whom I didn't know. Supposedly, this person described as wearing an Afro hairdo lived at my address. The name used was not Hebrew, but the description fit that of a typical female disciple who had taken off her turban and white garments.

Without our permission, Judith had begun issuing the addresses of supporters and believers as references for mothers on welfare. I quickly confronted her and demanded that she stop using my address. I didn't want to be a part of any deception, black or white.

DISCIPLESHIP

After I had begun to wear white daily to work and to the temple, the subject of discipleship was echoed again. There was a need for more laborers. The Temple was now receiving positive reports in the newspaper. One headline in the Miami Herald read: ***"Yahweh's Worth Twenty Million Dollars!"*** The Temple had acquired numerous buildings, apartment complexes, motels on the famed Biscayne Boulevard and had opened grocery stores in the community. The Chamber of Commerce was now showing interest in its enterprises and businesses and political leaders were calling for private meetings with Moses Israel.

The local Urban League even voted Moses Israel the recipient of their Economic Empowerment Trophy at their annual awards banquet. And if that could be topped, Moses Israel was featured on the Michael Putney Sunday morning talk show on local network television. Everyone, disciples, believers and supporters were happy for the acclaim and the respect that it brought. We felt vindicated for our hard work. I too was very proud. It was in this euphoric mood that Judith approached me about becoming a disciple.

"Mary Ilana, have you recently thought of becoming a disciple?"

"Sure I have."

"Then why don't you? It's obvious that you are a true believer and supporter."

"Well I would have a difficult time being held accountable for every move that I make. I like being free and spontaneous. Your lifestyle would be too restricting," I said with a smile.

"Oh, you wouldn't have a problem with that. You see, you are self-driven and highly motivated; the others are not. We require them to report their whereabouts to help them develop self discipline. You don't need that. Plus I could use you on my staff. You are a professional and it's obvious that you can conduct business. I need someone I can trust with money to help me purchase supplies."

"Thank you, but I wouldn't fit in. I'm too reclusive."

"I realize that, but we can work things out. Give it some thought."

Yes, I thought about Shalisha, Toellette and Hadahsah who were skilled professionals with college degrees. They possessed class, grace and charm and were very independent and successful in their endeavors prior to becoming disciples. Like Areille, they too thought that they would be privileged after becoming fulltime workers. Now they discussed their frustrations with me. Shalisha's "tales of woe" were particularly poignant.

One class night Moses Israel announced that he would begin teaching a new series on "How to become an Entrepreneur" at 5:00 a.m. to accommodate supporters and believers who had to go to work. I attended and often stayed for Morning Prayer which began daily at 6:00 a.m. One morning, after the scriptures were read, personal supplies were distributed to all disciples. I was seated next to Shalisha. As her team was called forth to receive their monthly rations, I watched her carefully. When she returned, tears rolled down her cheeks.

"Look at these things Mary Ilana. Every month I have to put in a request for more panties. These things tear up after the first wash. Look at these plastic shoes. You would think that Judith would buy better and softer shoes for us being that we have to stand and walk so much. Look at my feet. I've never had calluses, corns and bunions before. Hell I need a pumice stone to scrape away the dry skin. I couldn't get one, so one day when I was so disgusted, I picked up a rough rock from the street to scrub the soles of my feet. Hell, I need a pedicure," she lamented.

I looked at her compassionately. She continued.

"I've forgotten how toothpaste tastes and how deodorant smells. All we get is this: alcohol, mineral oil, a bar of soap, baking soda and a box of twelve sanitary pads. God forbid if I have a heavy menstrual flow and have to change my pads more than twice a day. Girl, don't give up your job and become a disciple. I love working for the cause but this kind of stuff makes me regret my decision. Judith is so unfair. Look at her and her cronies. They kiss her behind so that they can get more and better supplies than the rest of us."

Shalisha sat back and wiped the tears from her eyes. I reached over and held her hand. I was sure that I would not make that mistake. Discipleship was a form of bondage.

For disciples, all things were supposed to be in common, all things except Judith's that is. Judith controlled everything. I remembered a directive she gave to a supervisor concerning a sister on welfare.

"Sister Judith, I received a notice that a representative from the county agency is going to make a scheduled visit to Rachael's apartment. What shall I do?"

Judith ordered, "Have the grocery store manager stock the apartment's refrigerator with food and put other necessities in the cabinets and on the shelves. But after the visit, retrieve the goods and return everything to the grocery shelves. Warn Rachael not to touch or eat anything."

I couldn't believe my ears. In that same meeting the directress of the school stated, "The VCR in the auditorium is broken. What shall I do?"

"What happened to it?" Judith asked in disgust.

"I'm not sure but it's destroying the tapes. May we borrow one of yours so that we can review Moses Israel's lectures in class?"

"What do you mean? Too many things are in need of repair. Ya'll too careless over there. No, I won't let you use mine. Just go without one until yours is repaired."

"Who is going to repair it? We don't have any money." There was no response.

What? Did I hear Judith correctly? Yours! Mine! What about "OURS?" Weren't all things in common? No, I could not become a disciple.

"Snap, snap," Judith motioned with her fingers realizing that I was in deep thought.

"What do you say, Mary Ilana?"

"I'm not ready for discipleship yet, possibly when more independent, success oriented people come into the fold. Then maybe I'll give it some serious thought."

I changed the subject as Judith had begun eating a snack that she'd just gotten from the food co-op on the side of the building. She loved to eat and had problems controlling her weight. She obviously didn't adhere to the strict one meal a day diet either. I thought of how thin and emaciated the other disciples looked from not eating while working very long and strenuous hours.

As Judith ate, I thought to myself, "I like Bally shoes, Bali bras, and Henson panties." No way was I going to give up shopping. I wanted to stay in the mall as long as I wanted.

I knew that Judith disliked me and would treat me as she did the others if I submitted to her rule. I would not fall victim to this servitude.

Being married to Chico had totally made me immune to any form of pressure or persuasion. Never again would I be in self imposed bondage or servitude.

The Second Day: On the Sea

It is nearly noon. I close my notepad and stand to stretch. I remember that tonight's event is "The Captain's Dinner." I'll wear my beautiful black velvet dress. I wish I had a date to dine and dance with afterwards.

It now occurs to me that the ship's photographers will take pictures of each passenger shaking the captain's hand. Should I avoid that phase of tonight's events? Should I wear my tinted glasses tonight? Should I …'No Mary,' I hear a voice in my head, start accepting yourself within and your beauty will show without.

I realize that I am not alone. The Spirit of Truth is abiding within. I affirm, "Tonight I will enjoy myself. I will enthusiastically participate in activities. I will have fun! I will have my picture taken tonight!

"Mary enjoying a show after the Captain's Dinner"

THE THIRD DAY: PUERTO RICO

"Mary in Puerto Rico"

Having had a wonderful time last night in the supper club, I awaken feeling refreshed. The comedy routine was hilarious. I laughed so hard that the muscles in my stomach ached. Laughter is good for the soul. I feel as if I've lifted a heavy burden from my shoulders. I'm sure that it's this introspective process that's helping me to relax. I feel less guilty about my actions. That is, those actions that affected me only, but the decisions I made about the children still plague me. I'll concentrate on them today.

It's going to be a short day on board. We dock in Puerto Rico at noon. I'll have to hurry. I quickly dress and go to my favorite spot. Taking a few minutes to meditate, I pick up my pen and begin to write.

THE UNIVERSITY

After a few years of acquiring dilapidated buildings and restoring them to their previous luster, the purchase of a "real" school was eagerly anticipated and welcomed. Everyone, followers, supporters and disciples, worked very hard to renovate and restore this building with the same zeal that the other buildings had received. It was an ideal site because it actually was an abandoned church, which was used as the auditorium; with a school that had numerous classrooms on the first floor, a cafeteria and a playground. The second floor was converted to a dormitory which was carefully and very strictly monitored by a group of women assigned as dorm mothers and guardians.

But there was something different about the attitudes now. There was a higher positive energy level that flowed through everyone. We were parents who wanted the very best for our children; and they were ecstatic.

As the temple expanded nationwide, many disciples sent their children to be boarded. Like many of the local believers and supporters who had earlier enrolled their children in the temple's day school, I eagerly inquired about how my kids could be boarded in what I thought would eventually become a "most prestigious" educational center like the former Academy of the Assumption near Brickell Avenue. That Catholic school was a residential Montessori center whose students were from elite families throughout the country. My niece Starla, Liz's daughter, attended that school during her primary grades.

I also thought of the Clara Muhammad School on 7th Avenue at the Muslim Mosque. Their students were most articulate, well mannered and had positive self concepts. I wanted the best for my kids and wanted to be a part of the team who would develop the school's curriculum.

Earlier, I'd withdrawn my kids from public school because I'd been experiencing some major academic and social difficulties with my daughter Renee. Since the divorce she'd rebelled against me thinking that I was the cause of Chico's leaving. As her GPA decreased and she continued to fail the yearly Stanford Achievement Test, she began identifying with the rowdy group in middle school and had to spend time in internal suspension.

Thinking that the anesthesia that I'd been administered during surgery while pregnant with her might have caused some of her academic problems, I denied repeated requests for permission to have her tested for special education classes. Not wanting her to be labeled a slow learner, I borrowed a battery of tests from the school psychologist and administered them to her; then asked him to interpret the results. I was happy to hear that her scores were well within the range of normal intelligence; but there were some indications of process deficits in the area of auditory sequential memory; thus reading comprehension would be challenging. She was great in math and in tasks where the materials were presented visually.

I immediately enrolled her in Fran Ross' Tutoring Service in the Carol City Shopping Center to target her deficits while I constantly reinforced her areas of strength. As I devoted more time and energy to her, Juanita, obviously thinking that I favored Renee, became more verbally critical of Renee's shortcomings; thus their blooming sibling rivalry intensified. Their constant bickering and negative remarks toward each other were exhausting. I needed relief.

I thought, like my Catholic school's training, the temple's strict code of student conduct for behavior would surely help me get them through their adolescent years safely. However, I always wondered if it was the right move for Juanita who excelled in all of her studies. Would the temple's curriculum be challenging enough to command her attention and sustain her interests?

Finally, Lonnie's asthmatic condition would surely improve since he would have to adhere to a strict diet based on biblical laws at the temple. I made my decision. I had to keep them together.

Disciples did not have to pay tuition for their children because they contributed their common lot to the temple. However, I was assessed a weekly contribution for lodging and food.

The students were well disciplined and eager to learn. Initially, the teachers organized a weekly presentation for the parents. On Friday nights, we assembled in the auditorium to see our children perform with pride. When we gathered for this purpose, all envy, jealousy and strife vanished. Our motto, "One God, One Mind, One Love and One Action" was in total effect. The love of our children was the magnet that held us together.

As the newness of the school wore off and everyone continued their long workday schedules, attendance at this weekly event diminished. Soon the enthusiasm dwindled and the programs ceased. Instead of a weekly event at the school, the children recited a series of "discourses" on biblical topics and expounded on them during class nights and at the three annual feasts.

While they recited, I could hear pitch variations and inappropriate loudness levels that were causing their voices to sound strained. I could hear the hoarseness after a period of time. I began to focus on how they practiced.

I observed that to memorize such long speeches, they had to say them over and over and over again every day. They were often competing to hear themselves above the other children's voices. Thus they began talking louder, faster and with higher tones. They were not drinking enough water to lubricate their vocal cords, thus the strain and hoarseness. I pointed this out to the directress. Nothing changed.

Determined, I asked for permission to conduct a speech and language screening on the younger children. When the request was granted, I eagerly gathered my Peabody Picture Vocabulary Cards and my Goldman Fristoe Articulation Test and began to test. Several kids were identified with minor misarticulation patterns. Some stuttered but too many had hoarse voices. To help the students, I told each one to request a drink of water whenever their throats hurt and gave them tips on pitch and volume control through proper breathing. They respectfully followed my advice.

During the testing, I also identified language problems, specifically vocabulary. As the cards were flashed the children were unable to identify many of the pictures. The basic vocabulary that most children learned by the age of three or four were not known to these children. Then it occurred to me that most of these children had been born at the temple, their parents were disciples. Their environment was very restricted. They had not seen television, listened to radio, been read to from pictured books, and had not visited any scenic attractions in the city. In fact, I realized that they had not been outside or off of the temple's properties, ever!

Since the children could only utilize books that Moses Israel authored or other biblical works which he approved, I selected chapters from the Bible that contained lots of nouns. The children needed to see what they were saying. The Book of Leviticus was perfect because it contained the divine dietary laws. The names of many animals were listed. I cut and pasted pictures to compose booklets. With the help of a friend in business, I bought a case of copy paper and utilized her office's high speed printer that collated and stapled the material. The children were excited when I presented them with the books. At the next feast I sold some to the parents from out of town to earn money to print my grammar book. I was happy because I felt useful, needed and appreciated.

Then the older children became the target of my concern. Could they read effectively? I wondered. Most of them had been in public schools prior to coming to the temple so I knew that deficits were possible. How could I determine if this were so when they never read aloud individually? All reading and reciting was performed as a group. They committed everything to memory. I decided to go over and observe them when the group read the scriptures each morning at 7:00 a.m. That meant that I had to leave home at 5:30 in the morning, observe the children, and then hurriedly drive across town to get to work on time; but I had to do it.

Aha! Many students were not in lip sync. Some lost their places and began to look around; their attention was not focused on the words. Some had memorized the verses and continued to recite beyond the passage in which they were to have stopped.

I carefully discussed my observations with Hadahsah, who had been a public school teacher, because I felt that she would understand. Somehow my genuine concerns were misinterpreted as "our children can't read, and our children have deficiencies." This was later reported to Moses Israel.

"How dare you make such a statement? All of our children are ten times better at everything and more proficient in all subjects," he reprimanded me verbally.

But rather than get angry, complain and become a problem, I hurriedly worked to complete the grammar book that I was writing. Like the texts that we used in Catholic school, references to the doctrine and beliefs were throughout each chapter's lessons. I made sure that every word was relevant to our history, culture and biblical heritage. Identification was essential.

I read and re-read, studied and re-studied. I spent every moment in meditation on how to take the knowledge available and rewrite it from a scriptural perspective. I fasted for insight and understanding. Ideas were flowing so quickly that I had to buy a computer to effectively store and edit information.

I continued to let my children matriculate at the temple's school because the benefits of the discipline far outweighed my perceived shortcomings of the staff and the curriculum. I knew that I could teach them the basics of any subject that they missed at home on the weekend.

Later, Chico, hearing of the change in schools, became angry and challenged me in court. He wanted the children back in public school but he didn't want to assume any direct parental responsibility for rearing them. Therefore, when the judge ordered us to see a conciliator to assist in solving our conflicts, I firmly held my position. Chico didn't agree with the recommendations and soon resumed his non-involvement in our lives.

About a year and a half after the school's opening, my actions had been sufficiently observed, and Moses Israel granted me the opportunity to teach the foundation of the Hebrew language to the students on Sunday mornings and on weekday evenings. Though I didn't speak or understand Hebrew, I taught basic Hebrew vocabulary and covertly helped the students to read phonetically by showing them how to transliterate the Hebrew symbols into the English alphabet for pronunciation. I was happy.

Several months later, the media ran a feature story on the temple's school. Finally it had achieved some notable acclaim. But the enthusiasm subsided when a reader submitted a "letter to the editor" the following week complaining about the misspelling of the word "stemming" which had been observed on the chalkboard behind a picture of a student shown in the article. The "double the consonant rule" had not been followed. Moses Israel was angry because of this perceived ridicule.

After that, correct spelling and other basic skills were to be emphasized and remediated as soon as possible and I was called in to conduct teacher training workshops. Though the teachers seemingly acquiesced to the techniques I presented, we all knew that none of that was to be actually utilized with the students on a continuous basis. Rote memory was the way, their only way, Moses Israel's way.

As I conducted these workshops, notes were taken and later given to Moses Israel to review. Predictably, a conflict soon occurred. I wanted the children to be more expressive in their presentations. There had been a misunderstanding of the word "drone" that I used in discussing vocal quality and intonation. In that context, the term "drone like" meant "in a flat monotone." I was not aware that the disciples were studying the scripture "Go to the ant, thou sluggard; consider her ways, and be wise." Drone, an associated term for ants had been used to label the sluggards within the temple.

Moses Israel soon summoned me for a conference, or more precisely, a reprimand. I sat calmly and listened to the charges. For my defense, I turned to the word "drone" in the dictionary and pointed to the two listings. One meaning applied to the ant and the other for a type of speech. My accusers were speechless. I politely stood and walked out of the door.

Shattered Lens

"Students at Yahweh's Educational Center"

THE ENTOURAGE

Now with mixed or shall I say bruised feelings, I attended another class. As usual I sat in the rear purposefully isolating myself from the others. The presentation for that night was a video of Moses Israel's recent trips. As I watched and listened, someone gently tapped me on the shoulder, then handed me a note.

"Shalom Mary Ilana," she whispered in my ear. "Sister Judith wants to talk with you. Please call her tomorrow at the hotel." As I turned to question the messenger, Miriam walked away.

The next day I telephoned the hotel and was told that Judith wanted to meet with me personally. I arrived at 4:00 p.m. To my surprise, she invited me up to the suite that she shared with Moses Israel. She was unusually friendly. Once I sat down she asked, "Mary Ilana would you like to travel with the entourage?"

"That's not possible. My job responsibilities are too great at this time. I can't afford to take extra leave."

"I thought about that. We can fly you in and out at various times to accommodate your schedule."

"We?" I questioned.

"Yes, the temple will pay for your airfare and hotel accommodations."

"Really! Why?"

"You represent the class of persons that Moses Israel wants to be surrounded by. Many supporters fly in from across the country to attend the events. Whenever your schedule permits, you can stay longer. The average trip is from five to seven days."

"It appears from viewing the videos that the host congregations pamper the group royally."

"Yes, and unlike the summer bus tours, we ride in a caravan of all white Ford Towncars and live in the best and most exclusive hotels in the city."

She paused then asked, "Do you have a major credit card?"

"Yes, why do you ask?"

"We need one to be able to rent cars. We tried to leave a deposit large enough to cover the total cost of the cars once, but the rental companies' policies require a major credit card. Many of the followers have discarded their cards. May we use your card?"

"How much of a limit do you require? It seems like you rent a fleet of cars." She laughed.

"Oh, about two thousand dollars will do. You don't have to worry about having your credit line tied up. We'll pay the bill in full as we turn in the cars. What do you say?"

"I don't doubt your ability to pay."

"Then you agree."

I nodded my head affirmatively.

"Welcome to the entourage."

As I left the suite, I laughed aloud knowing that Judith's behavior was too good to be true. Why couldn't she just be straightforward with me? I knew that she disliked me if only because she couldn't control me. So to just say "we need your credit card" would have been fine with me. The request was not unusual. I'd allowed friends and family to use my cards in the past; but this is great because I will get to travel free.

As I left the building, the thought to proceed with caution kept flashing in my mind. Again, I ignored it.

As I drove home, I remembered a lesson Moses Israel taught on how he expanded the organization. He announced, "I am the first Black man to establish twenty temples around the country simultaneously. Though, the Nation of Islam has numerous nationwide mosques, it took them years to accomplish that. I did it in one day, even though the elders were initially without a physical structure to call a temple. What mattered was that the elders were there "spreading the word" and wherever the "word of Yahweh" is, so there is a temple. "Know you not that you are the temple of God, and that the Spirit of God dwells in you?" he quoted to prove his point. The congregation shouted praises to his accomplishment.

After the lecture, he would then give a report of the elders' progress in each city. The competition to be the top city was rated by the amount of money sent to Miami, not by the number of new disciples added to the roster.

Now after years of this procedure, the format was changed. Recruiting members was more important. Flyers were distributed and tickets sold. If a certain percentage of attendees were guaranteed by the host temple, Moses Israel consented to go to that city as their keynote speaker at the convention center or municipal auditorium. A gift, presented by the city's elder, would have to be given to him for sharing his knowledge with the audience. This scripture was quoted to demonstrate that the host group would comply with the biblical teachings:

The Third Day: Puerto Rico

"And he said unto him, Behold now, there is in this city a man of God, and he is an honorable man; all that he says surely comes to pass: now let us go thither; peradventure he can show us our way that we should go. But behold, if we go, what shall we bring the man? Behold, I have here at hand the fourth part of a shekel of silver: that will I give to the man of God, to tell us our way."

The movement to improve the temple's overall public image was implemented. A public relations plan was developed. Select members of the temples from around the country were trained to present positive information that would demonstrate that, as a people, we had common goals and objectives, regardless of religious affiliation. Indisputably, the emphasis was on the need for economic empowerment within our communities.

Armed with a carefully prepared text that proved the temple members had achieved an enviable status as entrepreneurs, these select members charged upon a targeted market of educated and industrious individuals to entice them to become a part of this successful movement. Moses Israel now wanted the professional class of African Americans to return to his fold. It was emphasized that as a part of the temple he could solve all of the problems that the other black leaders and organizations had been unable to do.

Everyone was excited and the responses were very positive. Our people were always searching for solutions and were seemingly receptive. Moses Israel now regularly traveled to the cities and spoke directly to carefully selected audiences.

"Moses Israel surrounded by his bodyguards"

A special group of disciples traveled with him from city to city. These members were thought to be the VIP's of the nation and generally perceived to be the closest to Moses Israel. They guarded and protected him wherever he went and were his ears and eyes. They were his royal court, the king's entourage.

An elaborate media presentation was produced. Video tapes of the temple's successful businesses and property purchases were highlighted. The hotels, apartments and villas were decorated and filmed. Captions of the amenities dashed across the screen. Community leaders and politicians who had privately visited Moses Israel were captured on video positively acknowledging their pride in the temple's business endeavors.

The video presentation was followed by a fashion show which featured well designed long white cultural garments. Except for the length of the garments and the matching head wear, many of the styles could be beautifully worn by any woman, regardless of her race, religious affiliation or cultural identification.

Moses Israel's message at these events did not directly focus on active membership or public identification with the group, but, rather, on how he could assist the aspirants in becoming prosperous entrepreneurs under his leadership and tutelage. For the skeptics, who were cautious because of their fears of having to become disciples if they participated in this partnership, Moses Israel would ask me and other supporters in the audience to stand. We were proof that you did not have to "quit your job" nor "give up your home' to be associated.

At the end of his speech, those who were interested in affiliating were encouraged to go to assigned areas and sign up. Since a lot of the mysteries about the group had been allayed, via the video, the fears of the aspirants diminished after viewing "white people of renown on film" smiling and praising the good works of this industrious group.

As I began to travel with the entourage, I realized just how much of the disciples' personal identities had been relinquished. Publicly, they did everything together as if they were one body, and whenever they were asked by Moses Israel to openly state their opinions, it was as if a repeat button had been pressed on a tape recorder. Every comment was the same. In every city, the faces of the guests were new, but the disciples' comments remained unchanged. After a while I was not impressed at all. I knew that everything had been carefully orchestrated and staged to conform to a predetermined image, real or imagined.

The Third Day: Puerto Rico

In December, we journeyed to New Orleans, Louisiana to attend a National Business League Convention. Moses Israel had been invited by the League's national president, Arthur Teele, a Miami businessman and political figure, to be the keynote speaker. The members of the entourage were excited.

During that week, Moses Israel sent some disciples as his personal representatives to each workshop that the league sponsored. At the end of the day, each disciple would report to Moses Israel.

"Sir, the League focuses on the procurement of government funds to accomplish its goals and objectives. They are too dependent on federal funding. Therefore unlike us, they are not self-sufficient. Many of their seminars did not start on time which caused some confusion later. Our staff however, is always very prompt and effective in organizing large group functions such as our High Holy Day feasts."

Everyone smiled and looked at Moses Israel for approval. Then they individually began to praise him for teaching the congregation about the importance of time management and for demonstrating how to accomplish goals without any funds from the government. Each one stood and cited more examples of Moses Israel's good works around the country.

I had not commented yet. As usual, I'd been observing their behavior. Because this was my very first seven-day trip with them, I wanted to understand and follow the proper protocol. I wanted to conform to their rules, if I could. Finally, I was asked to express my views.

"Mary Ilana, what have you got to say?" he asked.

"Well, I am pleased to see our people come together with one mind to effect positive changes. Though the members of the league are not as we are, they demonstrate the same desire to uplift our people economically." There was absolute silence but I continued.

"We have been taught that we are the same people. We are Judah, the elect, the chosen. So it doesn't matter that the league is utilizing another means of funding. What matters is that they are committed to positive change. In time as we all grow in the knowledge of who we truly are, we will all come together and be able to accomplish greater works."

Moses Israel just stared at me for a while. Then he stood up and said, "She's right! You all sit here and tell me what you think I want to hear. You haven't done anything on your own yet. None of you came here with money or possessions. Everything that's been done was accomplished with my money. I have done it all. But you go to each meeting and find fault with what everybody does. I don't want to hear all of the negative reports.

What have you learned from the meetings that we can use? That's what I want to know."

The entourage appeared shocked. They held their heads down like little kids who had just been scolded.

Moses Israel looked at me and asked, "What do you think about government funding?"

"I think that we deserve to get what's rightfully ours. We pay taxes and we've not received reparations for our slave labor." I paused to gauge the atmosphere then continued.

"After slavery we were promised forty acres and a mule and we still haven't received compensation for four hundred years of servitude. We should be demanding more while working toward self-reliance."

I could tell by their looks that I shouldn't say anymore. I had a lot to learn. The women in the group were very cold towards me and purposefully excluded me from their general conversations for the rest of the week. I learned very quickly that only one voice was accepted. After that trip, every opportunity to discredit my statements or to assassinate my character was taken.

The women who consistently accompanied Moses Israel on these trips were disciples whose primary function was to serve him. These were the same women who were also his constant companions at headquarters. They were most dedicated to him. They personally served his meals, braided his hair, gave him manicures and pedicures, facials and body massages. When he was engaged in lengthy business conversations or while he was teaching openly, they intermittently served him beverages or made sure that his water glass was always filled. They preceded him as he left buildings, opened doors for him, and surrounded him protectively while he talked with public officials. They kept their eyes on him and understood his body language and gestures and were quick to provide him with whatever it was that he indicated nonverbally. They were his devotees.

Not only were these women Moses Israel's servants, they also catered to Judith, but not with the same level of enthusiasm. They were her personal valets. It was obvious after close observation that they didn't care for the way Judith talked to them. She spoke with authority but without respect and seldom demonstrated appreciation by smiling or thanking them for services rendered. Judith acted as if everyone was beneath her and she didn't hesitate to prove that point while in the midst of a crowd.

I felt like an intruder. I was not accustomed to being in their company for extended periods of time. They lived communally and I lived in my

The Third Day: Puerto Rico

private residence. I wasn't allowed to assist Moses Israel personally because I had not been "trained," so I remained quiet and observant.

I traveled with the entourage on five additional trips. I liked the ambiance of the luxurious hotels and the sightseeing. I went to New Orleans, Philadelphia, St. Louis, Los Angeles, and again to Philadelphia the following year. Because of the continued disputes over my independent thinking, I decided not to go with the group anymore especially after the incident in Philadelphia.

Just prior to that last trip to Philly, I received a certified, registered letter from my gynecologist and obstetrician, Dr. Aden informing me to seek medical assistance from an oncologist, a cancer specialist, for my daughter Renee. This was the first time that I'd ever personally received any literature from him concerning this matter. I'd read about the effects of the diethylstilbestrol in medical journals years earlier and had taken preventative measures by changing our diets, eating natural and organic health foods, and taking vitamin and herbal supplements.

This letter brought back all of my fears. I soon was an emotional wreck and as usual I didn't share any of my feelings with the group nor with my family. I suffered in silence not realizing the effect my reticence would have on my mental and physical state.

Therefore, my behavior in Philadelphia seemed more bizarre to the women. I was unusually pensive, very quiet and extremely detached. I was unable to eat much because I had a nervous stomach. I was mentally preoccupied with my life and wasn't paying them or their conversations any attention.

All that I was thinking about during their criticism of me was my daughter. I selectively tuned them out. Though I was physically in their midst, my mind was worlds away. I was just there to sign the rental agreement for the cars.

One morning I was standing near the door of the hotel's suite. There was a knock, I opened the door and a white waiter entered the room with a service tray of rolls, coffee and tea. As he rolled the cart to the center of the room, I stood with my hand still on the knob holding the door ajar. When he turned and left the room, I closed the door and resumed my stance along the wall without saying a word to him. I was unaware of the entourage's stares because of my mental meandering.

Suddenly I was crudely brought back to the present moment by hearing my actions being verbally admonished. All eyes were again focused on me.

Moses Israel said, "You are not my disciple. I teach my disciples to be friendly and to reflect my attitude. You didn't speak to the waiter. Was it because he was white? Or did you think you were too good to speak to him? If you can't demonstrate my attributes then you don't need to be around me. You aren't an asset to me or the women's group."

What the hell was going on I thought? What had these women conjured up this time? Why was he so agitated? Where was his mercy, his ability to discern, his sense of fairness? What were the charges against me? Who were my accusers? Was I going to get an opportunity to defend myself? No! Court had been held and the verdict was guilty. Where was the "one law for all in Israel;" or was this just another one of his teaching strategies?

However, he was correct on one point, I was not an asset to the "Women's Group." After several years of attending classes, I'd finally been invited to a closed meeting and given an overview of their version of "The Order of the Eastern Stars." I was familiar with the tenants because my mother had aspired to become a "Worthy Matron" in her chapter. After my induction into this sisterhood, I was reminded of my pledge to recruit other women from the community to join; but I didn't. Who would I ask? It's not like I was going to invite friends over for a Mary Kay, Shaklee, Amway or AVON demonstration and follow up with a list of enticing rewards if they became salespeople.

For the next two days I was excluded from all of the meetings in Philadelphia, so I missed my meals. Unlike being on the summer tour, I wasn't in the city where I could stop at a fast food restaurant and purchase food. I was becoming dizzy and lightheaded. My tongue became thick and sluggish. I had to keep myself together. I had to make it home.

On the fourth day, I got up and showered before the others awakened. As I came out of the bathroom, I went over to my suitcase to gather my underwear. I dropped the towel so that I could dress. Suddenly a strange sensation came over me, so I looked around the room. Initially, I thought that I saw another sister, who was not wearing her turban, standing in the corner by the window; but it was Moses Israel. He turned around and scanned my body from head to toe. I was completely naked so I immediately ran back into the bathroom and closed the door. He said, "Come out of the bathroom Mary Ilana. I am your Father. You don't have to be shy."

I refused. He waited. When I finally opened the door, another sister handed me my undergarments. I put them on, came out and finished dressing. He just watched without saying anything. I was very nervous. For the next few days he just stared at me, but he didn't deride me anymore.

When we returned to Miami, I wrote a letter asking for a private meeting. He promptly consented. I knew that this would be a great opportunity to let him know about my behavior in Philadelphia. I gathered my certified letter and some literature on the drug that I had taken prenatally. I wanted more than anything to use this opportunity to seek his knowledge on healing. Though I seriously questioned his behavior, I remembered that he'd often stated that God had revealed to him the properties of all of the herbs and their curative powers and that one day, he would share this knowledge with those of us who were faithful.

I knew that I was a good person and had studied diligently. So would Moses Israel share with me what I needed to know to help me and my daughter? I prayed that he would. I was feeling so desperate and didn't want to miss an opportunity to learn all that I could. Obviously, my Catholic background still had me believing that I needed an intercessor between me and God.

We met at the temple's motel on Biscayne Boulevard and sat outdoors near the pool. We talked for about an hour.

"I apologize for not speaking to the waiter and for presenting myself as being unfriendly to the disciples."

I shared my past with him, the spousal abuse and the eye surgeries. And yes, my apprehension of men, black men that is. I let him know that in spite of all of the gossip that the sisters spread about my wanting their men that I had abstained from intercourse for the past few years.

"When you ran back into the bathroom in Philadelphia, I could tell that you are quite sexually inhibited."

"Is that a statement or a question?" I evasively responded.

"Both."

"Well, yes and somewhat. I'm rather old fashioned in my values, morals and mores. I'm not quite "with it" yet," I smiled. "Even my divorce lawyer laughed and called me a "prude.""

He chuckled. "Are you afraid of men?" he asked.

"I'm not afraid, I'm more fearful of my being deceived by them. They have too many hidden agendas. I've done almost all of my socializing with men in group settings. But don't misunderstand; I've had some romantic rendezvous since my divorce, but nothing steady or serious. But nor am I the typical woman of the world or the harlot that the sisters characterize me as. They misunderstand my relationship with the brothers. I treat them with great respect and they are protective of me, like my biological brothers and I appreciate that."

He seemed fascinated with my explanations, but I was beginning to feel very uncomfortable as his eyes penetrated my soul.

I'd seen that look in his eyes before in the hotel in St. Louis. The entourage had dispersed and the suite was very quiet. Everyone was asleep. 2:00 in the morning is my special time to be alone. Even when I go to bed late, my body's clock will alarm and I habitually wake up. I turned over and opened my eyes and to my surprise he was standing over me. He leaned over and whispered into my ear, "It's good that you sensed my presence. That's very important." Then he turned and walked away.

What did he mean by that? The next morning around the same time I observed one of the women in the entourage reentering the bedroom butt naked. She quietly pulled her night gown over her head and quickly slipped back into bed and pulled the covers over her shoulders. The same thing happened the next morning and the following morning but with other women. They were programmed to do something in a very covert manner. I didn't want to believe my intuitive feelings, but my gut was rumbling. Were they his maidens? I smiled thinking, "He surely ain't no priest. He's got a lot in common with the preachers that he mocks."

"Mary Ilana, are you daydreaming?" as he waved his hand in front of my face.

"Pardon me. I was remembering." Our conversation continued.

"As far as healing goes, this is the remedy you've been seeking. Eat plenty of red and purple foods, like red cabbage, beets, and purple grapes with seeds, blueberries, and raspberries. Eat raw, live foods only for a month or so and drink plenty of freshly squeezed fruit juices. The fresh fruits and the vegetables are to be eaten separately," he instructed.

"Thank you for your counsel and understanding."

As I stood, I thought that he would have given more information on spiritual healing since I'd read that remedy in "**Back to Eden**" but I was most grateful for the reassurance.

As I turned to walk away, he said, "Mary Ilana, I want you to spend a lot more time around the temple. I want you to get to know me better. Get to know Judith. She'll teach you a lot. I've noticed how nervous you always are in my presence. Now that I understand you better, everything will be all right. You don't have to get permission from anyone to see me again. Just tell one of my guards and it will be arranged." He paused then put his hand on my shoulder.

"Why don't you come over and sleep at the motel some nights. We always have extra rooms."

He leaned over and kissed me on my cheek, then quietly quoted this scripture in my ear: "Everything is made for my pleasure so present your body as a living sacrifice, holy unto the Lord and remember that "Thy Maker is thy husband." I smiled remembering that he had quoted that scripture to the women who had not been chosen in the marital line during the feast. Now I understood its subliminal message.

He turned and walked towards Jesse Obed, the bodyguard who was standing nearby. They stood in the parking lot and waited for me to get into my car. As I left the property I looked back at him. He had that same stare in his eyes that he had in Philadelphia and in St Louis. Intuitively, I knew that some of the gossip that I'd heard about Moses Israel's intimate relationships was not mere rumors at all.

I grimaced thinking, "Shouldn't the Son of God have been able to discern that the last thing I wanted was another meaningless sexual encounter?" I sighed.

Instead of becoming more visible and active around the temple, as he suggested, I decided that I'd become more detached and distant. As I drove away, I concentrated on how to take the kids out of school without being perceived as a hypocrite. Chico's wrath was no longer an issue.

THE 70TH FLOOR

Summer was near and I was concentrating on taking a vacation with the kids. While relaxing, the telephone rang. It was Ruth, Judith's secretary.

"Mary Ilana, Moses Israel wants you to meet with a prospective candidate for membership in the women's group at Sun City Motel tomorrow morning. Can you make it?"

"No, I'd rather not! Isn't there anyone else available to do the presentation?"

"You are his choice. Won't you go?"

"Well, just this last time. In the future you'll have to find someone else. What's her name?"

"Celeste."

"Tell me about her."

"Well another sister approached her about becoming a member of the sisterhood, but Moses Israel didn't want anyone who did not have educational and financial credentials equal to Celeste's to encourage her to join. Celeste is a business woman who understands how to procure funds by bidding. The temple wants to enter into that financial arena. Celeste's involvement is important."

I arranged to dine with her for lunch on Miami Beach. We talked for hours. We were very much impressed with each other. I was happy to have someone with whom I could positively relate.

Celeste was a very wise woman. Though she was only two years older, when talking with her I felt like an adolescent. She was very sophisticated and well traveled. As a graduate of a very prestigious, private Black college in Atlanta, with a degree in business administration, she'd become a successful entrepreneur who owned and operated a wholesale distribution company. She was witty and very sharp. I thought her keen sense of perception rivaled the best minds in the country. She was articulate, straightforward, confident and cocky, for sure. Obviously African American, at first glance you knew that she was of mixed racial lineage. Her grandmother was pure blooded East Indian. Celeste had naturally straight, jet black, silky hair; beautifully even-toned olive skin and very large, black, deep set eyes. She was tall and of medium build. She looked as if she could have been Gandhi's granddaughter.

The Third Day: Puerto Rico

Our meeting was successful. Celeste joined the group and the report that she submitted to Moses Israel was so positive, that I was personally asked to accompany the entourage to Atlanta to room with her. Reluctantly, I consented but I vowed that this would be my very last trip.

Atlanta, Georgia, a beautiful southern city, epitomizes the height of African-American people's progress and achievements in America since slavery, Reconstruction and the Civil Rights Movement. There we are empowered economically, politically, socially and educationally. It's a thriving metropolis just waiting for superman to come and remove the remaining obstacles, spiritual blindness and lack of knowledge of self that prevent us from gaining complete and permanent control over our destiny and affairs.

The potential for a significant temple impact was in Atlanta. To conquer this city's bourgeoisie by positively converting them to the Hebrew Israelite ideology and philosophy would surely set a nationwide precedent that all other cities would hasten to follow. The temple's local chapter organized an event at the city's famed Foxx Theater for Moses Israel to speak. All was ready.

The entourage arrived at one of Atlanta's finest hotels, the Westin Peachtree Plaza. A luxurious suite had been reserved on the 70th floor. Upon entering this plush setting, we gasped at its beauty. Truly only the chosen, the very elect deserved such rich accommodations. The ambiance and amenities helped ease my past agony.

The entourage quickly gathered in the suite's large reception room awaiting the arrival of the city's representative to officially welcome Moses Israel. The usual proclamations were presented by the vice mayor, after which he asked, "Are there any questions or comments?"

Silence filled the room. Everyone stoically looked toward Moses Israel and then to Judith, the second in command. The newest addition to this entourage, Celeste, who like myself was not a disciple broke the silence by asking a very simple, yet appropriate, non-threatening everyday question.

"What's the population of African-Americans in your city?"

Little did Celeste know that she had violated the eleventh commandment: Don't speak or think; just listen and smile! Only one voice was ever heard. Celeste was educated very quickly. Nonverbal signals reverberated around the room. The stares from the disciples were enough for her to know that all was not well. I looked at Judith and read her thoughts by observing her body language.

"How dare Celeste break with protocol? Who does she think she is? I'll teach her soon enough."

The change in mood was so overwhelming that even the city's representative hesitated before voicing the numbers from the latest census report. "Are there anymore questions?" he asked again.

"No! That will be all. Thank you for coming," voiced Judith.

With the formalities over, the entourage quickly and quietly dispersed. The routine was fixed. The roles were rehearsed. Another city, another audience, but the same message, the same video and the same fashion show.

Still, I was happy that I'd come this final time. I seriously believed that one day our people would wake up and unite. I didn't see any other group working as effectively toward that goal as were the members of the temple. Every organization had its own agenda, but the temple recognized us as one people and embraced everyone.

I still wanted to be a part of the group especially knowing that the same negative behaviors that I encountered at the temple were as prevalent in the churches, work environments and in other social cliques among our people. So even though the schemes and wiles of my Hebrew sisters had pushed me to the limit and my tolerance level had far exceeded its threshold, I prayed for strength to withstand any unforeseen eventualities. But as I looked at the women, I sensed a malicious intent that had no previous match. They had come prepared. Little did I know that their remarks over the next seven days would be enough to completely turn me away.

The next morning, the entourage assembled around Moses Israel. "I am very excited about the potential of recruiting a great multitude of my people here. I want you to understand me very clearly. I no longer want anyone from the ghetto. The poor and downtrodden have rejected me, and I'm tired of the problems they cause. Like Cain, they were given a chance to prove their ability to rule but they failed. They can be servants in the new world order. The scripture reads, there will always be some poor and needy among us and it's written that only one-third will be saved. Our mission in Atlanta is to find the elect, the chosen. Let's clean house to make room for the profitable servants," he ordered.

An elder stood and said, "Many of us have undesirable persons among our ranks across the country. We need guidance on how to purge them."

"No longer are the poor, uneducated, and unskilled to be accepted into the esoteric group. They can come to the temple to hear the lessons, but they are not to be given any "high wisdom" reserved for the elect. That will be done privately in the brotherhood and sisterhood meetings."

A sister stood and boldly asked, "What must we do about people who do not conform or participate but just come to class and pay tithes thinking that they have done all that is necessary, like Mary Ilana?"

Suddenly Moses Israel turned to me and asked, "Mary Ilana, who do you pray to?"

It all happened so fast, but without hesitation I answered, "To God, the Father, Yahweh."

"Then what about the Son?" he inquired.

I quoted scripture. "No one comes to the Father lest he go through the Son."

Did I say something wrong? Moses Israel became furious. He leaned forward and pointed his finger in my face, as I was seated very close to him. Then his face turned as red as a beet.

He shook his finger and said, "Praise me! Drop the "P" and raise me up! I and the Father are one."

I was speechless. My eyes widened and my brain went into high gear again as adrenalin pumped quickly through my system. My pulse and respiration increased. I knew that he was frustrated with me, but this time it was different. It became so quiet in the room that you could hear a pin drop on cotton. Why was he so perturbed? Why were my actions and words constantly irritating him? That look of fury in his eyes reminded me of Chico. Would Moses Israel do the same thing to me? Never before had I been afraid of him, but now I was really scared.

After staring at me for a while, he stood and left the room. His high ranking elders followed him. Everyone stared at me in disbelief that I had spoken such words. I just didn't understand their attitude. What had I said wrong? I'd only quoted a well known scripture that I had often heard him quote.

The group dispersed after realizing that Moses Israel had gone to the hotel's spa. When we gathered again later that evening, Moses Israel never looked my way or spoke to me again.

That night in my room, I asked Celeste, "What did I do wrong?"

"I spoke with him after the incident and he said that you had likened him to a priest or rabbi. He said that he was no intercessor or mediator to God. He is God himself."

"Was he talking in parables?" I questioned.

"He meant it literally."

I laid back on the bed and thought, "The cat was out of the bag." He now realized that I did not worship him as God, the Father. I had only perceived him as a servant of God. I had regarded him as a teacher and a messenger only. That's why I had secretly continued to call him Moses Israel, the author.

Celeste was relaxing on the bed. She looked up and just stared at me then said, "What are you doing around this motley crew, Mary Ilana? You are not like them. What goes with you? What is your story?"

We talked about my life, my initial reasons for being associated with the group and my relationship with men.

She laughed. "Men are a breeze. You just have to guide them like sheep while you make them feel like they're the shepherds." We laughed.

"Let's talk girl talk, honey. What's going on here anyway? Judith's on my case. She just keeps rolling her eyes at me, and the other women are just as bad. They act like a harem in heat. They seem so threatened by my presence," she said with a smirk on her face.

"They treat me the same way," I replied.

We looked at each other and smiled. Certain topics were better left unspoken or not discussed openly. Itching ears were everywhere. The conversation was continued but on a more scripturally sophisticated level.

"Are you familiar with the book of Esther?" I asked.

"Yes, I've read about the bath houses of the king's women. They purified themselves with precious oils and fragrances for a year, right?"

I interjected, "Yes, and during that year the older women taught the younger women how to minister to the king."

"Hmm!"

Suddenly Celeste stood to dramatize the scene saying, "And then each virgin anxiously awaited her turn for the king to extend the golden scepter towards her."

"Yes, it's a matter of protocol and extreme formality," I said pompously.

We fell out laughing and screaming as we reenacted the story pretending to be beckoned by the king.

"Now let's get serious, Mary Ilana. The "Man" is as mad as hell at you. What did you do to anger him so?" she insisted.

"I just stopped coming around as he requested. He said that Judith could teach me a lot and I decided that I didn't want to learn anything from her."

The Third Day: Puerto Rico

"What was she going to teach you? Judith's not that smart," Celeste laughed.

"That's obvious to almost everyone, but she is competent and most importantly, she gets the job done while keeping the disciples in line. You know that Judah is hardheaded, stiff-necked and rebellious."

Celeste's mind went into high gear. She slowly and deliberately repeated the account of my conversation with Moses Israel about being abstinent, having limited experience with men and being old fashioned. Then she said as if a light had come on in her head.

"Girl, do you know what you did? You disobeyed his orders. The golden scepter was extended to you and you didn't follow protocol. You obviously were to become a vital part of this entourage and he wanted Judith to train you to serve him."

She paused and stared at me again.

"Well, I'll be a monkey's uncle. You have more nerve than most. Or prehaps you are just that naive. What more will I learn this week?" she said. This trip is going to be very in - ter - esting."

I could tell that Celeste had itching ears also. We smiled, then laughed, then sighed. I was in serious trouble.

As Celeste fell to sleep, I mentally replayed our conversation and thought of its implications. It had been nearly a year since I was asked to spend more time at the temple. Instead I decided to become an entrepreneur by starting a home based tutoring service. I wanted a center with lots of equipment and learning aids. I dreamed of establishing a private school like Marva Collins.

To accomplish this, I'd been receiving technical assistance from a new disciple, who was very skilled in business and computers. For approximately four months prior to the trip to Atlanta, when Abner had free time, we spent it together. I was very impressed with his knowledge. He had worked for McDonald Douglas as a systems analyst prior to coming to the temple. He was apt and articulate and I enjoyed his company very much. He was very kind, but too much time alone together led to other actions unrelated to business. What the hell? I enjoyed breaking my years of abstinence. But the word got out about Abner being with me as the temple's "crime watchers" spied on his whereabouts. I sighed because I knew exactly why Moses Israel was pissed with me. The sisters must have told him about Abner.

I was more frightened the next day when Elder Amos pulled me to the side and said, "Moses Israel expressed just how very angry he was with you and mentioned that he should have pushed you out of the window from the seventieth floor to hear who you would pray to as you fell. Be careful Mary Ilana. Some of the disciples take everything he says literally and feel that they are chosen to carry out his will."

My heart rate accelerated. How many times had I heard him ask, who would kill for Yahweh? Almost everyone would raise their hands. Who among the entourage would try to impress him by demonstrating their loyalty? I was a long way from home. I had five more days to go.

Why don't I just leave? I could charge my airfare back to Miami that day but there was no place to go. Moses Israel often warned us that when Yahweh wanted to get you, there was no hiding place. God's death angels were everywhere. Though he had taught the scripture, "thou shall not kill" from a metaphorical perspective, I now believed him literally.

Figuratively, kill meant to: assassinate the character; deprive of life spiritually; give an unfavorable report; spoil the chances of accomplishing goals; shatter hopes and dreams; deny; destroy the active or essential quality; ruin; tire or exhaust; impede markedly; de-energize and produce fatigue. Hell, I'd already been over killed. The visible death angels, his ardent disciples that surrounded him in Atlanta had only one option: to take the breath of life from my physical body.

It became more and more obvious during the week that Moses Israel was still angry with me. It shone in his eyes. I needed to be cool and logical for the next few days and I needed a sure win strategy to get out of this predicament when I returned home. I knew that God, the Totality of all beings, the Mighty Fortress, was the only force that could help me now. Like a good Catholic I prayed without ceasing daily.

CRISIS INVESTING

While returning to Miami from Atlanta, flying thirty-three thousand feet above the ground, I looked out the window at the clouds and thought of a Catholic catechism lesson on judgment day. When you died, if you were not able to go straight to heaven, you might get a second chance to prove your worthiness by going to Limbo. I felt as if I were now in Limbo, too far from earth but not close enough to heaven.

I turned around in the plane and looked down the aisle at the group piously arrayed in white and visualized them as dark heinous creatures waiting to throw me into the pit of Hell. To keep from crying, I laughed as I reflected on a lesson that Moses Israel taught on the "Mark of the Beast."

He stated, "The book of Revelations is now being unsealed by the lion of the tribe of Judah. I am here to unravel all of its mysteries at this crucial point in our history. This knowledge is necessary for our survival during the perilous times ahead."

"The One World Government is in the process of being organized. The European Common Market is only a few nations short of its goal for ratification. The World Bank in Brussels, Belgium has assigned every person an identification number which, when the proper time comes, will be imprinted via laser beams onto the right hand or forehead. There will not be a need for currency or credit cards at that time. Computers and bar codes will monitor all of our transactions."

"Big Brother is preparing for this smooth transition by cooperating with the banks, the selective service system, the social security system and the telephone companies. The asterisk and the pound buttons on the telephone are to assist in all electronic transfers and transactions. A campaign to have workers channel their payroll checks through direct deposits is in progress. Shopping at home via computers is another gimmick that will precondition the people's minds to accept the new order."

"The Trilateralists, covert members of the government who support the new order, are behind all of these undertakings. The economy is the key to it all. The banks are going to fail. Give your tithes, offerings, and donations to the temple so that you can receive blessings and our storehouse will be filled in the day of trouble."

I wondered why it appeared that the preachers and their families were the main ones to directly benefit from the monetary blessings of the Lord. Every church member knew the scripture on tithing, Malachi 3:6. And everyone who tithed expected the windows of heaven to pour them out blessings. But there had to be a conflict in its interpretation because most tithers seemingly expected their reward in the "sky in the great by and by" after death. In the "here and now" they suffered financially as the churches always had a plan, purpose or program to constantly extract more money. So was the preachers' prosperity just an earthly "symbol" to help the congregation to visualize their heavenly reward?

I wasn't opposed to tithing, I just wanted my reward in the "here and now" so I invested in tax deferred annuities, savings bonds and bank savings accounts. They were safe, tangible, and redeemable here on earth. Of course I gave an offering whenever I attended a church service. I felt it my responsibility to help defray the costs of maintenance on the edifice. But never would I support a church that was not directly helping the people. I wanted to see church sponsored banks, credit unions, nursing homes, low cost housing, grocery stores and schools. Our people needed those things now, in this life.

The members of the temple, through Moses Israel, were talking about "heaven here on earth;" they were actually building, buying and renovating property. Scripturally, he taught that a day of famine was coming. Therefore, economic empowerment was constantly discussed. Current events related to the stock market's gold and silver reports were "telecasted" at each class via a "YHWH" news team. Books were suggested for us to read to verify these prophesied events. I read almost everything printed: ***The Mark of the Beast***; ***None Dare Call it Conspiracy; Numismatics; The Trilateralists and Crisis Investing.***

After educating myself, I decided that I would tithe and support the temple's efforts so that "the storehouse would be full in the time of trouble."

"How can I begin to tithe?" I asked an usher since I'd never seen a collection basket or envelopes circulating during class.

"After class, stand in the line that forms outside of Judith's office."

The next week, with my check book in hand, I got in line. Once inside the office, she said, "We do not accept personal checks."

"I'm sorry but I only write checks. If you want my offering, or want me to purchase groceries from the market, you'll have to accept my checks. I seldom carry cash."

"Well, we'll try you out for a while," Judith said realizing that I was not going to give her cash.

"How can you lose if I'm paying tithes?" She didn't respond.

For two years I accurately recorded the contributions on my income tax return and thought nothing of it until I received the notice from IRS a year later.

I gathered my receipts as requested and asked Judith to provide me with a statement on the temple's letterhead. My request was denied. I didn't understand. I resubmitted requests three times. What was going on?

"The temple does not have tax exempt status. Your contributions were to Yahweh who doesn't care about man's rules," she arrogantly stated.

"Repeat that please. I still want a statement on the proper letterhead." Again, an emphatic "no" was Judith's harsh response.

I kept my scheduled appointment with the IRS.

"Are you purposefully disobeying my orders?" the auditor unsympathetically asked. "If so you are placing yourself in jeopardy of incurring the penalty for perjury."

"I'm really trying to get it. Hopefully I'll have it soon."

It had been a month since my initial request. Again I asked for a statement adding more information hoping to stir some emotions in Judith. Her negative attitude was more adamant than flint.

This time she sent a very strong message to me. "I don't care if she has to go to jail. The temple comes first."

I returned to the audit and provided copies of all of my contributions and transactions at the temple. I had been very methodical in recording each check as "B" for boutique purchase, "G" for grocery, "FO" for feast offering, "T" for tithes.

I was again admonished by the auditor; but I remained calm. My actions were in accord with the Divine Law so I knew that all would go well for me. I had tremendous faith that I would be delivered out of this emotionally taxing situation. I had justly "rendered unto Caesar," as I had faithfully paid my tithes. I waited and waited for a response. Finally, my contributions were accepted, but with a strong warning about contributions to groups without 501(c)3 status in the future. This was a modern day miracle.

When hearing of my success with the IRS, Moses Israel heralded the victory in his lecture, but never mentioned the temple's refusal to assist me in this battle. My perception of Moses Israel was becoming like that of other preachers and Judith, his cohort was likened to Jezebel. I thought, "I must remember that church is a business and businesses primarily operate for profit."

I had contributed to the temple's storehouse in accord with the scripture on tithing; but would that matter now that I was in a crisis? Unlike the bank, I couldn't get credit or withdrew any of my funds. Instead of feeling positive and optimistic as I did when I began to tithe, I now felt stupid.

My thoughts returned to the present moment as I felt the vibration of the landing gear being lowered. As the plane began its descent into the Miami International Airport, I again looked around at the entourage. I prayed for another miracle because today was my day of trouble and I needed all of the blessings that were to be bestowed on me right now, here on earth.

As the wheels of the jumbo jet touched down on the tarmac, I vowed, "never again."

As the entourage proudly walked through the terminal, knowing that every curious eye was fixed on them, I felt totally detached. I no longer wanted to identify with them. My desire for group acceptance had been totally extinguished.

As the caravan of white cars exited the ramp and turned south toward the temple, I thought of home. As soon as I got out of the car, I hurriedly gathered my bags and rushed to my car which had been left in the parking lot.

"Mary Ilana! Mary Ilana!" Amos yelled. "Can I catch a ride with you?"

"Yes, but hurry!" He quickly got in the car and closed the door. I cranked the engine and backed out.

As I turned the corner onto Unity Boulevard aka 27th Avenue, I sighed, thinking unity! What unity?

Then Amos spoke, "Mary Ilana, after that escapade you pulled in Atlanta, I talked with Moses Israel privately. He said that he had been patient long enough with you and has had it up to here with your disobedience," demonstrating a hand to forehead gesture.

"You were invited to attend staff meetings. You came if you wanted and left as you pleased. He offered you an opportunity to help manage the motel on Miami Beach, and you went over three times then stopped without an explanation. Why?"

"Cause I didn't like Judith's attitude towards the disciples! She didn't exhibit the same "spirit of hospitality" that I had been reprimanded for in Philadelphia. While working with her one day, she misidentified me as a

The Third Day: Puerto Rico

disciple as I entered a room wearing white from head to toe. She blasted me for not doing something that she had ordered. Realizing her mistake, she apologized by saying, "Oh, I thought that you were Shera."

I thought, "What difference did it make?" Shera deserved to be spoken to politely also.

"That same day, another disciple, Hannah, approached Judith with some old smelly blankets that were found in the motel's laundry room. She asked what to do with them."

Judith responded after smelling them, "I don't care, you can throw them away."

"As Hannah walked away, Judith yelled out loudly, "Wait, wash them and give them to the disciples who live in the plant. They will take anything."

"I wasn't shocked by Judith's attitude but I knew then that I could not work with her at all. I believe in treating people respectfully especially when you are in charge." There was silence in the car.

"Well what about this situation?" Amos continued. "When Moses Israel restructured the definition and duties of a disciple so that the rules were more conducive to people like you who were not willing to give up their total independence, you purposefully missed all three meetings that explained the options which would have allayed your concerns."

"I remember! Nehemiah forewarned me after the first of the three meetings. He told me that as Moses Israel discussed the revisions, he stirred everyone up emotionally about the benefits of discipleship. When they were excited and jumping for joy, he had them to raise their hands if they thought that the new plan was a good compromise. Naturally when the hands were up, he told them to keep them up to take an oath. Then a pledge form was passed out by his staff for them to sign on the spot. Afterwards he lectured on the negative consequences of taking a vow to God and then breaking it. I was not going to get caught up in that frenzy. If I had gone to one of the meetings and had not raised my hand, he still would have badgered me for not being faithful and trusting. In class he called me lukewarm, remember?"

"So you had been warned," Amos chuckled.

"Yes! You see Amos; I realized a long time ago that Moses Israel is a master strategist. He thinks and plans ahead then methodically takes action step by step. Through any given context, he could get disciples to do almost anything and justify it with scriptures. Just think! Did you ever hear him actually say to anyone that they must quit their jobs and come and work at the temple or to sell their property and give the funds to the temple?"

"No!"

"Right! He just taught the lessons, read the scriptures, and then asked who would obey. You see ya'll don't listen. You just jump up and down and give high fives whenever he says something profound, which is always." I sighed deeply.

"Amos, I'm frightened. What does all of this mean?"

He said, and I quote him exactly, "I'm going to kill her if she doesn't conform. I want her on my staff as we move forward."

"Did he mean it literally or figuratively?"

Amos laughed then said, "You are hopeless. You're just too academic."

Even now my damned questioning would not allow me to fully comprehend my plight.

The sound of other vessels passing brings me back to the present. We are about to dock. I quickly return to my room, place my notepad on the bed, and get my miniature tape recorder. I am flowing with memories and I don't want to lose any thoughts while I'm in the city. I grab my purse and hurry to the upper deck.

As I disembark, I hear, "Welcome to Puerto Rico," the eager vendors shout gleefully. "Step right over here and have your picture taken on the canvas of your choice."

I immediately spot the appropriate canvas for my portrait. It is a huge million dollar bill. I stand in front of the monitor and smile. As the computer generated photo appears on the canvas, I relax. My eyes look full and bright. I feel terrific.

As I stroll off into town with the crowd, I see jewelry shops on every corner. I purchase a gold medallion with the symbol #1 to wear around my neck. I continue to shop but am mindful of the time because I've purchased a tour package that will take me to a nightclub in New San Juan to see a Flamenco show tonight. I'll have to return to the ship by 7:00 p.m. to get dressed.

The show is full of energy, delightful and very colorful. The tour van returns to the ship at midnight. According to the itinerary, we will dock in Saint Thomas at 8:00 in the morning, so I go directly to my room and prepare for bed.

THE FOURTH DAY: ST. THOMAS

"Mary in St. Thomas"

Clink! Clank! Clunk! The sounds of the anchors lowering awaken me. I quickly dress and rush to eat breakfast. I am so impressed with the view that I ask a passenger to take my picture.

I hurriedly disembark and take a cab into town. I visit Bluebeard's Inn and Megan's Bay before I begin my shopping spree. In a few hours, I'll return to the ship, which I hope will be virtually deserted. I want to continue writing.

THE SACRIFICIAL LAMB

The unfair reprimand in Atlanta was the last straw for me. Finally I knew without a doubt that I was not an acceptable member of this group. I felt disconnected from them spiritually, culturally and ethnically. I was so angry and dismayed. I had always known that I could not conform to their communal lifestyle. Nor could I just blindly accept every precept taught without researching and questioning.

I'd always justified my actions scripturally by believing that I was being made stronger in character, or that I was more blessed because I was rebuked. Now, none of those rationales made sense. Something was wrong or I had been wrong all along. I realized that though the temple had been a temporary safe haven from an abusive husband, I'd placed my family in a very dangerous environment. Now I had to protect my kids even if it meant losing my life.

As I reached my decision, I thought of the rumors concerning the fate of members who had left the temple. Those rumors had never affected me because I wasn't a disciple and had never taken and oath or pledge. I'd only acknowledged my Hebrew name. I believed that we were the "people of the book" and supported the movement. But now that I was seriously ending my association, I was worried because those disciples who interpreted Moses Israel's words literally would not ask about my status or classification if they decided to come after me. I prayed and prayed for a solution.

A few weeks earlier, Juanita said, "I don't want to attend summer school at the temple. I want to go to Cleveland and be with Aunt Eurie and my cousins. Can I fly up with Latrisha in June?"

First I hesitated to consent. Then it occurred to me that that was the perfect solution. The previous year, several out-of-town students returned to their hometowns for summer vacations. Moses Israel was upset when they returned in the fall with new thoughts and interests. So he voiced another edict, "School will now be year round without a vacation. Any parent who does not follow this attendance policy will risk having their child permanently expelled."

Remembering this, I consented to let Juanita go to Cleveland, but I needed a solution that would be controversial when she returned that would put all of the blame on me. Moses Israel had often said, "When the parents leave so do the children because they can only be as sincere as the parents. The fruit doesn't fall far from the tree."

The temple's focus had drastically changed over the six years that I'd attended bible classes. My personal safety, unity and historical relevance had attracted me, but now the focus appeared to be more on total obedience to Moses Israel, who had now openly proclaimed that he and only he was the indisputable Son of God incarnate.

Disciples were now worshipping him as God Almighty. His name had changed again. He was now Yahweh Ben Yahweh. Around the temple, the disciples referred to him affectionately as "YBY," but I continued to secretly refer to him as Moses Israel, the author and teacher.

Some disciples would do almost anything, based on their interpretation of the text, to uplift their status within the nation. I couldn't risk my children's future any longer. No one, not even my kids, could know what my thoughts and plans were. As I prepared myself to become the sacrificial lamb, a scapegoat was presented, Chico. He was finally good for something.

I smiled and prayed that circumstances would work in my favor.

As agreed, Juanita escorted Eurie's granddaughter Latrisha to Ohio. Lonnie spent the summer with my brother Bennie's three sons. Renee, a recent high school graduate, was eager to attend college. She registered to take the GED because the temple's school was not accredited. However, because of the additional home schooling I provided, she passed the test on the first try and quickly applied for admission for the fall term at Miami Dade Community College. Always being a daddy's girl, she drove my car over to Lillie C. Evans Community School where Chico was the night administrator, to show him her two diplomas.

"That piece of paper from the temple doesn't mean shit. You're eighteen now, leave your mammy and come and live down south near me. I own two condos. You can live in one of them and attend Miami Dade's south campus. Here's a check for $1500 for passing your GED. Don't give your mammy a dime of it; if you do, I'll never give you a cent more."

Renee returned home and placed the check on her dresser and went to bed. The next morning as I entered her room, I saw it and out of curiosity picked it up, but before I could make a comment, she jumped out of the bed and onto my back and tussled to retrieve the check.

"Give it to me," she screamed. "It's mine. You can't have it."

"What are you talking about," I angrily shouted as we fell back onto the bed.

"Daddy gave me the money."

I immediately understood. This was the perfect situation!

After I knocked some sense into her, I said, "Since you had the audacity to pounce on me you can pack your bags and go to Chico now. I will not have you or anyone else abuse me. This was your first and last attack. Get up now and get dressed. I'll take you to grandma's house. You can call your dad from there to pick you up. You are not welcomed here anymore." Inwardly, I cried as I dropped her off.

During the summer, Juanita and Renee talked daily. Renee enthusiastically informed her that, "Daddy has lots of money and his nursery school is doing so well that he quit his job as an assistant principal to work full time in the business. He just bought me a brand new Hyundai Sonata and moved me into a condo that he owns in South Miami."

"Really?"

"Yes, and he has given me a credit card so that I can buy anything that I want and he pays the bills."

"It sounds like he is rich."

"Yeah, everyone talks about his money and influence."

"What is his house like?"

"It's a two story with five bedrooms. It has a screened in patio with a big swimming pool and a bricked barbeque grill."

"Wow! I can't wait to see it. Give me his telephone number so that I can call him."

While in Cleveland, Juanita developed a close relationship with Chico via telephone after Renee told her that Chico had purchased a new car for her graduation and cotillion. Juanita became excited about the possibility of Chico showering her with gifts also.

At the end of the summer, Renee picked Juanita up from the airport in her shiny new car. When she got home she called me at work. "Emah," Hebrew for mother, ""May I visit Tamar today? She lives in Overtown. I can ride the bus to her house. She gave me directions."

Tamar was a classmate of Juanita's who she'd stayed in contact with during the summer.

"No, Juanita. You've never ridden the public bus and you are unfamiliar with that area. Stay home until I return from work."

Juanita was bold. Saying no to her was a challenge. She disobeyed me and went anyway. She'd planned to be home before I returned but her timing was off because she was not familiar with the bus schedules.

Later that night we debated furiously. I listened carefully to her defense but held my position. But most importantly, I learned a lot about how the curriculum had changed at the temple's school for the older students.

"We only have class for two hours a day. Then they select a few students to go to the sewing center or the business area for technical training. Most of the students are frustrated because of unfairness and favoritism and they're being utilized as "helpers" in the various businesses. I do not want this! I want to study so that I can go away to college. I want to become a lawyer."

I knew that this was the time to act quickly. I had to use my alternate plan of action. I did not want her to return to the temple's school for her junior and senior years because I'd searched her backpack and discovered love letters that she had written to Zachariah, a sixteen year old classmate from New York. The contents, if true, convinced me that she had lost her virginity when they secretly rendezvoused in the restroom earlier in the school year.

I knew that she would defy me again, even if she was attending public school. As my mom would often say, "Once girls begin to smell themselves, you have to watch them like a hawk." I too had secretly disobeyed my mother who had kept tighter reins on me in high school. Yes, I found a way to meet with Chico several times before he left for college. Now I couldn't trust Juanita to obey my orders either. Only Chico would be able to control her. I was under too much stress to deal with her attitude and she needed to be protected from herself.

"Ok, don't unpack," I said arrogantly. "Just go straight to your daddy's house since you two have become so friendly over the phone this summer. I'm tired of taking care of ya'll with just the few dollars I receive in support. You're older now and I need time for myself. Renee, put Juanita's luggage in your car. You can come back for Lonnie's clothes tomorrow. Go now! Get out!"

My performance deserved an Academy Award. I knew that if I had called Chico and asked him to take Juanita and Lonnie, he would have refused just to spite me. He didn't want them to live with him; he just wanted them away from me and out of the temple. Finally we agreed on a common issue. As they got into Renee's new car and speedily drove away, I cried profusely.

I don't know how Renee discussed my actions when they arrived at Chico's, but he accepted them into his home. A week later I received a court order requesting a hearing for a reversal in the primary custody and child support. Chico had vowed that one day he'd turn the children against me and I decided that this day was as good as any; but would he succeed?

Inwardly I rejoiced. Outwardly, I sadly told everybody, family, friends and coworkers, that the kids had been taken from me. This drama also satisfied the ones in the chief seats at the temple. They too rejoiced at my dilemma. It didn't matter, I'd accomplished my objective: to have Chico validate my story by spreading the word around town that he'd taken custody of the children and reenrolled them in public school.

MARKED FOR DEATH

Alone, I concentrated on saving my life. Steadfast in my decision to gradually end all ties with the group, I appeared supportive yet distraught. I didn't want to make any more enemies. Therefore, when Celeste called and asked for assistance on a project for the women's group, I consented.

"Mary Ilana, help me write a proposal that will incorporate the goals of various women's organizations within the community with those of the temple's sisterhood."

"All of the ideas that I've submitted in the past were rejected as being too worldly," I informed her.

"I have an idea. Let's rewrite them."

"Ok, I'll give them to you. You're good with words so maybe you can restructure them. Meet me in the café at the motel on the beach tomorrow."

"Fine, be on time."

After hours of discussions over lunch, a multifaceted package was prepared and ready to be presented.

Celeste said, "I want you to accompany me to the meeting."

"No!" I said while moving my head from side to side.

"I understand your reluctance but I feel that your continued involvement will be a great way to make amends with Moses Israel," she stated in a consoling tone.

"I'll reconsider if you get his approval first. I don't want to get there and be embarrassed." Celeste now had direct access to Moses Israel.

"Ok, I'll talk with him personally," she promised.

After receiving permission, we strategically planned our performance. In the meeting, I would sit directly in front of Celeste but would not speak. She would always refer to us as a team by using the pronouns "we, us and our" constantly.

The next week, everything went according to the plan and we were successful. "We," actually Celeste, were granted permission to host a major event that should capture the imaginations of middle class, success oriented, professional women. Because Moses Israel wanted this project to be perfect, Celeste was given an unlimited budget for its implementation.

The sisters soon realized what had happened but it was too late to stop the action, so they planned their counter attack.

The next day around 10:00 a.m. Celeste called.

"Guess what? We were so dynamic that the women fumed after you left the building. They realized that it was your initial proposal and later told Moses Israel that you were negatively influencing me to get your ideas implemented. I saw them huddle together and heard them plotting their revenge. Can you imagine?"

She continued with the conversation, but my thoughts focused on the word "plot."

As I pondered, I finally understood the reasons for their viciousness. They were fearful for their positions. They were disciples who had devoted their lives to Moses Israel. Though I believed in spirit, I wasn't dependent on nor committed to Moses Israel, the man. I still had my job, my house, my car and my bank account, so to them I was a free woman.

They were bound and shackled by their oaths and saw no way out of the choices that they had made to become disciples. They couldn't imagine their living conditions and status improving unless they impressed him. They wanted to maintain their "chief seats and high positions" in the synagogue.

It didn't matter who was hurt. They were only looking out for themselves. They had lost their focus. Their goal was not in helping the masses of our people but rather in self-preservation and self-aggrandizement. They wanted me, and the other believers and supporters like me, completely relegated as insignificant. Our independence was a threat to them. They wanted our voices and ideas silenced and our erroneously perceived social status within social organizations diminished. They didn't want us to positively influence the professional women within the community. That would be too simple.

They wanted to do the improbable by demonstrating their wisdom, knowledge and understanding of success and prosperity as taught to them by Moses Israel. Celeste and I were educated by the system. They wanted to show us college educated women how inferior we were. After all, they were Moses Israel's elite group, members of his entourage, his scholars, and his handmaidens. They wanted all of the power and reward.

I refocused my attention and continued to listen intently to Celeste's conversation.

"You won't believe this but after you left the meeting, Moses Israel openly shared with us bits and pieces of the private conversation you had with him after the trip to Philadelphia."

"Just what did he say?" I fumed.

"He told us about your past abuse and how it had affected your relationship with men. I think that he was attempting to diffuse the anger among the sisters in an effort to help them understand you better. Instead those silly women heard another opening for them to tell him about your relationship with Abner."

"Oh no, Celeste, this experiment of yours didn't work." There was silence for a few seconds. "I understand the women's attitude but I don't understand why he is behaving so mundanely? Surely he has transcended jealousy and envy."

"Mary Ilana, what did I tell you in Atlanta? Men, all men if they are walking, eating and breathing, can't handle rejection and you continue to openly defy him. You'd better get your act together. His last words about you after hearing this news was, "Mary Ilana is so negative."

After moments of silence, I say in an unforgiving tone, "How can he say that he's a spiritual counselor and breach my confidential statements. I don't trust him anymore," I sigh.

When I hung up the telephone, I thought and I thought. Why did Moses Israel call me negative? I had to understand his words and the context in which he had spoken them. In studying his teaching style, I knew that his use and choice of words meant more than what the average listener perceived. I remembered the lesson in which he had us to provide several definitions of the word "take." Collectively, we came up with approximately ten meanings. Then, he had us to turn to the word in the dictionary, and to our surprise, there were one hundred and ten distinct usages. We were amazed. Then he humorously said, "I am the word; you can't limit me or my heavenly father."

Mindful of his techniques, I went to my bookshelf and pulled down the dictionary and turned to the word "negative." As I read the definitions, I couldn't personally relate my actions to any of them. My eyes quickly scanned the page. Suddenly, there it was; the word "NEGATIVISM."

I read aloud: "The belief or attitude of any negative thinker; atheism, agnosticism; The denial of traditional beliefs without proposing constructive substitutes; psychologically, it meant a type of behavior characterized by resistance to suggestion: when the subject fails to do what he is expected or asked to do."

Yes, I finally understood. Through my actions, I had denied that Moses Israel was exclusively divine or more prophetic than other biblical characters or current members of the clergy. I was a skeptic, who was most resistant to suggestions without questioning and I didn't conform to the temple's collective mindset as demonstrated by my behavior. I remained a free thinking individual while in the midst of them. Yes, I was a nonconformist. I was a negator. I was the enemy. Now, I was very scared.

GETTING MY "HOUSE" IN ORDER

I was so distraught that I forgot to eat regularly for days. My lightheadedness and dizziness returned. I started losing weight. My thoughts were rambled and my speech became sluggishly inarticulate.

Expecting the worse, I went to Office Depot and purchased two forms, a *Last Will and Testament* and a *Quit Claim Deed* for the house. I quickly inventoried my belongings, organized my official papers, typed the forms and went to a local check cashing outlet, stood in line and waited to have the papers notarized.

The line was very long and moved very slowly. This gave me time to think. First I laughed, and then my eyes began to fill with tears. This was not the finish that I'd expected. I got out of line, remembering that I had a friend, Elise King, a registered nurse, who lived nearby in the Brentwood development. She was also a notary official. I made a brief stop in the pharmacy to get a box of Sominex and quickly drove to her house with blinding tears rolling profusely down my cheeks.

Elise perceived my anguish, notarized my forms, without reading them, and quickly consoled me. She telephoned daily to monitor my emotions. She understood what was happening psychologically and physiologically, but I never told her my story. I didn't want anyone else involved.

I really wanted to talk with my sister Liz, but I was afraid to call her. Liz always knew what to do. I missed my children. Chico threatened to take away their possessions if they visited me. I felt so all alone. I was without hope, without motivation and without a desire to live. Everything looked dark and gloomy. But I had to confide in someone trustworthy.

I called my college classmate, Vern, a licensed clinical social worker. I openly discussed everything with her.

"Vern do not discuss this matter with anyone, especially my family, unless something happens to me. You're the only one I can trust. I want you to know where I keep all of my important papers and documents."

I then started crying. "How did this happen to me?"

We cried together as we journeyed back in time to our college days remembering our dreams and plans.

Meanwhile, at the temple, a massive move to "evict" those disciples who were considered undesirables was underway. They were no longer needed to pass the word, or to bring in a financial quota. The businesses and properties, in which they had worked so hard to renovate, were now producing incomes. The disciples who were once proud to be considered "house," those who lived communally, were now told to "pick up their beds and walk."

Moses Israel began to teach on Lazarus, the beggar. The theme was the "Lame Man." To gauge his mood, I purchased class tapes and listened carefully knowing that his teaching style and choice of words would provide clues to the next phase of his master plan.

"Those of you who do not produce for yourselves will find yourselves sitting outside of the gate of the temple begging for crumbs of bread. Take off your white robes, comb out your afros, and get a job. No more free meals and lodging."

The "house cleaning" process had begun prior to the trip to Atlanta. The term TMS was used as a label for disciples who demonstrated "temple mentality syndrome;" meaning those stuck in the dependency mode. They had believed that God, through the Son of God, Moses Israel, aka Shiloh, Yahshua, the Grand Potentate and Yahweh Ben Yahweh, would always take care of their needs, wants and desires.

There was much stress and anxiety. Many had discontinued their educational or technical training when they became disciples, and because they had contributed all of their earnings to the "common fund," all of them were now without savings. Many of the women had numerous children to support and their husbands had either left the temple or couldn't be contacted.

Moses Israel was relentless in highlighting this theme, **"From Poverty to Riches"** for several months. The same emphasis as was **"Working for Yahweh"** that was preached to the professional class five years ago which accelerated their exodus from the temple, was now being stressed for those who had forsaken all of their worldly possessions and had become fulltime workers across the country.

Unless they could become "profitable servants," they were no longer welcomed with open arms. The pennies that they had pooled together were not enough anymore. The table had turned and the doors swung outwards. Discipleship had run its course.

The anticipated return of the professional class was positively heralded throughout the nation. Disciples who did not meet the criteria to qualify for admission into this desirable caste began to feel betrayed. They scrambled here and there, to and fro to better their educational and economic status.

They didn't want to be left out. Now they considered my not having sold nor shared my property, or quit my job a good move.

The same disciples who teased and looked down on me as if I were not as devout because I refused to become "house" were now more pleasant towards me. Some of them called asking for advice and professional references for job applications.

When they complained about their plight and started to discuss the unfairness of their situations, I didn't respond. Nor did I laugh or seek revenge for the many injustices that they had perpetrated against me. I understood their frustration, disappointment and anguish. Instead I demonstrated compassion without sympathy. I empathized with their plight but I didn't allow them to exploit me in the name of unity, sisterhood, nationhood or God.

THE CRUCIFIXION

Having become persona non grata, I felt lost. Feeling the pain of ostracism, I remembered the movie, "*The Last Temptation of Christ.*" After being nailed to the cross, the Christ reflected on his life as he looked out at the crowd. I too, began to reflect on my life, my goals and objectives, my accomplishments, my motivation, intentions and now my failures. As I bore my cross daily, I too, like Jesus, could hear the terse remarks of the spectators as I journeyed up Calvary. They shouted, "Stone her! Ha, ha, Ha! Goody for you! How foolish! Stupid! Give us Barabbas!" Their merciless harsh words seemed to reverberate in my mind daily as I walked among neighbors and co-workers.

This was a cross that I had not intended to bear. I'd envisioned Utopia, the days when the lion and the lamb would sit together by the stream peacefully. The time when there would be equality and justice for all; the time when peace, happiness and prosperity would flourish and the world would be free of sickness and disease.

Isn't that what almost all religions teach? Are we not taught to expect a deliverer; a great gathering of the chosen; a day of judgment; a reward in heaven? Aren't these beliefs common in the various Christian denominations? Isn't that why we have so many types of churches because of different interpretations of the same holy book? So why was I being harshly criticized? Why were Christians laughing and throwing stones? Where was the understanding and the compassion? But most importantly, I wondered why was it so difficult for African Americans to believe that they too could possibly be God's chosen people, if there were "a" chosen people? Had slavery, Jim Crow, and various forms of discrimination so demolished us that it was impossible to ever conceptualize any significance to our existence and our struggles? I questioned and questioned, but there were no answers!

Harriet Tubman, Sojourner Truth, Phyllis Wheatley, Jane Pittman, Rosa Parks and Marva Collins and many other notable Black women had been my inspiration. I too had wanted to carry and pass the torch of freedom. I now knew that I'd lived my life in a fantasy state. I'd been a book worm and a dreamer. I'd been one who pursued knowledge for its own sake rather than for its practical applications. I was very hopeful.

I was not optimistic anymore. Pessimism was overshadowing my being. My aura was gloomy. I'd lost hope and my faith in God was waning. I was no longer motivated and I resigned to live the rest of my life alone.

I was on an emotional roller coaster daily. It was easy to conceal my feelings though. Very few people suspected that anything was ever wrong. For years I had been an itinerant speech and language pathologist rotating among various work locations daily. So it was easy to smile for three and a half hours at my morning school, but lunch time was agonizing. I cried profusely as I drove to the next school. After reaching my destination, I'd wipe the tears away and smile again for three and a half more hours only to resume the crying spells as I drove home to my lonely house.

Going to work became more difficult. Staying home was even worse. With the children gone and no one to shop for, I stopped eating regularly. My knees trembled and I often felt faint. Water would pour out of my skin as my body tingled. I was unable to speak clearly because my tongue became lethargic. It felt as if it were glued to the floor of my mouth. My thoughts were rambled. There was a malfunctioning of my nervous system; the axons and dendrites were misfiring or not synapsing properly. I needed to eat and rest.

I'd lived my life for and through my children and now they were gone. Though Lonnie later returned to my household, I knew that life would not be the same. My love and yearning for my daughters was overwhelming. If only I could talk to them, things would be better for me; but that was impossible. Chico's promise to turn them against me was working. He provided them with a material kingdom that they couldn't resist and I couldn't afford to duplicate. "My God, my God! Why have YOU forsaken me," I lamented daily.

The emotional pain was almost unbearable. I felt hated, misunderstood, and condemned by everyone in the temple; in the schools that I worked; by the African American female principals who covertly persecuted me by denying my many requests for transfers into their schools and who constantly wrote me up based on hearsay without first conducting diligent inquiries of the facts or contextual circumstances, thus thwarting my professional growth and kept me having to write letters in my defense. Finally, by a few African American speech pathologists who shunned me at workshops for fear of what "the others" would think of their association with me.

Professionally, it would have been completely intolerable for me to cope with if it had not been for Ethel Williams initially and Jacquelyn Glaze later. However, Bob Grasso and Sally Corak, who are white, were always there with a smile, a wave, a compliment or a kind deed or gesture at every staff meeting, workshop or in-service training.

I felt socially alienated. It was as if my name had been stricken from the book of life. I was seldom, if ever, invited to parties or events unless someone was trying to sell their quota of tickets.

There was only the unconditional love of family, but I had not shared my plight with them. What a dilemma! I didn't want to live, but was afraid to die.

THE DEATH WISH

With everything in order, my insurance papers, Last Will and Testament and my property deed, I waited for what I thought was the inevitable. I was restless. I pondered what went wrong. I lamented. However, being a true believer in the scriptures, I knew that my duty was to observe the laws of God without fear no matter what the consequences. In late September, when the Feast of Tabernacles was held, I returned to the temple to attend as prescribed in the Book of Leviticus. Just prior to that was the Day of Atonement which I celebrated at home alone. A complete fast, no food or water, for twenty-four hours was obeyed. I lie prostrated on the floor for hours asking Yahweh, The Heavenly Father, for forgiveness of all of my past sins.

I had not realized how physically weak I had become; otherwise I would not have gone without water. The next week, I developed cystitis and thought little of it as I drank cranberry juice. I went to the bookshelf, got my copy of *"BACK TO EDEN"* and turned to the list of herbs for the condition. Golden Seal was my choice. For a few days, I took several dosages daily; my body reacted terribly. I decided to detoxify that herb from my system by taking another pre-formulated combination of cleansing herbs. My body began to tingle so I increased that herbal dosage and drank more water.

I knew that something more serious was wrong though. My body just didn't feel right. My thinking was impaired. Morbid thoughts constantly entered my mind. I'd lost my desire to live and was depressed and lonely.

On December 8th, I awakened with a sense of despair so great that I prayed for death but I had to go to work because I was backlogged in my testing. As usual, I had not eaten breakfast at home so I went into the school's cafeteria and bought some cereal. As my stomach growled, I began to feel gaseous; there was an awful bitter taste in my mouth that I'd never experienced before.

I was afraid to go into the therapy area because it was isolated in the teacher's workroom in the kindergarten building which was detached from the regular school. I was sure that I was gravely ill. I walked to the main office and asked Pam, the registrar, to check on me later; then went into the school's clinic and sat on the bed. I remember getting up to rush into the bathroom to vomit, but obviously I didn't make it. At approximately 9:15 a.m., I passed out. The registrar found me on the floor. As I slowly regained consciousness, I whispered in her ear my need for a blanket. I was very cold, my clothing was wet and my pores were profusely secreting perspiration. I can't explain it but the physical sensations that I felt prior to my passing out were gone and instead of morbid thoughts, I felt peaceful.

Pam wanted to call the paramedics, but I convinced her that I was fine. When I was able to walk, I drove home and called Liz, who now worked at Miami Heart Institute in the intensive care unit. I explained the sequence of events and of my herbal use but purposefully omitted how emotionally drained I was.

"You are very blessed," she said. "Your heart probably skipped a beat because of the lack of sodium and potassium in your system. You most likely suffered from a "P" wave. You could have died. Make sure you drink plenty of Gatorade and go see your doctor soon."

"Thank you. I love you Liz."

"I love you too, Bebe."

When I felt better; I called Donna, an aspiring herbalist and told her what had happened. She rushed over with her natural healing books. As we talked, I realized what I'd done to myself. She read the section on Golden Seal.

"Though Golden Seal is considered the best medicinal herb in the herbal kingdom because of its many uses and properties, it is also considered one of the ten most dangerous herbs because of its effect on the nervous and endocrine systems. You should not take it daily because it accumulates and stores in your liver."

She handed me the book. There it was: "Golden Seal has the ability to lower blood sugar and should be used by diabetics but not by persons with hypoglycemia. Golden Seal has the ability, upon entering the bloodstream, to regulate liver functions.

Warning: Do not take either during pregnancy or continuously for a long period of time without some periods of rest."

I'd taken self-healing too far. Most revealing was the fact that I'd subconsciously programmed myself to die and Golden Seal was the lethal weapon.

IN THE TOMB

For nearly two weeks, I was confined to bed too weak physically to walk without tiring easily. My body continued to tremble and I kept fading in and out of consciousness. I was so frightened and alone. I hadn't let my family know how terribly I felt physically and they still knew absolutely nothing about my situation at the temple.

Unlike the sorority sisters of Delta Sigma Theta who assisted me during my divorce, calling the temple's sisterhood to ask for comfort was unthinkable. I was now "persona non grata." Their philosophy was "all that happens to you is "God's will." If someone died, became ill, was hurt or experienced misfortune, it was discussed openly in class as an example "for all of Israel to hear and fear." Illness or any misfortune was a sign of faithlessness or unrighteousness.

I quickly refocused on my physical condition as I tossed and turned in bed. I prayed the prayers of contrition as I remembered them from my Catholic upbringing. It was just me and God, face to face in the confessional booth of my bedroom. There were no intercessors. I placed the call to God myself. It was direct dialing, person to person, without operator assistance. It was not a long distanced call. This call was placed from the inner chambers of my soul.

After making spiritual contact, I relaxed and put all of my trust in God. Whatever happened now would be acceptable. I fell asleep peacefully but was soon awakened by strange sensations engulfing my body. A vibratory force of energy started swirling around within me. I became light-headed and felt euphoric. Was I going into shock again or was I hallucinating? This force of energy oscillated in my toes and began to surge up my body as if it were trying to leave through the top of my head. It did and I was very surprised to see my body lying there on the bed while looking down on it from the ceiling.

Was this judgment day? Was I preparing to meet Saint Peter at the Pearly Gate with the record of my life? No, I'm not ready to defend all of my actions. I prayed again confessing all of my transgressions. I loudly confessed my secret faults.

I cried, "Let me go to Purgatory and work this thing out." Was I plea bargaining with God? YES!

Was this a dream? No! This was actually happening to me. Was I having an out-of-body experience or was this the result of a herb induced illusion? It felt real.

This scripture resounded in my head as I reentered my body, "Fear not them which kill the body, but are not able to kill the soul: but rather fear him which is able to destroy both soul and body in hell."

I pondered this great lesson which I didn't fully understand, but realized that the soul was separate and distinct from the body. My cup was running over with divine ideas that bombarded my mind as fast as the speed of light. I felt reinvigorated, revitalized and reenergized. I sensed that the Creator was not a "form" but pure radiant energy. No longer did I feel like just a physical being. I was not afraid of death anymore. "Oh death, where is thy sting? Oh grave, where is thy victory?" I uttered joyously.

After having experienced the radiant energy of God's essence flowing throughout my body, I knew that I would live, but I still didn't want to be alone.

After writing these episodes, I realized just how deeply I'd been affected by the events. If I had continued counseling after my divorce or had shared my thoughts with someone whom I trusted about my experiences at the temple, maybe they could have provided another viewpoint which could have challenged my thinking. Instead I suffered in silence while appearing highly organized, extremely professional, very confident, and beyond reproach.

THE FIFTH DAY: ST. MAARTEN

The wall of silence is slowly being removed as I roll away the stones through my reflective writing. My blinded eyes can see more clearly. Light is replacing darkness in the crevices of my mind. The blinders that I've been wearing for so long are finally being removed precept upon precept, line upon line, here a little and there a little.

The scene in St. Maarten is different. I look for the ship's logo which heralded your destination to take a picture, but soon realize that it is not available at this port. I see a caravan of taxicabs parked waiting patiently for the passengers to descend.

I pool with two strangers to tour the sights. The guide proudly points out the vacation homes of notable celebrities and the luscious golf courses and resorts. He gives us a history lesson on the island's colonization as we cross the French side of the bridge onto the Dutch side.

Finally we stop at a market. What a contrast! This is actually the way the locals live. Not in the mansions or in the resorts, but as hagglers trying to sell their wares. I get out of the cab and begin looking for bargains.

THE TAROT READING

After regaining my strength, I visited my girlfriend Linda and shared my out of body experience with her. Linda stared at me then cautiously revealed that she has had similar experiences.

"Really," I said excitedly.

"Yes, I also have a friend who has the ability to channel. He discerns messages from disincarnate beings," she responded.

"Oh you mean like Edgar Cayce, right?" I said with skepticism.

"Well sort of like Cayce but this guy can also tell of your past lives, and discern your future through tarot card readings," she added.

"Well I'm not into that kind of thing. There are specific scriptures that forbid those practices. I'm afraid of that."

"What's there to be afraid of? No one can hurt you. It's just like reading the horoscope in the newspaper. If you believe in it you can use it as a guide for your daily living. If you don't, then it can't affect you," Linda reassuringly expressed.

"How long have you been into this and why have you never revealed this to me?" I asked.

"I've been seeing him for about three years. I didn't tell you because you weren't ready."

Linda got up and went into her den returning with transcripts of several readings that had been channeled for her. As she discussed them, I became more curious. I wanted to know what might happen to me since I had left the temple. I wanted to know about my health. I wanted to know about the safety of my children.

I sat quietly as she showed me books that dealt with the subject, but I was thinking about the laws and statutes in the Torah and of the commandments of God. I didn't want to lose the spiritual bonding that I had just established. I thought of scriptures that would help to extinguish my curiosity like: "Surely the Lord God will do nothing, but he reveals his secrets unto his servants the prophets." But my inquisitive mind got the best of me as I agreed to meet with the tarot reader.

I stayed focused on the "Light" as Rolando spread the cards on the table. Linda pressed the pause bottom on the tape recorder and waited for him to signal that he was ready to begin. Arturo, Rolando's friend watched.

I thought, "What if I don't like what I hear? What will I do? Perhaps I should stop this madness now." But it was too late. As he pointed to the first card and nodded his head, the recording session began. I quietly listened.

"I don't know if this holds true for your whole life, I haven't looked at all of the cards, but the theme of the reading will be rejection of previously held desires and goals, and not so much reevaluation. It's not so much that you have to think, "Well if I don't want to do this, what is it that I want to do?" If I don't believe in this, what is there to believe in?"

"What you're rejecting and accepting were both already there. Your new beliefs and new goals are not something that you have to think about. They've been there all along but you've been sort of squashing them because you've chosen this other way and this other realm that you wanted to master. You always knew that it was something else you wanted to master so it's not a great deal of introspection involved in the process right now. It's simply a question of your taking the first step."

He paused to study the cards, then said, "There's a bit of destruction involved in that process. The rejection involves really pulling things down."

"What do you mean?" I asked.

"Pulling down previously constructed things and just starting this other path. I don't know what it means. I'll have to take a look at your karma."

My eyes widened.

"You've got a karma involving religion and politics simultaneously which is really weird. Some sort of leadership position what involved spirituality and political management of a small society near a village a very long time ago. It may have been in the Middle East. It was in the Middle East. What's good is that when those two things coexist, usually there is corruption and manipulation; but that's not the case with you. You have a pretty good karma. It actually involves a lot of self sacrifice on your part in that life. There wasn't any hypocrisy there."

I smiled.

"You learned a lot in that life and you may have ignored certain worldly pursuits in which you're involved in this life." In order to fully learn the lesson in this life you chose to be involved in illusion, sort of like to make sure you didn't lose anything. The physical world is really an illusion.

HUH! You've embraced the physical world and the intellectual world in this life."

"It's been a long time since your last incarnation, a very long time. It's interesting. I think our souls have qualities. People don't usually realize that just as people have qualities, so do souls. Your soul is very methodical."

I nodded my head in agreement.

"Let's get into your past. There is something tragic that happened at the beginning of this life. Something tragic that has gone a long way in shaping you. That's very significant."

I broke my silence and asked, "Shaping meaning influenced?"

"Yes," he answered.

I thought about the injury to my eye and of not having a father in my early life.

"There's a tremendous resistance to change in you. I don't mean to insult you," he chuckled.

"Please do," I laughed.

"That tremendous resistance to change, there is another word for it. It's called stubborn."

I grinned.

"Remember, I told you that you were following this one way of doing things and you were in the process of rejection."

"Yes, I remember."

"Stubbornness is what keeps you from changing, not fear."

"So, I'm rebellious huh?"

"Yeah," he said emphatically. "Your karma is changing. There was a move that was significant in your life; a move from one house to another."

"House in the spiritual sense or the physical sense?"

"House in the physical sense," he stated. It may have involved your meeting someone that was significant in changing your outlook. Think about that."

"Is there a time reference?" I asked.

"Yes, this life; but not at the beginning," he said.

"Could that move have been from my parent's home to my marital residence?"

"Yes! Certainly! Something spiritual was given to you then."

"That sure was a move," I laughed. "I needed God to help me through my abusive marriage. I prayed daily."

Linda screamed with laughter. We laughed so hard that we had to stop the tape recording. The reading resumed moments later.

"OK, something is confusing; you'll have to help me out. Were you recently involved with a man who was not as smart as you?"

I was thinking that none of them were as smart as me so I asked for clarification.

"What do you mean in terms of college degree or intellect?" I asked.

"Not as, well it's not a question of a degree but of sophistication," he clarified.

"Was he worldly?"

"Quite possibly," he replied.

"Then how recent?" as if there had been so many men to remember.

"It was very recent. Like within the last couple of years."

"Yes."

"Well that's really significant."

"Why?"

The reason it was significant was because there was a lot of clarification in you as far as your ideal relationship with this man."

"Did this cause me to grow?" I asked.

"Yes, to grow, rethink and refocus," he said.

I thought of John Kelley. He was very smart but appeared to be so humble. He was well traveled yet as simple as the boy next door. Through him, I began to trust some men. If he had not been Chico's friend, I would have fallen deeply in love with him. He'd kept his promise to protect me and the kids. He will always be a good friend.

I refocused on the reading.

"You think you're losing control of things right now. You think that things are kind of slipping through your hands. Concentrate on your abilities as a woman. The feminine powers, they are very strong and you can deal with taking care of yourself in a spiritual sense." He points to another card.

"There's a spiritual path that's opening up for you right now that involves much more of the feminine than the masculine. It involves much more of nature and the earth mother type of belief system than organized Christian religious systems and there is a tremendous opening for you in that area. Yes, there is a great opening in spiritual beliefs that involve fertility and the earth mother tradition."

I was clueless.

The Fifth Day: St. Maarten

"There's a great deal of blockage right now; right now this instant in your life. It is tied to what I just told you about the feminine power. The path that you are about to, or that's opening up to you, involves the feminine mother tradition and a lot of subtle spiritual feelings. It's going to be very subtle hints and feelings that if you tune yourself into them they will be very helpful to you especially at night."

"The night?" I questioned.

"Yes, in meditation. Yes much more so than the day. That's interesting. A lot of people are helped by the sun and by meditations that involves bright lights or energies that involve bright lights. But with you the things that I get involve starlight, night breezes, outdoors at night."

I thought that was very interesting because I am a nocturnal person. Between two and four in the morning, I'm up reading, exercising or meditating.

"There's, huh, this exact moment in your life goes back to that past life spoken of. These lives are tied together. Think about it a lot, about politics and religion, about being so good and self sacrificing. It is very significant."

I thought of the six years that I studied at the temple.

"There's a relationship coming up that you're not prepared for, a romantic relationship."

I interject, "You mean in this life I'm not ready yet after all of the rejection?"

Linda laughs!

"You may think you are but you're not ready because it's going to cause you pain. You are going to cause yourself pain more so than the other person."

"So I'm masochistic huh?"

"No because you are too analytical! Don't stick it to yourself so hard. You are missing the tools right now of emotional defense and subtlety. You will have them but it will involve some suffering, self imposed suffering. You tend to do that a lot."

"Yeah, I have."

"There is a relationship on the horizon and I was looking forward to whatever," I paused. "But you're correct. I'm either extremely emotional or too analytical."

He interrupted. "No, you make the worse mistake. You try and keep both. You try to analyze emotions, motives, and feelings. Just be!"

I sat back and took a deep breath.

"There is going to be a splintering of yourself in the next twelve months. Many changes will occur, changes that you will explore which will cause you to change how you look at the world, and how you experience the world relative to religion and politics."

"The lesson that you came into this life to learn involves shifting the way you look at yourself and the way you view the world. It involves opening up the heart without fear and tuning down the brain, your mind." He points to another card.

"I see a great combination, a romantic combination."

"Oh, I can't wait. I'm so horny now."

"This will take care of it. I see a great deal of separateness from other people when you get involved in this relationship, a bit of seclusion. There will be one person whom you'll talk to a lot about this relationship but only one person. The rest of the world you'll shut out."

"I tend to do that now."

"Yes, but you'll do that even more then."

One more card is placed on the table.

"I see a distancing with family members at this time, a great distancing. There's a great, I see the word "harvest" in mind that's awaiting you, spiritually and worldly. And that more than anything is what you have to know. It's all there waiting, but you have to take it. In order to do that you must listen to your guide, to very subtle influences and more than anything else, to your heart and not too much on your mind. Follow your intuition. That's it."

"Thank you. It was rather intriguing. How much do I owe you for this reading?"

"Nothing; this is a gift from God. I give freely as I receive freely."

CLOSE ENCOUNTERS

After the tarot reading, the thought, "there is a relationship on the horizon" kept resounding in my mind. As time passed, there were two persons with whom I had close encounters: Julius and I'll call the other one Job. Which one will sweep me off of my feet and replace the pain with joy and pleasure?

JULIUS

In April I met Julius, a realtor and school social worker, at a Chinese restaurant near the Miami Dolphin Stadium. As we talked I gleaned that he wasn't a native Miamian who might have known Chico. If only for that reason, I wanted to get to know him better. We communicated for two months until I left for my summer vacation.

When I returned in the fall, he quickly discerned that something was bothering me, but I was very reluctant to open up. I didn't want him to change his judgment of me by revealing my past religious association; about my abusive marriage; or that I was feeling very empty without my kids. However as time passed, he became more convinced that I was troubled and encouraged me to talk freely.

"Mary, I work in marketing because my undergraduate degree is in business but I also have a master's degree in counseling. I've done family counseling before so I have the skills to help you if you let me."

I relaxed and began talking about relationships. He countered my views by explaining them from a male's perspective. Then I mustered up the nerves to tell him of my experiences at the temple.

"You don't fit the profile of someone who would be involved in such an infamous group. I'm fascinated. You are very interesting."

Great! He wasn't turned off after learning that I had attended the temple. I thought, "Could Julius be that friend I so desperately yearned for?" I wondered.

Weeks later, I called and invited him to my home and purposefully wore a one piece royal blue Danskin bodysuit. I had a very nice figure which I often concealed by wearing loose clothing, but this night I wanted him to see me as a woman. I wanted to be desired again and I knew that he was interested if only sexually.

When he saw me in that bodysuit he couldn't believe his eyes. "Damn girl, you're so fine!" he exclaimed admiringly.

I modeled for him while saying, "Many prophets and righteous men desire to see what your eyes are seeing."

He laughed so hard. I had a way of humorously interjecting scriptures for special effect. Julius's laughter helped bring back the humorous side of my personality. We laughed, talked and became romantically involved that night.

Soon we were inseparable, but deep down inside I felt like there was someone else in his life. He was very evasive when I brought up sensitive topics and I didn't know where he lived. Like his clients, I'd only been given the phone number to his pager.

In March, Julius called. "Mary, I want to see you. Will you come over to my house?"

"What house?" I questioned.

"I've just purchased my own home. I was renting before. I'll explain when I see you. Get dressed. I'm coming over to pick you up."

I quickly dressed and waited in front of the house for him. When he arrived, I hurriedly got into the car and kissed him on the cheek. After driving a few blocks, I became aware of the silence. Julius, who was very talkative, was unusually quiet. What was he hiding? Should I wait for his explanation?

Finally I asked, "Are you going through withdrawal pains? Did you just break up with someone?" I asked.

"Everything is fine. That's not the problem. I have a lot on my mind tonight. I just wanted to be near you. You have a calming effect on me."

I wasn't satisfied with his response. Too many times in the past I didn't heed the inner voice of caution that echoed warnings in my ear and later had to suffer the consequences of my inaction. This time would be different. I decided that I would begin to detach from him and slowly end the relationship.

The next week, Julius called.

"Hello Mary."

"Hi Julius, how are you?"

"I'm at Cedars of Lebanon."

"You're in the hospital?"

"Yes, I was driving along the expressway the other day when my nose began to bleed. I quickly exited and went to the nearest hospital. My blood pressure was extremely high and I was on the verge of having a stroke."

"Are you Ok now?"

"Yes, I'm fine. I'll be released as soon as my doctor completes his rounds. I'll call you when I get home. See you soon."

With this news, I felt better and reasoned that I was too hasty in deciding to end the relationship.

When he came home, I comforted him, but the sensation that he was indeed hiding a deep secret overwhelmed me.

Finally he said, "Mary, I won't be able to make love to you as often as you would like. There are days when I have E.D."

"What's that?"

"It's short for erectile dysfunction. I can't always get it up because of the medication that I am taking."

I assured him by saying, "It doesn't matter. I am used to abstaining for long periods of time."

He smiled, but I knew that he wasn't being truthful. We had been intimate for months and he hadn't experienced any sexual inadequacy. There was something else that he dreaded discussing.

JOB

Job, like the biblical character, was very humble, patient, prosperous and highly intelligent; though functionally illiterate. He'd leased an apartment in an exclusive country club area and flew into the United States on Monday morning and returned to his Caribbean island home each Friday afternoon. While in town, he studied during the day and attended adult basic education classes at night.

The assistant principal, Mrs. Cooper knew of my tutoring services and introduced him. Initially, I thought that he was a stutterer because of his hesitations. However, after feeling more at ease around me, he told me quite fluently that he couldn't read or write effectively because he'd stopped his formal education in the primary years.

"I have an incredible life story and the business community wants me to share it, but they don't know that I can't read or write very well. So I need a private tutor and someone to assist me with my journal."

"I can tutor you after my regular workday if you're at my home promptly at 4:00. We'll discuss the journal later."

"What about the fee for your services?" he inquired.

"Wait until I assess you, then I'll have you sign a contract. We can start Monday. Here's my address and telephone number."

"Thank you!"

Job arrived promptly at 3:45 and we began at 4:00. In his presence I felt a flow of energy surge up and down my spine. I decided to observe him carefully. His voice was very soft and melodic. He spoke slowly, deliberately choosing each word. His statements were very clear and concise. I found him mentally intriguing. Physically, Job was a giant among men. He was very tall, approximately 6'5", dark and handsome. I was instantly attracted to him.

One afternoon, Job sat quietly and stared at me. His eyes were very dark. I felt that he had an unusual gift to "see" into my soul. It's as if he could read my mind and my secret thoughts.

Finally he spoke, "I am a dreamer. I have visions in the night and I pray and meditate often. I want you to learn to be still, go into the quietness of your bedroom and ask God for guidance. I perceive that you are hungry for the truth. But be careful of some people on your path because the devil is so smart that he uses religion to deceive. Beware of religion and of false prophets, seek God only. You can make peace with God for yourself. You believe and know God in your heart but you've not accepted Him as your guide. You do a lot of things that you think are right but they may not be God's way. Also keep some thoughts and comments between you and God only."

When he left, I immediately wrote his words in my journal.

My contractual relationship with Job started three months after Julius moved into his home. Though I wanted a long term romantic relationship with Julius to evolve, I found myself looking at Job wondering what it would be like to have a relationship with him. But Job was very businesslike. He never ever gave me any indication that he might be even a little bit interested. But that didn't stop me from thinking. I wanted to feel like a woman again and there was something about Julius's character that kept me doubtful of his sincerity.

Job was so fine. At times I would be so into him that I lost my concentration and had to ask him to repeat himself. As time passed, I became more fascinated. Though I helped him with his journal, he always managed to be elusive and private. He only told me what he wanted me to know and when he wanted me to know it. He was the most calm and controlled man that I'd ever met. Nothing seemed to bother him.

The Fifth Day: St. Maarten

One day he sensed that I was not as attentive. He asked, "What's wrong? You're not concentrating."

"I'm just tired and need a vacation. My girlfriend Linda and some of her coworkers went to Istanbul, Greece and Italy last weekend. I was planning to go with them but cancelled so that I could continue with our sessions. I'm just thinking of how much fun they're having now and wishing that I were with them."

Job suggested, "Why don't you visit my island this weekend and relax by the beach. The water and sun will be good for you. You're a Pisces, aren't you?"

"Yes," I laughed. "How did you guess?"

"I didn't guess."

I stared at him and said, "Yes, a weekend retreat is just what the doctor ordered."

"Good. I'll make all of the arrangements. I have to return home tomorrow on an early flight. Your ticket will be at the counter. Don't disappoint me. I've got a goal to accomplish and I need you alert and relaxed. I'll pick you up at the airport."

On Friday morning I packed my garment bag and placed it in the car and went to work; stopped by the beauty salon for a wash and set then proceeded to the airport, parked and boarded the plane. Airborne, I realized that I didn't have Job's telephone number or address. I panicked. What was I to write on the immigration card?

"Mary," I said to myself, "Here you are 32,000 feet in the air and you don't know vital information about this man. Girl, when will you ever learn not to be so naive? But for some reason, my soul felt good about him. I felt safe in his presence. I relaxed.

I quietly remained in my seat until everyone else got off of the plane then followed the passengers to the immigration lines. I felt that I would not be allowed to enter the country. But as I was standing on the yellow line waiting to hear the call, "Next please," I heard, "Pssssssst! Pssssssst!" An immigration agent signaled for me to come to his station. He took my cards and started writing the necessary information in the blanks. I was very surprised but now more curious. Job was still nowhere to be seen.

"Welcome Mary. Job is waiting for you outside. You will be living at the Holiday Inn," he said with a big smile. Sensing that I was nervous he said, "Relax, everything is fine," he grinned. "Job's a great guy."

Sure enough, Job was standing outside of the doors dressed in raw silk and fine linen. He was a handsome sight for my sore eyes to behold. He drove me to the hotel in an awesome burnt orange BMW 700 series, and checked me in. When my luggage was unpacked he said, "Come with me. We're going dancing."

I was pleasantly surprised. Job was so much fun to be with. He continued to amaze me. This was not the "straight-laced, business only" man that I worked with. He was full of laughter and smiles. He was also the best dancer on the floor.

We laughed and talked. Job ordered virgin drinks for both of us. Surprised, I asked, "Why don't you drink alcoholic beverages?"

"I haven't had an alcoholic drink since I was 25 years old."

"What happened then?"

"I heard the voice within. I don't drink so that I can focus. The voice instructs me. That's how I've been able to conceal my illiteracy. I stay focused and I memorize everything that is important."

We talked a while longer then the music changed from fast disco to slow and romantic. The lights were dimmed simultaneously. Job took me by the hand and escorted me back on the dance floor. I hadn't slow danced in years. His being six feet five inches tall was just what I needed. I laid my head on his chest. As the music continued and the songs became slower and more romantic, Job pulled me in closer and tighter to him. I was in heaven, a complete mental, emotional state of happiness and bliss. I wondered if Job were my soul mate. His presence felt so good to me mentally, physically and spiritually.

We returned to the hotel around 3:00 a.m. Job insisted that we walk along the coast before retiring. Back in the room, we talked about his country. Suddenly Job asked, "Do you want me to make love to you?"

God yes, I wanted him to stay and to make love to me passionately but I replied. "No thank you. I'm very tired. It's been a very long day. I want to rest."

"OK, I won't see you again until Sunday, I have much business to take care of but I'll call you." He handed me a card. "Call this cab company and ask for this driver and have him to take you to the downtown district tomorrow. Do some shopping. Don't worry about the bill; I'll take care of everything." As he left, he politely kissed me on the cheek. I was impressed with his manners.

The next two days I walked along the seashore. I rested, prayed and meditated. As I lie on the sand, letting the healing waves of water rush up and down my body, an oddly shaped seashell landed on my stomach.

I picked it up and decided to keep it as a token to remember the night we danced.

On Sunday, Job returned to take me to the airport. In route he took me on a guided tour of the island. He was a gracious host. Surprisingly, he shared his life's story in more detail. Truly he was a prosperous and most astute businessman. He was the owner of a construction company that built hotels and condos on the island. He also owned boutiques and restaurants. Because of his character, I was convinced that there had to be more Black men of high integrity and moral values who would lovingly uplift and respect Black women. Job had set the bar to a higher standard. I would never accept less.

Comfortably in flight, I imagined how a relationship with Job might be, but I knew that I had to get myself together to interact with him on a personal level. He was a MAN in every sense of the word. More pussy wouldn't alter his brain waves. He was more goals oriented than I was and his life was proof that God was no respecter of persons. I sighed. I would try to be cool around him.

THE SIXTH DAY: ON THE SEA

I have become more sociable. Last night, I promised a group from Tampa that I would join them after breakfast for a round of cards in the casino. I like playing cards, especially Whist. It reminds me of life in the dormitory during college and of the house parties I attended after graduation. I'm going to have so much fun.

Later, as I walk to dinner, I feel more enthusiastic. It will be the "Last Supper" that I'll spend with my dining mates. They too have become more relaxed in my presence. As I take my seat, I realize that tonight will be different. The waiters quickly begin serenading the tables with festive melodies. Soon a fantastic culinary lights display begins. The atmosphere is cheerful. Everyone is smiling and laughter can be heard.

As I quietly enjoy the moment, the couple from India gets my attention. The husband says, "Mary, I've noticed that stone that you are wearing and want to know if you are aware of its properties."

I did, but I wasn't sure that I wanted to discuss the reason why I was wearing it with him. So I responded, "It's just a symbol of the very large diamond ring that I imagine I'll wear one day."

To my surprise he says, "I am a Geophysicist. There is energy flowing through that stone. Just as the energy from a quartz keeps a watches' moving parts working, so does the stone that you are wearing possess and radiate energy. That energy interacts with your physical energy. I've noticed a profound positive change in you since the beginning of the cruise."

How perceptive! I look at him and smile.

THE AGATE

Committed to getting my professional life back on track, I eagerly helped Desiree Perkins and Cynthia Cochran, two Speech Pathologists, to charter a local chapter of The National Black Association of Speech, Language, and Hearing Pathologists (NBASLH). Until we had enough members to nominate and vote on officers, I volunteered as the treasurer and quickly went to the bank with the non-profit certificate to establish an account. We were very excited as we mailed out recruitment notices for our first chapter meeting.

It was a success with many recruits in attendance. We collected membership dues and I was given the checks to deposit; which I promptly did the next day. However, a few weeks later, a two day countywide in-service workshop was held at William Turner Technical Center and feeling redeemed, I decided to sit with the group. I immediately sensed that something was wrong. Their attitudes were so negative that during the break I asked Cynthia what was the problem.

"We'll talk later."

"No, I want to talk now. I'm sure that their negative vibes have to do with me."

"Well, after our initial meeting, a few of them started calling around. They don't want you to be the treasurer. They think that you will give our dues and funds to the temple. I tried to assure them that you are trustworthy, but they have their doubts."

"Thanks for letting me know. I'll take care of the situation."

At lunchtime I went straight to the bank, withdrew the funds and closed the account. The next day at the break, I circulated among them and returned their dues, having each one to sign that they were in receipt of their refund. I was dismayed but not thwarted; deciding not to seek an office or participate in any of the group's social functions. My involvement would be limited to activities that enhanced my professional growth.

The local chapter received a correspondence that NBASLH would be hosting its national convention in New Orleans in April. Desiree and I promptly registered for the event and confirmed flight and hotel accommodations. I anxiously applied for professional leave and submitted a proposal to the national organization to have a table to display my community service project.

The convention was super and I was having a wonderful time. I saw many college classmates for the first time in over fifteen years. At night I participated in the many planned social activities. I especially enjoyed walking through the French Quarters and shopping at Riverwalk where I watched the famed steamboats entertain tourists. On Saturday morning I went to a jazz festival and purchased unique gifts from various vendors.

The most significant and rewarding part of the convention was one of the breakout sessions that I attended. It was facilitated by a professor from Louisiana State. *"How to use your Skills and Training as a Speech Pathologist to expand your Career Choices"* was the topic. Upon entering the room she handed us a sheet of paper and asked us to write our obituary. We all looked puzzled but quickly complied with her instructions. The purpose was to determine what was important to us; and what might we be remembered for. That exercise was a life changing event for me. I immediately knew that I would dedicate my life to children as a mentor and tutor.

Realizing that the convention ended a day earlier than our scheduled departing flight, Desiree quickly called the airlines to inquire of its standby policies. We hurriedly packed, checked out of the hotel, and made a mad dash to the airport.

Exactly one hour after returning home, my friend Donna, the aspiring herbalist who had no prior knowledge of my recent trip, knocked on my door. With her was a friend, Patricia, who had flown to Miami from Chicago to participate in a New Age trade show. Donna wanted her to conduct an astrological and gemstone reading of my life.

After a candid discussion, I reluctantly consented so that I could compare her impressions with those of the tarot card reader; I would tape record the session so that I could study it later.

Patricia began with this introduction, "This astro-crystalogy reading will be a combination of an overlay of your astrological influences as well as the energy and information that come through from the gemstones in front of you. There are approximately 109 stones in the set. As you see some are very large, some are very small, very smooth or rugged. It does not matter if you've selected one that looks like this or that. None of that really matters. What matters is that you allow yourself to be very fluid and don't try to rationalize or intellectualize the reason for selecting a stone. If you're attracted to it, even if it's for no more than curiosity, just pick it up. Each stone has an individual statement that it wants to make."

"Patricia"

I begin to select the stones. Patricia continues to elaborate.
"I'm working with your higher Christ consciousness and my higher Christ consciousness. At that state of mind we are one. We'll be able to attune with the consciousness of the crystals. There is no set number, so just pull to your heart's content. In the mean time, I'm going to give you some information in terms of the challenges that you were born with."

"With an 18 degree Pisces sign, you're in what they call a second decadent. Every ten degrees brings about another decadent. So you're in a water element of Pisces expressing through Cancer meaning that you would take that Piscean energy into the home environment. You like to have a very private condition in your home. In other words, you enjoy your own privacy. It is your place of solitude."

"You also have a very intuitive way of approaching life. You go more with your feelings than with your intellect. You have a very nurturing nature. Family and home are very important to you. Emotionally, you were very close to your mother and it carries over in your need to be a nurturing parent yourself."

"However, when things upset you, you tend to wear a mask. So you tend to go into a shell and not want to talk about it at all and it's basically because it comes so easy for you to be able to sense the needs of other people, it's difficult for you to understand that when you need something, other people don't have that gift."

I thought, how accurate and smiled.

"You're also very detached in the way you communicate with others. You don't like anybody to know that you have a clinging side to you, but because you respect each individual's right to be free and to express, you don't like to give an account of what you do. So you try not to put that burden on other people. So it comes across to other people as you're more detached than you really are. You have a lot more emotions involved but they don't pick that up."

I didn't interrupt, but I was impressed with her insight.

"Your friends are very important to you. You work very well behind the scenes."

I nodded affirmatively.

"You're very psychic and you have to work hard at understanding those sensitivities within yourself because you have a lot of openness to other people's feelings. So it's important that you're surrounded by very positive people because when you are around negative people they drain you. You feel yourself going through insecurity or not feeling appreciated, not feeling loved or respected for what you are doing and it's basically because you're an emotional sponge and you pick up all of that lack of love that other people have for themselves. You sense it right away and it's very easy to transfer that over and get it confused with your own feelings."

My eyes widen but I remain silent. I didn't want to give her any clues.

"You're also very disciplined in the sense that you are a self-disciplined person, not so much as you allow anyone else to restrict you. You know when it comes to doing what you want to do, you do it. You like being in authority."

"That gets to be a conflict because you're a very free spirit and you, hmm, there's an adventure side to you where you want to go out and experience. But there's also a very reserved and conservative side to you. You need to cautiously approach everything you endeavor to come involved in."

"You have a Karmic responsibility to teach and to give service. You're a stickler about order and that is your biggest challenge to constantly have order and you'll find ways to make it appear to have order even if it isn't. But that's a karmic lesson."

Wow! This is unbelievably true of me, I say to myself.

"It's a lesson you have to learn. Running away from the lesson doesn't help. It's a lesson that your soul is here to learn about the difference between learning to discern and discriminate; analyze and criticize and because you were an extremist in those other lives, because you so easily picked another person apart in other lives, in this life every time you just try to openly critique or analyze a situation to discern and discriminate, it will be taken or perceived to the extreme and the hardest lesson is that you will do that more to yourself than to anybody else."

"So you have to learn how to look at yourself and become detached. Use your ability to detach yourself and learn to observe a situation so that you can go on. You know rather than trying to make yourself fit into somebody else's expectations or mode of the way they think you should be, you're not here for them, but for yourself to learn and evolve and you're here to teach some things."

Finally, I break my silence.

"To teach what?"

"Yes, she said, Virgo is the teacher."

"Like what?" I voiced curiously.

"Hmm," she said, "One of them is about self respect and the importance of a good reputation and doing that through a spiritual level or a higher mind. It might be done through groups and organizations. I see a lot of Aquarian energy here; so New Thought groups or churches. Anywhere people come together under a pledge with one focus. If you don't come out as the teacher you will come out as a worker, coworker or servant, gladly doing service to that group."

"Is that future or past tense?" I asked. I was thinking of all of the time and energy I'd devoted to the children at the temple's school.

"It's a lifetime, if you'll look you'll see a pattern of service and it involves more than one on one cause you'll go from the extreme of being alone to associating with a group."

"Yeah, I have done that," I interjected. "I'll be with a group and if I get too much static or hear too much noise, I'll withdraw. Like now, I'm in a form of reclusion."

"You call it reclusion, I call it solitude. Anyone with this much water; Ha! Water is the spirit, the emotions and you have a lot of water in your chart. Your sun is Pisces; your moon is Cancer; that's water. Your Mars is Pisces and even without knowing the houses that they're placed in, there's enough energy right there to keep you in a spin between you trying to stay grounded and not being flighty with your emotions."

"What? What? Did you say flighty?" I laughed so hard.

"That's the term everybody uses. They say I'm flighty or moody." I stopped to reflect. She waited a few moments then resumed.

"You have an unusual relationship when it comes to your brothers and sisters."

"Yeah, I do!"

"Also you have an unusual way of communicating, a new age way of communicating. Even when you teach you try to come up with a way of bringing your ideas together. Sometimes people are not ready for some of your concepts and don't understand you. You have an unusual way of communicating and you're a stickler for being a disciplinarian starting with self and working outward. You're very goal oriented and other people who you interact with are not."

"Is that why I'm misunderstood a lot?" I asked. "Sometimes I don't understand myself." I smiled.

"Yeah, you are misunderstood a lot because of the communication thing, because Uranus is sudden and unexpected so there's a sudden and unexpected way that you'll express yourself."

"It's just like these stones. You think you're choosing them but that stone over there is just calling you. Why don't you just pick it up and stop my head from hurting."

I pointed to a stone and said. "Are you talking about this one?"

"Yes," she said.

"For some reason I keep looking at it while thinking no because it's too big and clunky; but it just keeps messing with my eyes though." I laughed.

"Didn't I tell you to don't analyze or rationalize? That's right! I'm clairaudient so I know that you weren't through trying to pick up stones. That's why I hadn't started reading the stones."

"Yeah," I laughed. "I'm attracted to all of the weird looking ones but I didn't want to pick them up. So I may as well pick them all up. "I'm serious," I smiled.

"See how that intellect works. You're thinking there is no rationale to these stones, no consistency and it doesn't fit, it's out of order and even though it keeps messing with me, I'm going to ignore it, you say."

"That's how you're doing parts of you and parts of your life, OK. If it doesn't fit or if it's not comfortable, not right or not perfect, so what? That's why some stones are like that. Some parts of us are not perfect and not polished. When I tell you what that particular stone is about you're going to flip, fall right over," she stated.

"That stone was just ringing at me. I should just pick up all of these weird ones that I'm trying to avoid. I keep going towards purple: I like purple," I exclaimed.

"Purple's very regal, but there are other reasons for it. Your Neptune is in Libra which says that partnerships are important to you but you've had a difficult time being able to attract and draw partners who understood you, or that you clearly understood, because what you saw is not what you got. Only after the commitment did that side that you didn't know before, that side came out of the person."

"Again this is ongoing throughout your lifetime because there are strong lessons you chose to learn in terms of fairness, honesty, deception and truth."

I thought of Julius and commented, "I was dealing with deception today. Why do people purposefully and maliciously deceive?" I asked with a puzzled tone.

"In your case, if you understood that some of the things that are happening are not going to make sense, because they are not happening to you "Mary" because of something that Mary did. It's happening to Mary because of something that your soul did in another life time in another place. Your soul made a commitment to come back to deal with this unfinished business."

"There is a law of cause and effect and these same people who are in your life today now being ungrateful are the same people who you may have been ungrateful to in time. So your soul has to be allowed the opportunity to experience that feeling, that hurt, that disappointment that you left on someone else. So when you came back you feel that hurt, that disappointment this time for your soul. It's not punishment. They're just lessons. If you don't you're going to keep drawing another experience back."

"Each time they appear different but somewhere along the way you'll see a string through each one of those relationships that the persons are not loving themselves and then taking it out on you. But because you have not learned the lesson of seeing things for what they are rather than seeing things for the way you would like them to be, you keep on drawing that same lesson to you. Call a duck a duck. Call it what it is. Love is Love, sex is sex, money is money and stop trying to put all of this in one pretty basket and it will save you a lot of headaches, particularly in relationships and in partnerships. Listen to your higher mind." Patricia stopped to drink a glass of water.

"You've got some heavy lessons to learn about family, children and romantic relationships."

"I've still got more to learn in this life?"

"Yes! You're still in this life time called Mary, OK. Sure you can learn them as you evolve so that when they come you'll recognize them. It doesn't stop the lessons from coming. It shows you a different way to handle the lesson; that's what makes the outcome different. That's what you came here for. Now, let's switch so I can get over here closer to these stones."

As she moved closer to me, I pondered her remarks and wondered how many more lessons I had to learn.

"That very stone that you didn't want to touch here means "I want to know the truth at all costs." You see how you played with that. That's those fish swimming in the opposite direction. You thought, "A lot of responsibility comes with that truth;" but your inner psyche said, "I want to know the truth no matter what it costs."

"Yeah, I've been saying that to myself."

"And you're also petitioning and meditating for direction towards the white light. So it's not about the decision you're making; but you're taking it to a higher source." She paused then picked up another stone.

"A lot of people depend on you. A lot of people have needs and expectations of you, but it's like they've got you going backwards. They are pulling you apart but you are allowing too much of it."

"You need to have a love affair with yourself."

"Yeah I'm in this relationship," she interrupts me.

"No not now, you need more time to learn to love yourself."

"Well I try to deal with him, thinking of Julius, but every week I've got to clear house, you know, my mind. I'll give him so much time then I'll pull out, I don't see a future with him. I feel that he is going to bottom out on me." Sigh!

The Sixth Day: On the Sea

"This is so deep. You see this stone right here, that nice little square. That's the love stone. See how tiny it is and see that little hole in the top of it."

"Yeah, OK"

"The way you've got that one placed shows just really that. You're measuring love out in a nice little neat package. You're saying to the men in your life, "if you act like you've got good sense then I know how to be a lover."

"Yeah, I'm at the point where I'm tired of foolishness," I sighed. There was silence for a few moments then she continued.

"This stone shows that you're trying to find order and flow to your life. It shows a lot of stress; it shows interaction with children, people, groups, organizations, friends and family; everybody's got a little piece of you and when they're finished, Mary's saying "Where is mine for me, Mary, the woman? Ok!"

"That is so true," I said. "My favorite song is ***I've Never Been To Me***. I love Nancy Wilson's version. I listen to it often."

"Your ego and your pride are involved and you're feeling sad because these same people are not giving you the props to help you feel good about yourself."

"I see a lot of healing here, a lot of natural healing and your ability to transfer healing to others."

"Really?" I asked. "I've been seeking healing but I've been doing it, well, I'm taking yoga classes for stress."

"Yes, I see that."

"And I've been meditating. I have a healing prayer also. I've stopped naming and claiming ailments."

"I see diabetic tendencies here in your blueprint."

"Well, let me explain. I can name it without claiming it now. The doctor said hypoglycemia. I don't claim ownership though," I laughed.

"You seem to be of the theme, "Physician heal thyself."

"Yes that's where I am."

"What I see here are the nerves, the digestive system and detoxifying. Those are the areas that your stones are saying. You're also concerned about toning up the body, muscles and changing habits or thought forms or people. You're in a big transitional stage now."

"These two stones say that you need an inner place of peace. Not just physical peace but inner peace."

"Yeah I do need inner peace."

"Also there are some people who do not like what they see as far as the spiritual change that's taking place in you, and if they could block you they would. But they can't. You just need to be aware of them."

"Do you have any inkling of who these people are?" I asked.

"No, but you do, or will."

"They do not want my soul to unfold?" I inquired.

"Yes, they do not want you to make a change because they are not changing or growing," she stressed.

"I know a whole house full of people." The disciples at the temple, I thought. I looked at Donna knowing that she read my mind. We screamed with laughter. After we regained our composure, Patricia continued.

"You have two projects to do; both projects are of a personal gratification and will give you a feeling of self worth and accomplishment. But you're procrastinating; you're putting it off. All you need to do is to have courage to do it. You're saying "when I get more time, more money or more resources." Your spiritual guides are saying, "There are no doors in your way. Your fear is getting started.""

"I thought about writing a book about my abusive marriage and my journey through the temple."

"Yes you should get started on it as soon as possible. The other project focuses on you initiating something, and once you do initiate, the energy of this project is going to be great; because other people you didn't expect to ask for help or that you wouldn't think about asking for help are going to offer help. But you do have to be aware of their egos. It's not going to be so much of a power struggle but more of ego tripping. So be sure of your intents and your goals."

I thought about Julius's persistence in my affairs and remarked, "I see a connection between this reading and the tarot reading."

"Yes, but this reading was necessary for reinforcement. Your self-awareness is now higher," she added.

"Your digestive system is where you are holding onto emotional garbage. You are eating the right foods better but you're holding onto junk. Though you won't partake of certain physical foods you're still allowing yourself to eat emotional garbage. You've got to start rejecting certain garbage that comes into your mental body because it's building up a storehouse of emotional ills that you are repressing. That's not good."

"You're right. I'm holding in a lot and I've been doing so for nearly fifteen years since my divorce from Chico."

"Yes and its messing up your stomach and it gives you side effects like allergies and asthma and low blood sugar. They're coming from the emotional memory bank. Learn how to release it, bless it and send it back into the nothingness in which it came from because it is not allowing your foods to properly liquefy so that the energy is not there to let the solar plexus do what it's got to do." She paused again.

"Yes, you're a bit anemic also."

"I'm not claiming it," I laughed.

"And you're straining your eyes a little too much. So read in better lighting. You're very spiritual and psychic and you have a lot of angelic protection. I see a lot of divine petitioning. Stop intellectualizing so much. You accept the protection but you're not following the spiritual guidance. You have to force yourself to let your higher self pick and choose for you because you have to analyze and rationalize everything. There's a higher God-Self within you so the more you say "Let there be light" you've got to let that light shine. Get Mary out of the way. Listen to the inner voice so that you may become a more perfect channel for God to express through. Does that make sense?"

"Yeah, it does," I reply.

"That's why you were knocked off of your feet and had to have a near death experience just to get you to stop intellectualizing in order to teach you and to get you to the highest part of you. OK. Since you came back into consciousness you're remembering now, aren't you?"

How did she know about that experience? I wondered. She looked at me and just smiled.

"This is incredible," I said in amazement. "A year ago no one could have gotten me to get a reading of any sort and now I believe that there really are people with certain spiritual gifts and powers."

"When you decided to pick up that stone that you were avoiding; you made a commitment to start growing spiritually. Everything and everyone who you need to assist you in your growth is going to come to you. Pay attention and learn to listen. That's it for now. Let's end here."

The next morning, Linda, Donna Josephine and I assembled on Hallandale Beach to observe Patricia as she conducted a Chakra balancing ritual. I was so intrigued.

Later, I purchased a stone from the trade show where Patricia was an exhibitor. The agate, a form of quartz, was to be worn for protection. It was suppose to attract strength, protect my body from stress when placed on the solar plexus, and help to enhance my dreams. I took the stone to the jeweler and had it encased in 18 karat gold; purchased a 22" inch gold chain and placed it around my neck. It became my signature piece of jewelry.

"Hallandale Beach, Florida"

THE HEALING PROCESS

Mentally I was still ecstatic about my tarot and gemstone readings and about my close encounters. They helped me to redefine my purpose and gave new meaning to my life. I read more and more. I reread that which was previously read from a new perspective. I was growing by leaps and bounds. My cup was running over. But physically I was still dealing with a challenge.

My blood sugar was low and every two to three hours after eating I was swimming in the head and feeling weak in the knees. I became cold very quickly. One moment I was happy and the next I was crying uncontrollably. The mood swings were sporadic. I still needed medical assistance. Though I continued to get annual physicals and blood chemistry laboratory analysis, I absolutely refused to take prescription drugs.

Believing that most medical doctors were not properly trained in nutrition and did not believe in the use of herbs or other natural healing techniques, I sought help from an herbalist at the *Institute of Chinese Herbs and Nutrition*, but continued to read my Bible hoping to decipher the code that would unlock the secrets of spiritual healing. "Physician heal thyself" kept circulating in my mind.

Concentrating on healing as I drove home, I thought of going to a bookstore to purchase another positive thinking book. I was on "automatic pilot" as I exited the freeway and subconsciously drove through the light. As I traveled west I read a sign on an office building which read U.T.C. What does that stand for I thought? Then it occurred to me that this was the location of the New Thought group that I'd visited years ago when Les Brown conducted a series of seminars in Miami. I quickly turned into the parking lot out of curiosity wondering if they had a bookstore.

I opened the door, entered the foyer and was pleasantly greeted. I could see a bookstore to the right of the door. I inquired.

"You can browse through the books and when you're ready to purchase call me," said the clerk as she guided me through the selections.

After searching the shelves, I still wasn't quite sure which books to select. As I pondered, another woman approached me. Knowing that I was an unfamiliar face, she pleasantly asked, "May I assist you?"

"Yes, I want a book on spiritual healing."

She pulled several from the shelf and briefly explained each. She handed me a tape entitled, **"YOU CAN BE HEALED!"** by the Rev. Dr. Johnnie Coleman.

"I remember reading about her in Ebony magazine a few years back."

"We are affiliated with her ministry. I am the minister, Reverend Mary Tumpkins. Please join us for Sunday Service. You have my personal invitation."

I had not been in a traditional church setting in years and I hadn't intended to start again soon, but I politely said, "Thanks for the invitation."

Later that evening, as I prepared for the night, I said my prayers, got into bed, turned on the tape player and listened. I was most inspired by the story of Johnnie Coleman's personal healing.

I turned over to rewind the tape then sat up so that I could be more attentive. Numerous techniques for healing were discussed. I thought, "This makes a lot of sense." As I continued to analyze the principles, I became very excited. Now totally awake, I started to rewind the tape over and over again so that I could take notes.

"Healing is not a process but a revelation. Healing is understanding. Healing is already in God's Mind, so you must change your thoughts through prayer and meditation. What you think is what you get. Healing is from the inside out."

After elaborating on each principle, she began to instruct the audience on how to give themselves a spiritual mind treatment.

"If the body is to be well you must begin by curing the mind; your spiritual body is precisely where your beliefs of the physical body seem to be. All is thought. Your health, be it good or seemingly bad is your individual state. Your mental attitude determines where you are and whatever you are. Inside of you is the Great Physician. It is your thinking that should be healed not your body."

Suddenly I knew what I had been doing incorrectly all of these years. I had been mentally dwelling on the possibility of becoming ill from the diethylstilbestrol that I had ingested during pregnancy with Renee. Therefore, my body was producing the side effects. My mind believed what I had read in the medical journals was actually going to happen to both of us, thus mentally programming my body to accept the information as inevitable.

I continued to listen enthusiastically. Finally, principles for correct thinking were presented. *"Whatever the mind dwells upon, the mind brings into existence. The mind must be kept free of negative thoughts and influences through self discipline and established habits. That which you fear shall come upon you. There must be no talk of illness or disease."*

I realized that I had to stop worrying, naming and claiming any illness or condition that I didn't want in my life. I had to take total control of my body through my mind. I was responsible for my healing and could affect perfect health by practicing the principles of truth. But most importantly, I had to forgive everyone, even Chico and Moses Israel.

By the time she completed the forty-five minute lesson, I was in tears, crying, wailing and lamenting. As I listened to the musical renditions that concluded the session, I began singing along with the soloist. I rewound that portion of the tape over and over and over again.

When I awakened the next morning, I prostrated my body on the floor and asked the Creator to forgive me of all of my sins. Then I dressed and went to the gift store to purchase several Hallmark greeting cards. Later, after writing a special message on each one, I mailed them to everyone who I thought that I had offended and to those whom I thought had trespassed against me. Feeling optimistic, I decided to go to a more traditional church on Sunday morning for the first time in years.

REPROGRAMMING

As time passed and I began to heal emotionally, I reflected on how I had gotten ensnarled in this web of confusion. When had I lost my objectivity and become closed-minded? I remembered what Moses Israel so often asserted in class in reference to those who he thought to be infiltrators.

"If you stay in here long enough and listen to my teachings you'll be converted. This stuff is powerful."

That was it! Though I had one agenda, I had been subconsciously programmed to believe that almost every word taught was the only way, the only truth and the only light.

As I continued to rethink my position, I remembered that my goals and objectives were to discover who African-American people were historically, and to be able to write and lecture from that viewpoint. So I'd seen, believed and accepted only that which I wanted to see and hear. I'd closed my eyes, ears and mind to everything else. I'd studied from a particular reference point; therefore my understanding was based on that view only.

It was like wearing rose-colored glasses and seeing the world as being pink, or wearing yellow-colored spectacles and seeing everything as being "jaundiced" and then adamantly defending my views as being the total truth to someone who was wearing green-colored lenses.

It finally made sense to me. I had to take off the darkly shaded rims to see the world as it really is. I was beginning to think that I had just frantically awakened from a bad dream and that all of my experiences were illusions.

De-spectacled, without a hidden motive, and seeking only truth, I enrolled in classes at the New Thought Truth Center. My eyes opened wider as I removed the darkly tinted glasses that I had been wearing since high school. I finally realized how influential perceptions were in determining behavior.

The Spirit of Truth was now my personal teacher and spiritual guide. I decided to go with the flow. I was entering a new and different spiritual realm. The better living classes were very therapeutic. As I grew in understanding, I soon began to release my feelings of guilt.

The Sixth Day: On the Sea

The Truth Center began each better living class with this statement: "Jesus Christ is the teacher of this class. We open our minds and hearts to His teachings for He is our guide to better living."

Each scriptural message was then interpreted as "your personal story" describing different stages of your growth. Everything was "self." All of the passages, people, places, names and situations in the Bible were applied "first" to yourself then to others because there is only one God, one presence and one power expressing individually through various physical forms. That aspect of self is the same in everyone, unchanging, consistent, and eternal. No person had more of God in them than any other person, though some people may have attained a higher level of self awareness.

This concept of how to apply the information was not foreign to me because it too had been taught at the temple. The major difference was with the order. Moses Israel taught everyone to diminish "self" or individualism and learn to think collectively. That was necessary initially because African American peoples are such a divided group. Even wearing the all white cultural attire caused most of us to blend as one, thus forgetting our unique characteristics, personalities, talents and God given gifts.

I had forgotten me. My "self" was not expressing itself. It had been stifled and suppressed. This new understanding helped to allay my fears and strengthen my faith. I was no longer fearful.

So when Celeste called encouraging me to attend an important meeting at the temple, I went. Arriving an hour late, I cautiously walked into the auditorium. Moses Israel looked up, stopped teaching and openly welcomed me back to the temple.

"Shalom my daughter!"

Every head turned towards me in anticipation of another verbal reprimand.

"What's wrong?" he asked them. "She is still one of us. We need to learn how to love and forgive each other."

What? Had I heard correctly? A "hypocrite" should be forgiven? I wondered what was going on. It was obvious that my absence had been the topic of a lesson or two. Though shocked at his kind words, I wasn't yet impressed. I knew from studying his teaching style that he had long term goals and tonight's special meeting was just one of the objectives on his agenda to achieve mastery. The temple was now under serious criminal investigation. Could that be the reason? I took a seat and listened.

Moses Israel continued his lecture. "The Federal Grand Jury is conducting weekly hearings. Judith and I have to attend. Many of you may be called to testify."

Later he called the names of believers, supporters and followers who had personally contributed their times, talents and tithes to the temple. He openly thanked them. This was so unusual. He had seldom called anyone's name and personally given them credit. All credit had always been given to Yahweh. What was going on?

Then it clicked. The warm welcome; talk of love and forgiveness; and the acknowledgement of those who helped the temple were sincere; but I also heard a subliminal appeal to become loyal and friendly witnesses for the defense.

SUNDOWN

Around 7:00 p.m., I quickly return to the cabin to change my clothing and hurry to the upper deck. I take a stroll on the western side of the ship and look at the great expanse. To see the sunset out on the open ocean is a spectacular sight. It appears larger and closer than ever. It has a magnificent bright orange glow and looks so powerful, yet nonthreatening. As I watch it descend in the horizon, I marvel at God's creation. I take out my tape and record my thoughts.

THE DREAM

However infrequent, sleep was a time for me to release the thoughts and feelings that I'd repressed all day. I would awaken in the morning with vague thoughts and bits and pieces of dreams, but it was always difficult to fully remember the substance of the dreams. I thought nothing about that until this particular morning in June, when a dream was crystal clear in my conscious mind and memory. Details, colors, mood, and conversations were vivid and easily recalled. Was this a sign or premonition? An eerie and mysterious sensation agitated my soul. What did it mean? Why the dirge scene? Whose death was being predicted?

I later called Donna to describe the details and to discuss their possible esoteric meanings. All went well intellectually until I dreamed that ***dream*** over several times during that month. Each time was an exact reproduction of the first. All of the events were sequential. All of the conversations were precise. All of the details exact. Even the death scene was the same. Now I was more than intellectually curious.

In this dream, Moses Israel was dead. A funeral service was being held in a large outdoors open area similar to an amphitheater. His body was in the center of the stage. On one side of the open casket were those disciples from the temple who mourned his passing and on the other side of the casket were bodyguards. The guards were men dressed in black double breasted suits that stood erect and looked very menacing and stoic. They had a sinister "air" about them. They were not lovingly protecting the body as Moses Israel's usual bodyguards at the temple had secured his surroundings. These men were guarding the casket fiercely. As each mourner descended the steps and formed a line to view the body, the guards would watch them carefully. Their arms were folded as if they were concealing weapons.

Since I was no longer welcomed among this group of faithful mourners, I sat alone and waited until each one had viewed the body and left the area. I then went down the steps towards the casket. As I approached it, I noticed that Moses Israel's eyes opened. I was startled. He then communicated with me telepathically saying, "Don't be alarmed. Act as if nothing is happening. I need your help to escape the guards. Go to your car and drive to a place where you usually go when you want to meditate."

I didn't move. Why should I help him? I thought. Did he not want to kill me? His eyes reflected that he understood my feelings. I stood there a few more seconds and then left the area.

I drove to Linda's house. She lived in Pembroke Pines. I often go there and sit on the carpet in her den when I want to meditate. I called her on my cellular phone to let her know that I was coming. She heard the anxiety in my voice.

When I arrived, Linda opened the garage door and I drove in and parked alongside her car. Suddenly we were startled by the sound of the car's back door opening. A tall dark skinned man exited. Where had he come from? Puzzled, we looked at each other. Before words could be spoken, the man took me by the arm and entered the house and went directly to the den as if he had been in the house before. We sat on the carpet.

He then said very sorrowfully, "They all deceived me, Mary Ilana. I should have trusted you more." I immediately recognized his voice. It was Moses Israel's.

"Who deceived you?" I asked.

"All of them," he said as he began to call their names. They were the names of the people who were thought to be the closest to him at the temple. They were members of his entourage.

As I started to ask, "Why would they deceive you?" I awakened from the dream.

Five months later in November, I received a telephone call about 6:30 a.m. from Fredericker. She hysterically said, "Mary, turn on your television set. Something terrible is happening at the temple."

It was the morning that the FBI coordinated a nationwide raid of the temples and arrested sixteen disciples. Moses Israel was arrested in Louisiana, and Judith was apprehended in Atlanta. The grand jury had indicted them for various federal crimes related to the Racketeer Influenced and Corrupt Organizations Act better known as the RICO Act.

Later that day, a news report was broadcast showing Moses Israel's arrest in Louisiana. He was handcuffed and was being escorted to court by two men who wore dark suits. These men guided him by his elbows with their hands on each side. They walked erect, looked fierce and very stoic. They were as the men who guarded Moses Israel's casket in my dream. I thought about the situation for a few minutes. I felt that Moses Israel's body was going to be laid to rest for a long time. He was being incarcerated. The casket in my dreams represented confinement to prison for the rest of his life.

Two weeks later I had another dream about a lesson Moses Israel taught two years earlier.

He'd said, "What you think is pictured in your mind's eye. The images that are projected from your inner screen reflect your beliefs and doubts, and are observable in your actions and reactions. The imagination is powerful and important. Whatever you are taught during childhood will replay on this screen unless you edit the film. Sometimes all that is needed to upgrade the quality of the movie is more color," he chuckled.

Knowing his teaching style, I wondered, "What is the point of this analogy?"

He continued with the lecture. "One such image that has to be upgraded is that of Jesus. Jesus' existence and his teachings are not denied here at the temple, as many people think, but the image of his being a white man is vehemently rejected. The images that are painted on the windows of our churches, displayed in all of our Bibles, and that adorn the mantles in our homes are all false."

During class, Moses Israel would have several disciples to bring their Bibles down to the front of the auditorium and instruct them to display the pictures of Jesus that were portrayed in each. They were all different. In some pictures he was depicted as a blue eyed blond; in others as a straight haired brunette. Never was he shown as described in the bible as dark skinned with wooly hair. Everybody laughed.

"You see our minds interpret this to mean that any or all white men could be Jesus and therefore must be reverenced, bowed down to and then praised. The very name "Jesus" that we call on today is incorrect because in the original Hebrew the letter "J" still does not exist. His name was Yahshua. That's why he hasn't answered your mournful cries. He doesn't respond to that name. You need to deprogram your minds; you need a new image and a new name to identify with the Son of God."

Over the years Moses Israel had changed his name often. Each name, he taught, identified his current mission or focus. He would always hint that none of those names were his ultimate name. I reflected on the night that he identified himself as "THE" Son of God. He stressed the article "THE" which meant the one in particular and the one already spoken of.

The years prior to this night, there were no images of the Son of God in the temple. But after Moses Israel's announcement that he was "The

One," he allowed himself to be photographed and his picture was not only displayed, but was available for sale. A new name and a new image had successfully replaced the old name and image of Jesus in many minds.

I too bought a picture and took it home and placed it on my dresser along with other family photos. I could not openly display it in the family room where I tutored because it would attract too much attention from visitors and I didn't want to explain. I remembered how Merdene and the parents of my Brownie troop turned against me. Also, I had encountered so much religious prejudice from devout Christians who shunned me professionally and socially; judged me harshly and cast verbal stones at me daily for my believing in a different interpretation of the same bible that they read. I'd learned the lesson of broadcasting my personal practices with my professional endeavors.

After a period of time, the picture had become a part of the furniture. When cleaning, I just dusted around it as I did the other photos. I seldom thought about it. After I'd left the temple, I did not immediately remove the picture. Several months later, I noticed it and was greatly disturbed. To me it was now as a graven image. When I removed it, the scene in my mind was instantly upgraded to a higher quality and resolution, the "Word." Finally, the belief that you had to have a physical intercessor like a priest, imam, minister or rabbi who supposedly had a direct connection to the spiritual realm was completely eradicated from my mind.

THE RESURRECTION

Nearly six months had passed since the incarceration of Moses Israel and members of the temple. Though I had not associated with the group for over a year, disciples began calling for money to defray the costs of Moses Israel's legal defense. In the past they were able to count on me to give a contribution or to purchase a product to assist them in meeting their financial quotas, but I was not supportive any longer especially after my IRS audit.

I also felt indifferent because when some members of the New York congregation were arrested a few years earlier, Moses Israel openly refused to put up bail money for them.

He taught, "The U.S. Criminal "Injustice" System uses bail money to support their illegal practices and to put extra funds in the hands of the bail's bondsmen and crooked judges. Bail for the rich is lower than it is for the poor, who after risking all, usually lose their property and savings. The temple will not fall prey to this trick."

Moses Israel allowed the detainees to remain in jail and to be represented by the court appointed public defenders at taxpayers' expense. The congregation cheered as Moses Israel expounded on out maneuvering the legal system.

He also taught, "It is God's will that the incident has happened in New York to further highlight the injustices of the system and how it is again practicing religious persecution of Hebrew Israelites. The brothers are to remain strong and courageous in the face of this great spiritual test. Those who overcome this obstacle will be rewarded by the Son of God in the end."

However, the incarceration of Moses Israel had a tremendous affect on the disciples. Prior to that time, they were regimented and structured. Now that there were "no guides or overseer," some disciples began to drift away and return to their previous lives. This was not an unexpected occurrence. For months prior to his arrest, Moses Israel had been teaching that there would be a change in direction for the temple.

As the grand jury investigations were intensifying, he elaborated on two themes for the last year of his public ministry. They were the *"Lame Man"* and *"Train up Your Children."* If the disciples had studied his style of teaching they would have recognized that Moses Israel was preparing them to return to their independent, self managing lifestyles. Obviously suspecting that the grand jury might hand down an indictment any day, he gradually released the tight controls that were imposed on the disciples.

Now as I listened to pleas for personal help in their efforts to reestablish their lives, I couldn't help but to think of how sure they had been of their "places in the kingdom of Yahweh" and how condemning they had been of me for remaining "uncommitted."

I was committed to God, economic and educational empowerment for our people and unity. They just never understood that I could not be a robotic clone. But I understood their plight and encouraged them in their professional pursuits. I knew that we were all just actors in this great karmic and cosmic play called life.

I had survived their wiles and schemes to witness the day when this scripture was literally fulfilled. "Who so digs a pit shall fall therein: and he that throws a stone, it will return upon him."

My thoughts reflected on Judith who had dug so many pits for so many disciples. After her incarceration, her daughter Sara came to my home and sympathetically expressed her mother's feelings towards me. I listened carefully as she verbalized Judith's remorse for having maligned my character. What was the motive behind this indirect confession I wondered?

It was a clear request for me to serve as a character witness for Judith's bail bonds hearing. Judith needed someone with a good public reputation who was not a disciple to speak on her behalf.

Can you believe that? Wasn't it Judith who refused to help me with my income tax audit? Did she not state openly to her staff that she didn't care if the IRS jailed me? Had this period of humility caused her to be "resurrected" in her thinking also? Should I assist her in this plight? NO! I didn't want to get involved. A wise saying came to mind, "If you can't say something good then keep quiet."

The day after Sara's visit, Judith personally telephoned from the correctional institution. I was very polite and empathized with her unfortunate situation, but I felt no sympathy. She was experiencing her own karma. Judith phoned two more times, but the calls stopped after I made an appointment to speak with her attorney.

I emphatically asserted, "My conscience will not permit me to take an oath of truth on the HOLY BIBLE in a court of law and then perjure myself. How can I say that Judith is kind, honest and deserving of bail? Will you convey my regrets to your client?"

"I understand your position. I'll talk with her."

I left the law office thinking of Judith's predicament. Behind her back, disciples called her Judas and often paraphrased this scripture in a revengeful manner: "When Judith, who had betrayed them, saw that she was condemned repented herself saying, I have sinned in that I have betrayed the innocent blood." Had Judith sold her soul for the love of money? She had controlled all of the temple's funds.

I also reflected on Moses Israel's aka Yahweh Ben Yahweh, incarceration. As I read the newspaper reports concerning his complaints, as expressed through his attorneys, about not being served kosher meals or being given ample servings of food; being denied access to witnesses' names far in advance of the trial; his being "locked down" in the hole; not being given adequate self care products or medical treatment; and not being allowed money and other privileges, I truly sympathized with the situation.

He had often quoted scripture stating that "the son of man" would be persecuted. Was this situation predictably as it should be and his words were "not returning to him void" or unfulfilled?

My mind also thought about the concerns that the disciples complained of repeatedly over the years without remedy. They too had been denied some rights under temple rule. They had to go to the prayer room and kneel for long periods of time when they didn't make their financial quotas; their personal supplies were meager and they were sometimes denied funds for medical visits perceived to be unnecessary by superiors; their diets, contained white sugar and white rice and canned vegetables, which we were taught were not nutritious; if they missed their one meal a day for whatever reason, they had to wait until the next day to eat, and they were seldom able to openly defend themselves against the crime stoppers who covertly accused them of misdeeds within the temple.

Thoughts of the plight of King David, God's Beloved, soothed my mind. Even he had to suffer the consequences of his actions after coveting Bathsheba and having her husband Uriah sent to the front of the battle so that he would be killed. Yes, God is the same yesterday, today and forever. God is not a respecter of persons. In Israel there is one law for all.

As the trial proceeded and news articles proliferated, a very negative and unfair portrait of the disciples was painted. Like in any diverse group or in the congregations of any church, synagogue or mosque, most of the disciples were good, decent, benevolent, honest, sincere, and God-fearing.

Many were unable or unwilling to process the lessons on a higher cognitive level or could not determine if the lessons taught were literal or figurative and acted based on their understanding at the time. Some were just not consciously ready to receive higher concepts from any teacher and several were as "little children" seeking parental approval.

Others were only able or desirous of looking outside of themselves for solutions to problems on the physical plane, while a few allowed themselves to be used as "tools of destruction."

I press the stop button on the tape recorder and reflected on this experience. I do not want to ever associate my personal goals and objectives with any religious denomination again. I want to be free and independent to express myself as positively and creatively as possible. The Holy Spirit within would be my intercessor.

My mind is being filled with unlimited possibilities and my life force is being directed towards helping all children regardless of race, color, creed, national origin or religious association, to read, write and speak more effectively so that they might become productive, clear thinking adults who feel good about themselves.

Tonight I am being renewed in the spirit of my mind. I feel "born again" and "saved" from my own inner demons.

THE ELEVENTH HOUR

At 11:00 p.m. I return to my cabin and change into a warmer outfit to insulate me from the night's breeze, and hurriedly return to my usual spot. I have to resolve relationship issues tonight. I now know exactly what I want in a companion, but I have to be ready when "Mr. Right" appears or I'll repeat the same mistakes. Time is of the essence! Crisis intervention is needed!

A NEW NAME – A NEW TEACHER

Every day was very much the same for me. I followed a routine, but on this particular day in April, I deviated from my pattern and decided to do my grocery shopping immediately after work rather than on the weekend. Therefore, I did not take my usual route home. As I approached the store, I saw a familiar face sitting on the bus bench. We waved excitedly to each other. I had not seen him in nearly six months. I then turned onto the parking lot of the store and proceeded to get out of the car. To my surprise he had rushed over to open the car's door for me.

When I got out he said, "Wow! You're very tall."

We'd never been in close physical proximity before. I had only spoken with him from my car as I frequently passed his service area on the way to work. He was a street corner newspaper vendor. Often times he would quickly hand me a poem through the window of my car. He was a thoughtful writer and his words were always so relevant to what I was contemplating.

I'd never stopped to talk with him personally. Our communication had been through waves and polite greetings. I never knew his name and he didn't know mine. He often yelled to me, "How are you today?" I'd respond, "Fine and you too," as I continued to drive.

Today I asked, "What is your name?"

He responded, "You-too."

Because it was obvious that he was of mixed lineage, I thought his name to be foreign and asked, "That's different. What's the origin of it?"

He laughed then humorously said, "Everyday I ask numerous people, "How are you?" as they pass my area. They hurriedly respond, "Fine, and you too" while continuing on their journeys. Even when I don't ask, I hear them yelling, "and you too." So, I've adopted the nickname You-too since that's what I hear frequently. I spell it "U-2" and use it as a pen name for my poetry."

"Great story; now tell me your real name."

"My name is not important. Perhaps one day I'll let you know more about me, but tell me your name."

I cautiously responded, "Alice, but my first name is Mary, which is so common that I seldom use it now."

He said, "Mary connotes a very docile, subservient, and meek person. I think of you as a "Catherine" who is royal, assertive, and elegant; also a majestic ruler."

We briefly discussed the origins of names and their meanings.

"Here's my business card. Call me sometimes and we will continue the conversation. I see that your bus is coming."

Late that night the telephone rang.

"Hello, may I speak with Catherine?"

"I'm sorry, you have the wrong number," I responded and politely hung up the telephone. The phone rang again.

"Please, may I speak with Catherine?" the caller insisted. My words and actions were the same. The phone rang a third time.

"Please check your numbers more carefully when dialing."

"Is this 621-4282?"

"Yes, it is but there is no Catherine here."

He said, "I have the right party, she's just not fully aware of who she truly is right now."

Boy was I curious.

"Mary, this is U-2."

"Hello! I didn't recognize your voice."

He immediately began to expound on the importance of knowing who you truly are.

"Who you really are transcends your physical existence and cannot be limited to a given name and its multiple academic meanings," he stressed. "The actual "person" is invisible, intangible and incomprehensible to the five basic senses. The physical is just an outward expression in human form of the real essence that is made in the image and likeness of God. That essence of being, called the Self, is the same in everyone. It has no form other than when it chooses to clothe itself in fleshly attire called a body."

"Are you a preacher?" I interject.

"No. Sometimes I am a student, but tonight I am a teacher."

"Ok, that means that I am the student."

"Yes! So what can you infer from what I've discussed already?"

"I was thinking of the mystery written in the book of Genesis where after Adam and Eve ate from the forbidden tree, it states, "And the eyes of them both were opened, and they knew that they were naked; and they sewed fig leaves together and made themselves aprons."

"From my esoteric readings, I gather that the aprons represented the outer garments, or the bodies that they put on to cover their spiritual nature."

"Great! If I were grading you, I'd give you an "A.""

I interjected, "I have an academic knowledge of the scriptures and I have the ability to analyze them from various linguistic perspectives, but I have not yet been able to spiritually discern them. My thinking is trapped on the intellectual plane," I chuckled.

As our conversation continued, I gleaned another concept of the Trinity. He stated, "Let's call the physical aspect, the "**you**;" the mental or soul aspect, the "**I**;" and the spiritual aspect, the "**me**." "ME, YOU and I" are distinguishable throughout the Bible as the Father, Son and the Holy Spirit.

If these three aspects are properly identified and interpreted, your understanding will be enhanced. Every passage should be viewed from this standpoint and then related to yourself first. One of our missions in life is to atone or become "AT ONE" with the trinity. Let's practice on this scripture."

I was excited about being in this role and waited for his example.

"Come unto "**ME**" all ye that labor and are heavy laden, and "**I**" will give "**YOU**" rest."

Before he could say more, I understood the meaning and its application.

He cautioned, "Catherine, put the Bible and all other biblically related books down for a while. All of the knowledge that you need is within you. The Bible was written as a guide only, like a reference book, but it has also been used by unethical clergymen to control the minds of people for centuries. It is still being used for selfish purposes by those who want to gain power and control over the masses. Almost all of the men, who have proclaimed that they were the Son of God, eventually lost their aim and focus as the number of believers increased. Do you remember reading about Daddy Grace and Father Divine?"

"Yes! I remember hearing about them from the older people in the churches." There was silence. He gave me time to think.

"Be careful when reading the scriptures and interpreting them from someone else's perspective. Your guide is within you. Follow your inner voice. It's never about the messenger. The only thing that matters is the WORD of GOD that emanates from your soul."

He then briefly discussed the historical background of which the Bible had been written. The Holy Koran, the Bhagavad-Gita and the Upanishads, which I had explored and were in my collection of books, were also mentioned.

"You must realize that Truth principles can be found in all major religions. God is omniscient and omnipresent. HE inspired many men in many cultures to write of HIS Truth. Man has distorted the truth by declaring his beliefs, which are based on his understanding, as superior to others. That's why there are so many religious wars. It's not in the religion. It's in discerning and understanding Truth, then putting the principles to work in your life. There are those who never go to church who are much more spiritually aware than those who attend religious services weekly. God is, just as Truth is, no respecter of persons."

I lamented, "When did I become so confused? All that I wanted was to learn of God's ways so that I could do the right things in life. I just needed God to bless and protect me and my children after I divorced."

"You got trapped in the environment and started blending in like the predator. Did you see that movie?" he asked.

"Yes," I responded.

"Did you "see" it with a spiritual eye though?" he asked mysteriously

"NO! It's obvious to me that I didn't." We chuckled.

"You need to learn to see and listen to everything from a spiritual perspective first, that's reality, then for entertainment."

There was silence.

"Do you remember these songs: *"If you don't know me by now, you'll never get to know me."* "What about, *"Stuck on You," "Lean on Me," "Are you lonely tonight, do you miss me tonight?"* and *"Let it be Me."*

"Yes, I remember them all," I said as he named tune after tune.

"Each one has the words "you, I or me" within their titles or lyrics. All of the songs are a cry from the soul for us to listen to the voice within. Writers who are inspired to compose the words of these songs think that they are writing love songs on the physical level, but it's really the Higher Self utilizing them to get a higher, more spiritual message across. God loves us and wants us to return to Him from within."

He turned on his radio and placed the speaker near the headset of the telephone. "Let's just listen carefully to the next few songs."

I was amazed. I heard the soul's cry repeatedly.

"Now back to how you got trapped in the environment," he commented. "You tried to blend in with the people around you. You are a unique individual. There is no other you. You can't even be like anyone else. You are not God, but you are an individualized expression of God. You stopped being yourself. You thought that you were detaching from people by hiding your true self from others but in actuality you detached yourself from "ME" or the God presence in you.

Your "**YOU, I** and **ME**" got out of order. When you get back in synchronization, your health will improve. You truly had a severe case of PMS. Your physical, mental and spiritual being has been out of order for a long time."

We laughed so heartily. It was a good feeling. "Laughter is healing also," he said.

We discussed many subjects and I asked many questions. I even shared my out-of body experience with him. I'd read Ruth Montgomery's book **"Strangers Among Us"** and wondered if another spirit or soul could actually "walk in" into your body.

He responded, "Disincarnate beings can only channel through you if you allow them to. The dead know nothing. At conception, God put his Holy Spirit within you to guide, to teach and to warn you. What happened to you was an awakening of consciousness. You were so polluted by the environment that you had to separate to take a good look at yourself. Remember that the mind always protects the body. It also was detoxifying your system. You had to be decontaminated from the world of sense orientation to grow spiritually. The feeling of energy that you experienced was Light. God is Light, the true cleansing agent."

Next, I shared my tarot cards, astrological and gemstone readings.

"Were they accurate readings?" he asked.

"Yes they were very accurate. I was so surprised. I'm not so sure about the karma or past life experiences though," I said. "I have no memory; just feelings of "déjà vu."

"Then if you know that they were accurate of you then they were. Only you can be sure, regardless of what is said. Trust in yourself. God can give you a message through any medium or channel He chooses. You can learn from animals, small children, songs, television programs, billboard signs or radio announcements. There are many ways and persons used to convey messages. But you have to be open and receptive."

"You also have to have the ability to discern the information, the source and the motives. Try a spirit with a spirit to know if it is of God. Not all spirits are good. Satanic forces have great powers to deceive. They gain your confidence when some events and predictions actually come true. So always be careful and alert. Never let anyone think for you."

"It's getting late. Do you want to continue talking?"

"Yes, I am excited and I'm also a nocturnal being," I chuckle.

"I know that. That's why I called you so late."

He continued by explaining the history of the tarot from the esoteric writings, and astrology from mythology. "Gemstones," he stated, "are natural resources which contain all of the chemical elements of the earth which are also within every living being. But you must remember that nothing outside of you can truly help you. Only the inner voice, your intuition can be 100% correct in guiding you. You must place all of your trust in the higher power of the Holy Spirit. That is the true forecaster and predictor of your life."

I paused to think. "Why is U-2 in my life? Why are his comments so reflective of my experiences? I break my silence and again ask for his identity.

"Really, who are you?" I begged to know.

He laughed. "The next time you see me, pinch me. I'm flesh and bones just like you."

"I will!" I respond gleefully.

"All that I'll say is that I'm highly evolved spiritually and I was inspired to help you, but you don't need to focus on my flesh or my name. Stay focused on the WORDS. They are life. Your prayers are being answered. You asked for wisdom and understanding and I am here only to assist you. You have the knowledge. You're quite a bookworm, aren't you?"

"Yeah, I love to read but I can't find the answers that satisfy my soul in books anymore. I've grown somewhat weary of them. I just keep finding more questions than answers for all of the facts I gather," I sighed.

"I wish you could help me to understand men," I laughed.

"If you learn of your true self then you won't have any difficulty understanding men. On the spiritual plane everyone is the same."

"Yeah, but I'm dealing with this brother on the physical plane in the here and now who is mind boggling," I grinned. I was thinking of Julius.

"That he is and you need to understand that. He's confusing you. He is going to hinder your progress," he said in an admonishing tone.

"You sound as if you know him personally," I said.

"I know his mind. This guy is not for you Catherine! He is with another woman yet he's trying to hold onto you but he's doing it through deceptive means and for dishonest motives. He will always hold you back. He's very insecure. You need a man who can teach you and help you to grow emotionally and spiritually. Your friend can't do that. He's trapped in the environment too deeply. You can't help him. He's programmed himself for unhappiness. It's karmic and you can't change that for him. He has to do that for himself."

"Do we have to live out our past lives' karma in this life?" I asked in defense of Julius.

"No, as your consciousness is raised you can change your karma and have other experiences. You choose your path as you grow. But your friend is stubborn and very skeptical about spiritual matters and he doesn't believe in the power of self. He is materialistic and is controlled by his sense appetite," he replied emphatically.

"He's good, but he doesn't mean you any good. You can't raise him up. He's caught up in the environmental mind and lives in the world of effects and influences. He has become a chameleon," he said without hesitation or remorse.

Again I defended Julius's character. "You stated that everyone has the God presence in them, so Julius is intrinsically good."

"Yes, that's true, but he has to discover that for himself. You can't do that for him Catherine."

"Beware!"

I thought and I thought. I had been given similar warnings about Julius's character by my gardener who was like a father figure. I trusted and often confided in him. He was nearly seventy –five years old and was full of wisdom. One day, as I was writing a check to pay my bill, he interrupted me.

He said, "Mary, you are about to make a big mistake again."

"What do you mean, Mr. Chavis?" I asked.

"The young fellow that you are dating is a very deceptive man. He's a user and can't be trusted. You're a free spirit Mary and I know that you're lonely for companionship, but don't be mislead.

"I ride around town and I see him quite often with other women. You have a lot to offer lady; don't be fooled." he said as he took the check out of my hand.

I defended Julius. "Oh, he's a part time real estate salesman who entertains a lot of clients. That's probably who you see with him."

Mr. Chavis didn't respond.

A few days later, I told Julius about the comments. He grinned.

"You always attract these weird people to you. First it was the tarot reader, then the astrologer; who's next?" he asked without allaying my concerns.

I responded with an old cliché, "When the student is ready, the teacher appears."

"Well, if you want me you'd better grab me. I'm a hot commodity, an endangered species remember. There aren't that many African-American men out there of my caliber. Do you know the ratio of professional Black men to professional Black women?"

"Yeah, I do and it doesn't bother me. I'm not threatened by your statistics."

U-2 tapped his fingers on the mouthpiece of the telephone to bring me back to our discussion.

"Hello! Hello! You're wandering again. You learn best by experiencing life, Catherine," he said. Nothing that I tell you will matter to you until you go through it for yourself. So, it's rough sailing ahead for you, but now you have been warned."

"Wait a minute. I have a suggestion. Why don't you try emotionally detaching from the situation by putting yourself in a learning mode? That's where you function best. Be an observer. Just go along with Julius's game plan just to see what happens. Remain friendly with him. You'll learn more about him as time progresses."

"But remember, not all men have had the same experiences that Julius has had. So don't let what you discover about him interfere with the personalities of other men who you'll meet later. Everyone is unique and has a special purpose and role to play in your life."

It would not be easy but I found U-2's proposition to detach from Julius's experiences most challenging and intriguing. I'd be like a great mystery detective who was going to solve the case by getting into the mind of the suspect without revealing my purpose. I would continue to be a friend and confidant if Julius needed me, but when in his company I would ask poignant, probing questions to elicit responses that would reveal his motives. Julius liked to talk.

"Catherine," he interjects because he knows that my mind meanders, "since you are an educator, let me compare life to your profession."

"That should be interesting. Go ahead!"

"Ok, let's say that life is a school and as inhabitants of the earth, we alternate as its teachers and students. To learn satisfactorily, you must pay very close attention to its curriculum. Each experience is a course of study and every situation is a class in that subject. The lessons learned are invariably subjective to your individual perception and academic aptitude. Therefore, the cost of tuition is the price you will ultimately pay for acquiring wisdom, knowledge and understanding. Your consciousness is your report card and you progress at your own rate."

"That's a great analogy!"

He continued, "Your awareness determines whether you pass the course or have to repeat it, because there is no failure in the school of life. Upon completion of each course, you subconsciously preregister for the next. You are not always cognizant of who your new teachers will be, or of who the new students in the class will be, but in the school of life you can be sure that the lessons will be especially designed to meet your individual and collective karmic needs."

"This pupil-teacher progression is continuous throughout your life. When it is time for graduation, you may have achieved the status of "Summa Cum Laude" and will be eligible to enter the institution of higher cosmic learning or your name may just be as an inkblot on the scrolls that list the many who matriculated during your life cycle."

I laugh remembering my Catholic teachings about Limbo and Purgatory. "Can I be recycled to earn additional credits to improve my GPA?" I chuckle.

"You can recycle you mind in this life if you stop behaving emotionally," he adamantly affirmed.

"I want you to take this seriously. There are many methods that can assist you in exploring the great storehouse of information that is available. But the path that leads to this inner reservoir of knowledge is straight and narrow. There aren't any shortcuts."

"Many travelers tire quickly, become discouraged, fall by the wayside, take detours, make U-turns, jump off the edge or come to complete stops. While a few travelers let nothing stop them from reaching their destination. Their success is not always determined by the method chosen, or by their ability to literally and figuratively interpret the doctrines presented. Their belief and trust in the supreme power within themselves is the key to their growth and understanding."

"Yes, I am too pedantic aren't I?"

"I would say that you need to find balance. It's rather late and we've talked extensively. I want you to meditate on our conversation for a few days. I'll call you soon. Good night! Sleep well!"

"Thank you so much. I really enjoyed the information. Good night."

As I prepared for bed, I thought, "My journey is taking a detour tonight. I am going to take a nonstop, one way flight to my new destination, SELF-ACTUALIZATION!"

I fastened my seat belt, made sure that my seat was in an upright position and plugged in my headset. This time I'll only listen to the voice within.

BLOSSOM

Later in June, I ended my intimate relationship with Julius. However, he would call periodically and chide me about being brainwashed by another "guru" whom he now felt controlled my life. I denied that and invited Julius to attend a discussion group with me. He refused.

One night as I turned into the parking lot, U-2 approached to assist me with my books. As we proceeded to our designated study area, Julius drove up, jumped out of the car and declared authoritatively, "Mary, I'm tired of this. I want you to get in your car and follow me home right now."

U-2 extended his hand to Julius in friendship. Julius ignored him.

"I'm sorry Julius. These discussions are much too important for me to miss. I'll talk with you later."

"If you aren't at my house in twenty minutes, you can kiss me goodbye." He returned to his car and angrily sped away.

U-2 laughed. "I think he loves you Mary. He just doesn't know how to express it in a healthy way. He's going to do something foolish to get even with you, but he will only hurt himself. Be careful."

The next morning, I heard a car pull into my driveway. I peeked out of the bedroom window and saw Julius. Dismayed that his tactics had not worked, he placed a letter on the windshield of my car, got back into his car and speedily drove off. I immediately went out to get the envelope.

Dear Mary,

You are first in my life at this moment but if you don't stop seeing this guru and putting other matters first, I will be forced to totally discontinue my relationship with you. I need companionship. If you want me you had better strive harder to keep me. There are other women out here that find me desirable. You have until September 1, to make your decision. I will be faithful until then. After that I plan to go on with my life without you.

Love, Julius

What! Julius made a conscious decision on his own about ending a relationship? I don't believe it. Julius doesn't like being alone. Someone is influencing him to act. There has to be another woman.

Later that week, I visited the Caribbean restaurant where Julius and I frequently dined. There he was with Blossom. The look on their faces let me know that there was more to this relationship than just business. They both worked part time for Faith, Blossom's sister. I said hello to both of them, then sat and waited for my takeout order.

Julius had introduced me to Blossom a year earlier. I needed someone to help tutor and she had been a teacher in the islands. For several months she taught advanced mathematics. During that time she revealed a lot about her personality as she probed to find out if Julius and I were a couple.

After so many subtle inquiries into my affairs, I asked Julius about Blossom. "Julius, I think Blossom desires you romantically. She asks so many questions about us."

"She's not interested in me anymore Mary. When she first came from the islands a few years ago, she wanted me to marry her to help her get a green card. She was having a difficult time financially and didn't want to wait seven years to apply for citizenship," he said.

"Well why didn't you marry her?"

"She's not my type. She's just lonely now. She just broke up with Smithy. That's why I asked her to work for you. It's therapeutic for her. Plus she could use the extra money. She cosigned for his jeep and he left her with the payments. She'll have another man soon. She doesn't let any grass grow under her feet too long," he said.

Soon thereafter, Blossom met another guy, Fred a security guard. One day, after tutoring, we discussed their relationship.

"Blossom, tell me about Fred! You obviously are excited about him. You seem to brighten up after he calls," I joked.

"Oh, I met him about a year ago but I wouldn't date him because he had too many children by too many different women. He's not the marrying kind. He has difficulty committing to a relationship," she said.

"Are you going to date him now?"

"Yes!"

"Do you like him?"

"He's Ok. There's nobody else beating down my door." She paused to think. "I need to get over Smithy and it's easier getting over one guy when you have another one to take away the pain," she said despondently.

"I would think that it's best to wait before you get into something else. When you're emotional you make too many mistakes. I'm speaking from experience," I chuckled as I chronicled some of my mistakes. We laughed.

"Aren't you afraid of getting pregnant though? He definitely won't marry you either if you do. His track record proves that," I said out of concern.

"Oh, I'm not worried about getting pregnant. I haven't used birth control in nearly ten years and I've never gotten pregnant. I guess I can't conceive," she said depressingly.

My heart went out to her. I remembered the pain that I experienced when I had surgery while pregnant with Renee. The thought of not being able to ever have children was emotionally disturbing.

"Who knows, maybe one day God will bless your womb," I said to brighten up her mood. She smiled.

Then her cell phone rang again. She anxiously answered. Afterwards she said, "Mary, I'm going out to lunch with Fred."

"Good luck! Now I see why you're dressed up so beautifully today. Perhaps you'll be the one to change his heart," I said with a smile.

"I doubt it but I'll enjoy it while it lasts," she said as she left.

Later that evening Julius came over. "Blossom has a date with Fred," I gleefully informed him.

He laughed and stated, "It won't last." Then he began to chronicle Blossom's failed love affairs.

Now a year had passed and I'd not seen Blossom until that night in the restaurant. Yes, Blossom was getting over another failed relationship with Fred and Julius was her target again.

I felt that she'd been waiting a long time to capture him.

As I continued to wait for my order, Julius came over to talk. I knew that he wanted to explain but I said nothing. In fact I changed the conversation.

"I'm preparing to drive to Tallahassee to FAMU to visit an old friend."

Julius, also a graduate of FAMU, urged, "Let me ride with you. I know about your blood sugar level dropping and how it affects you. It's a long trip and you shouldn't be alone. My cousin Ann lives in Tallahassee and it would be great to see her again."

I agreed to let him accompany me on the trip. "Just remember that I'm not going to sleep with you Julius."

He didn't respond.

After arriving at Ann's house, Julius was full of laughter and became so loving and affectionate. After all he was very attractive and humorous. I decided not to resist his advances.

Well much to my dismay, after psyching me up to enjoy the moment, Julius experienced erectile dysfunction again. In utter frustration and intense heat, I decided to leave.

"Mary, where are you going?" he pleaded.

"I'm going to the Holiday Inn to spend the night! I didn't cancel my reservation."

Disgusted with myself and feeling stupid, I hurried out of the door. "I'll call you when it's time to leave. Have a good time with Ann."

At the hotel, I finally tried to sleep but my latest escapade with Julius kept replaying. To mask those thoughts, I began to reminisce on Job. My tension and frustrations subsided.

I remembered the day that Job was waiting in my driveway for our scheduled appointment. He looked at me in a disapproving manner as I drove up with Julius. Later he interrupted the session abruptly and stated in an annoying tone, "I thought that you had ended your relationship with Julius."

"I did. We are just friends."

"It's more than that Mary the guy is interested in you. Let me give you some advice. When you end a relationship, stop seeing the person completely. That's the only way, otherwise you're inviting trouble. Life is a straight forward journey. You shouldn't look back."

"I can take care of myself," I said rebelliously.

Job just stared at me as if he were irritated by my comment. "You are very stubborn like a wild boar and only a real man will be able to tame you. That guy is no match for your mind, especially after all that you've been through. You are playing games with him. You make him think that he's so terrific and smart, but inside your mind you're saying how illogical, shallow and superficial he is. If you continue with this game it will backfire on you. Julius is craftier that you'll ever be, and he doesn't understand women anymore than you understand men. Both of you are blind."

Job hesitated then quoted this scripture from memory:

"In the last days perilous times shall come. For men shall be lovers of their own selves, covetous, boasters, proud, false accusers, despisers of those that are good, traitors, heady, high-minded, lovers of pleasures more than lovers of God; Having a form of godliness, but denying the power thereof:

from such turn away, For of this sort are they which creep into houses, and lead captive silly women laden with sins, led away with divers lusts."

"Mary, don't be a silly woman. Julius doesn't mean you any good. He will defile your house if you continue to be with him," Job urgently stressed.

"What do you mean?" I asked.

"I mean your physical house; your body. He runs around too much and even if you marry him he won't stop. Though he is well over forty years old, he hasn't grown up yet, especially when it comes to women."

"Oh, so you're an expert on maturity?" I retorted defiantly.

"No. I'm a MAN and I know men better than you do; but do what you want to do. Let's get back to work," Job said abruptly.

I was furious. He understood me better than I understood myself. Because of his cool, calm, controlled and detached manner, I wasn't threatened by his arrogance. In fact I found him challenging and very sexually stimulating. I'd met my match, but I still didn't know how to relate to him. I fumed as I sought the words to combat his statements.

As my mental gymnastics continued, Job just calmly stared at me as if he were reading my mind. Suddenly my mood changed. My body reacted in an intense manner. My genital area began to secrete profusely as it rhythmically constricted and pulsated. My heartbeat and respiration accelerated, my mouth salivated excessively, and my temperature rose by several degrees as more adrenalin pumped into my blood stream. I was highly aroused both mentally and physically. Job looked at me and began to smile; he understood.

Suddenly, he grasped my wrists. I pretended to struggle. He stood and in one quick motion brought me to my feet, released my wrists and lifted me up into the air by my waist and placed me over his broad shoulder. He carried me to the master bedroom, laid me gently on the bed and stared down at me with one of those commanding, "Don't you dare move looks." I didn't budge. As he undressed, I saw a thoroughbred, of pure Mandingo lineage manifest before my eyes.

Job softly affirmed, "After today you won't have to wonder about how it would feel to have me make love to you anymore."

I smiled and replied as I anxiously disrobed, "Nor will you." Within moments we embraced in lustful ecstasy. Before long I was in heaven, a state of perfect bliss, as he passionately made love to me. He didn't utter a sound. He just gently guided me from one position to the next.

He was so gentle yet very powerful. I joyously screamed and moaned uncontrollably. For the first time this intense drama was no act; no faked orgasms. My speech became unintelligible. Obviously I was speaking in tongue; the Spirit had definitely come upon me. Finally I understood the glory of the "flow" that Ruby glowingly talked about. I had initially experienced it with Abner, but now it was happening repeatedly with Job.

After what seemed like an hour of sexercising, Job turned over on his back and smiled. He continued to hold me so caringly and compassionately while caressing and stroking my body. I felt good all over, inside and outside. My mind was so supercharged that I continued to have orgasms. Job just smiled.

He softly whispered into my ear, "You've just had a real man to make love to you, my beautiful virgin. Don't ever accept less. You deserve the best. You're a very desirable woman and a terrific lady."

Oh, God, how I needed him to say that. I selfishly wanted him all for myself but I knew that he was committed to another.

As I mentally returned to the present moment, I realized how much I missed Job tonight. The hotel was cold and lonely.

Job's words were echoing in my head. As I began to replay the sexual experience over and over in my mind, I smiled and started counting the number of multiple orgasms that Job had gently thrust through my body and soul.

The memory of his touch was a powerful anesthetic. For the first time I counted in an increasing order to go to sleep. 1 orgasm, 2 orgasms, three orgasms Z… Z… Z… Z… z… z… z…..

After returning to Miami, I decided to pull out of the experiment that U-2 suggested that I conduct with Julius. The writing was on the wall. I had better heed the message or suffer the consequences.

DAWN

Though it is late, I will not go to the cabin until I complete my journal. I hurriedly write and write until I begin to nod. I close my eyes to rest them, but fall to sleep in the lounger. When I wake up and open my eyes, I see the sun rising in the east. In my mind, I can see that this great puzzle that I have been assembling about my life is also taking shape.

INSIGHT

Every morning, after I thanked God for all of my blessings and for His daily guidance and protection, I asked Him to create a condition that would cause Julius to be transferred to a work site farther from my schools since the company had other locations. I didn't want to see him again. Julius knew my every move including where I often ate lunch. I knew that he would follow me, so I changed my pattern daily as I changed schools. I did everything that I could to avoid him as I began to take charge of my life by going to movies, concerts and plays alone.

Things were going fine. I had not seen Julius for nearly three months until one night, I heard a knock on my bedroom window. It was Julius. I refused to let him inside. He pleaded with me.

I compromised and went outside and sat on the car. He was behaving very strangely.

"Mary please read this poem on friendship."

I read it and asked, "What is your point?"

"You are the best friend that I've ever had and I don't want to lose you."

I became very quiet. He would say more if I didn't utter a sound.

"After you stopped being my companion, I started drinking and did something very foolish. I wanted to hurt you but I hurt myself."

Hmm, I thought remembering U-2's words.

"I started seeing someone. I didn't go out looking for her. We were at the gym. She was just getting over a breakup and we decided to spend some time together to help soothe our wounded hearts. After dating a while, we recognized that we were incompatible. But by that time, she discovered that she was pregnant." I was surprised because I knew that he was talking about Blossom who thought that she couldn't conceive. I continued to be silent.

"We've decided that we will just be friends with a kid. She doesn't want to get married either."

"Well congratulations. It doesn't matter what your marital plans are, you are now bound for life. Is there anything else you want to say, I have to go inside and get some rest. I have a long day ahead. I've got to screen three kindergarten classes tomorrow and this night air isn't good for my voice."

"Don't you want to know who it is?"

"Oh, I know. It's Blossom. I have seen you two out together many times, especially at the Stadium Diner on 199th Street. That's where you use to take me for breakfast also, remember?"

He looked shocked. "Will you ever forgive me Mary?" he asked.

"There is nothing to forgive you for. I'm happy for you; now I can go on with my life," I said without hesitation.

He just stared at me as if he couldn't believe his ears.

"Is there anything else you'd like to say?"

As I stood up to leave, Julius grabbed my hand and held it tightly. I tried not to feel a flicker of sympathy for him.

He was beginning to emote. I pulled my hand away as I wondered what the true story was. Something drastic had to have happened to cause Julius to humble himself like this.

"It's too late now. There has never been a time when it's just been you and me without your past affairs hovering over our relationship. I've always sensed your ambivalence. I want a life free of entanglements. You need to try to work things out with her now that she is going to have your baby," I admonished him.

"Our definition of friendship is not the same Julius." I handed him the paper with the poem; ran into the house and locked the door.

I had prepared myself for his announcement about Blossom, but I didn't expect him to tell me that she was pregnant.

One week later, Julius returned. Without opening the door, I told him to leave.

"Mary, please talk to me; something has just happened that might change everything."

I was curious. I had itching ears again. I opened the window to listen.

"Blossom is threatening to miscarry. I was with her at the hospital from 2:00 a.m. to 9:00 this morning. Things don't look so good," he said.

I didn't respond.

"I'd asked her to have an abortion earlier, but she refused, but now if ...."

"What are you saying?" I abruptly interrupted him.

"Mary, if Blossom miscarries, she will be all right. Now she knows that she can get pregnant. She's frustrated about this situation too. I can prove it to you. She wrote me a letter. You can read it. Rosa has already read it. Call her! She'll confirm that I'm telling the truth. Everything can work out if you will just trust me again. Just be patient Mary," he pleaded.

If I could have, I would have vomited on him. I so despised his behavior.

I reminded him of what had happened to me with my first child and the pain and agony that I went through when I lost Vincente and how my own husband wasn't caring and attentive to my feelings and needs.

"No! Mother fucker! Get out of here. While you expect a miscarriage, I'll expect a miracle. Babies are a blessing from God. Conception is no accident. Your actions were by divine appointment. Just like you had no control over that, you have no control over this. God Rules! Now I understand you better," I screamed. "You are only looking out for yourself." I forcefully shut the window and closed the curtains.

Julius got angry that his story didn't work and started ranting. I could hear him through the walls.

Realizing his plight, he fumingly said, "I'm tired of you anyway. You've been a pain in the ass since the day I met you. You're just a religious fanatic, a bible nut. I don't need you either." He raged on and on.

He was Chico in another body. I realized that he had not truly been the friend that he pretended to be. I finally got a glimpse inside of his mind. I realized that he wasn't angry at me, he was angry and frustrated with himself. U-2's assessment of Julius had been 100% accurate.

The next evening, as I drove to the Truth Center, Julius's harsh words kept reverberating in my head. I lost my concentration for just a second to shake my head as if I could cause the words to fall out of my mind. I ran a stop sign. CRASH! .....BAM!

I was unaware that I had been in an accident until I saw a crowd of people standing around my crumpled car when I regained consciousness. I'd blacked-out for a short while. I was frightened but calmness suddenly overshadowed me as I realized that the presence of God had protected me again from my foolish actions. I could have been killed.

"Is there anyone you want us to notify?" the police officer asked. "The ambulance and the wrecker are on the way."

"No," I softly whispered.

When the paramedics arrived and removed me from the vehicle, I looked at my car as they placed me on the stretcher and securely anchored my head. Who could I call that will come in time to direct the tow truck to my house? Friends and family were too far away to get here quickly.

Only Julius! He lives a few blocks away, I thought as I remembered my location. I didn't ever want to see him again but I had to just one more time. Like Chico was in a time of crisis when I wanted to take the kids out of the temple's school; Julius too was now good for something.

"Can you beep a friend to take care of my car?" I asked the officer.

"Sure."

Julius drove up as I was being lifted into the ambulance. "Mary, I'm sorry. I know I caused this accident. I'll make it up to you."

"Just have my car taken to my house. I don't want it at a pound where it can be stripped for parts before I can retrieve it. Here are my keys. My AAA card is in the glove compartment."

"I'll take care of everything," he said dotingly.

As I rode in the ambulance, hearing the blasting sounds of the sirens, I thought and thought until my head began to hurt. I was just beginning to feel the effects of the impact.

NO COINCIDENCES

After recuperating, I enrolled in several more classes at the Truth Center. On Sunday, I eagerly dressed and hurried to the church for the worship service. Arriving thirty minutes early, I decided to browse through the bookstore. I picked up a catalog from the Johnnie Coleman Institute in Chicago, a schedule for upcoming Better Living classes and several brochures and placed them into my pocketbook to read later. I then went into the chapel to be seated.

I was feeling so very good that morning. I better understood my spiritual goals and felt more compelled to further my studies. With my various religious experiences, I'd decided that I wanted to become a teacher of comparative religion at the university.

With a few more moments to spare I began to read some of the literature. A membership application was in the packet. I completed it just to pass the time but was not contemplating joining the church. I wrote a check for the offering and placed it into the envelope and inserted it into my Bible.

Service began promptly. The lesson was titled "Consciousness." With the sermon complete, the ushers quickly passed the collection baskets. I dropped my envelope into it and passed it along.

A week later, I received a letter from the church informing me of the dates for the new member orientation and spiritual baptism. I was surprised. "Subconsciously" I had also placed the application for membership into the basket with my offering.

I realized that my actions were not of my conscious will but of my super conscious volition. I didn't fight the feeling. The thought of being truly baptized this time for the right reasons and with adequate knowledge and understanding of the doctrine espoused would be exhilarating.

As the weeks progressed and I had time to think about this significant move, I became more excited. I invited my family to come and witness this event. Surely they would be happy that I was becoming a member of a religious community that, to them, was more acceptable than that of the temple.

Mom asked, "Is the baptism going to be held at the beach or does the church have a pool inside?"

"Neither. It is going to be a spiritual baptism, a mind thing," I said. She looked downcast and worried.

"Is the minister going to sprinkle you with some water?" she asked again as if she wanted clarity.

"No. There won't be any water at all. None! Nada!"

Mother almost collapsed. "What are you getting into now?" she lamented.

I tried to comfort her. "I was sprinkled with water as a child at the Catholic Church and I was fully immersed as a teenager at the Baptist church. Don't you remember? Reverend Shipp baptized me during the revival."

She looked up and smiled with relief. "Well as long as you've done it properly once, I guess this'll be OK."

"Praise the Lord," she said shaking her hands and head as she raised them towards the sky.

I chuckled silently.

As I left her house she called out to ask, "Will you ever do anything normal like other people?"

I just smiled at her.

"I seriously doubt it. I'm not like other people." I placed my hand over my lips and blew her a kiss, then waved goodbye. "Love ya!" I yelled.

She clutched her heart and closed the door. I grinned as I drove away.

I awakened Saturday morning and anxiously prepared for the morning's baptismal orientation activities. I arrived early. Members of the welcoming committee were happily preparing the reception hall for the guests and arranging a buffet breakfast on the tables.

Promptly at 9:00 a.m. Rev. Tumpkin began the orientation. We were given a packet with information about the church. She guided us through one of its booklets pertaining to their beliefs titled, ***"What We Teach"*** *and **"Things You Should Know about New Thought."***

The word free, free, free, rang continuously throughout my ears as she read aloud.

"Are there any questions?" she asked after going over the church's history.

"Yes, are the stories in the Bible literal or figurative? If figurative, how do they relate to us individually and to this doctrine?" I asked.

"The stories are both literal and figurative. They are literal in that they actually happened in the historical sense; figurative in their spiritual interpretation."

"Will you elaborate?"

"Briefly, many ancient writings describing the journeys of prominent figures are historical narratives. These are stories of events and personal experiences, factual or imagined, characterized by a tracing of causes and effects, and by an attempt to evaluate and interpret facts. Many of those narratives were written figuratively of the lives of the spiritually oriented people who once walked the earth."

I nodded to indicate that I was listening attentively.

"The Holy Bible, the universally recognized inspired narrative, was written as a guide for the patterning of our lives today. The chronicling of the lives of those outstanding biblical figures demonstrates how we too could identify and express the God potential within us."

"To ascend in consciousness, we must recognize and understand that perfect pattern written of and attempt to live our lives in the light of those examples provided and practice the universal principles of truth faithfully regardless of denominational affiliation, which so often divide us."

The minister looked at me as if she anticipated my next question and said.

"New Thought is not new, it's not new age, and it is not a cult. It's based on the principles taught by Jesus. It combines Theology, Psychology and Philosophy in a practical and metaphysical format to assist us in understanding our relationship to the Creator."

"Thank you." I felt a great sense of release; my soul was being liberated from doctrinal bondage. I felt free to participate with this church while living my life based on principles and not on dogma and creeds!

"Mary in Chicago, Illinois"

REALIZATION

The Baptismal Ceremony was spiritually performed one week later. As I stood before the pulpit, I looked back to see if anyone from my family had come to witness the occasion. I sighed, feeling so alone when I didn't spot a familiar face. Disappointed, I slowly turned around and listened to the minister.

"There is one body, one spirit, one Lord, one faith, one baptism, one God and Father of all, who is above all and through all, and in you all."

These words reverberated in my head. Instead of being totally immersed in a pool of water or being slightly sprinkled with water, the minister then laid her hands on my forehead and pronounced: "I baptize you in the name of the Father, the Son and the Holy Ghost, Amen."

After the ceremony the message, "A Day of Rest," was delivered. A metaphysical viewpoint of the meaning of the Sabbath was taught. As I listened I knew that I was just beginning to unfold spiritually and that there was much more work to be done. I would have to erase a lot of error beliefs that would thwart my growth. My responsibility as a new creature in God was "right thinking, right feelings, right words, right actions and right reactions." But most importantly, I would have to take full responsibility for all of my actions, past, present and future. I was ready for the challenge.

A few months later, in December, Julius came to my house approximately 2:00 in the morning knocking frantically on the door and windows. He had been drinking again. Reluctantly, I let him in to keep the neighbors from hearing the commotion.

He looked terrible and began to complain about the awful words that Blossom had been saying to him.

"She's so frustrated about being pregnant and not being married. She's having a difficult time with morning sickness and some other complications."

"She's just going through hormonal changes," I assured him.

"No Mary, its more than that. She's physically hostile and verbally abusive. I've seen her like that before when other relationships failed," he commented pathetically.

"Well why don't you marry her? You've always admired Caribbean women, so what's the problem? Isn't she the answer to your dreams?"

"No!" he blasted. "She knows that when these babies are born, my responsibility to her ends," he said. "I have to stand by her now that she is so sickly and her mother is terminally ill. She'll have to be committed to hospice care soon."

"I'm sorry to hear that. Give Blossom my sincere regards. It's good that you are helping her through this," I said without sympathy for him. But my mind was spinning in reverse. Did I hear him correctly? "Did you say babies?" I asked.

He sobered up.

"She had a sonogram a few weeks ago. She's going to have twins," he lamented.

"Why are you so sad? That's great. Must have been a good screw," I smiled. "Or was she taking fertility drugs?"

Julius didn't respond. He just stared at the ceiling as if he was praying for deliverance.

I couldn't help but laugh to myself. Though Julius had four adult children, he had just gone from zero to three dependents.

Suddenly he grasped my hand and said, "Mary I really care for you. We have so much in common. We went to the same university. We're both American," he remarked.

I interrupted him.

"What does that have to do with anything?" I puzzlingly asked.

"She doesn't treat me like you treat me. Her culture is different. You know that Caribbean people look down on Black Americans, especially African American Black men," he said.

"So why didn't you prevent her from getting pregnant?"

"You know Blossom said that she couldn't get pregnant. I thought so too," he cried.

"No Julius, she said that she hadn't gotten pregnant. You need to start listening to what people say."

"Well I ain't never going to marry her."

"It doesn't matter now, you are forever bound. Children don't know anything about marriage contracts. They just know that this is my mother, and that is my father. To them, that's family."

He paused to think. "Sleeping with her was like an insurance policy for me. I thought that I had lost you last summer. Shit this is too much," he lamented.

"Just stick by me Mary. I need your support now. Please stand by me like I stood by you after you left the temple."

I wasn't going to let him play this sympathy role on me or make me feel guilty with that "you owe me one" attitude.

"No! No! Do you think I'm a fool? Get out of here!" I screamed. "You're playing a game. Just leave."

I want you Mary. Marry me and let me move in with you. I can rent out the rooms in my house to earn additional income. We can make it. With our combined incomes it won't be a strain even with my paying her child support," he drunkenly cried.

I now had very little respect for him. "NO! I blasted him. I am not going to help you out. I can take care of myself and I'm not going to spend the next eighteen years helping you to support those kids. I ain't that crazy. I'm not getting caught up in y'all mess." I was so angry that I continued to rant.

"I'm not the one to supplement your incomes. I work hard and I've had to struggle all by myself since my divorce. I deserve better now."

I looked back at him and noticed that he was slumping over. I wanted him to leave but he was too intoxicated to drive. I just stared at him. Then I thought, "I should let him go. Maybe he'll get arrested and learn a valuable lesson while in jail." I quickly dismissed those evil thoughts as he staggered into my guest bedroom to sleep off his drunkenness.

But I couldn't sleep. I walked and paced the floor all night pondering what I did to deserve this again. I opened the bedroom door and looked at him. Killing him in his sleep wasn't worth it but the thought of doing so was appealing.

My anger soon subsided. I realized that this was my fault entirely as I remembered that U-2 said that I would bring this pain on myself. I sighed, returned to my bedroom and finally went to sleep.

As soon as morning came and I heard him stir, I went to him and said, "Get out and don't ever come back again."

As he walked away, he slowly turned and said, "When I went out with Blossom, I felt like everyone was looking at me saying, "Wow, what a prize he has on his arms!" I never felt that way when I went out with you Mary."

I was devastated by his remarks. His words penetrated the most vulnerable part of my soul. He had thrown the most vicious verbal punch and he knew exactly where it would strike.

Dawn

As he got into his car and drove off, he turned his head toward me and smiled. Yes, he had gotten his revenge for my rejection.

I was shattered but remained silent. Julius was not drunk now and fully understood the effect that his words would have. Yes, they hurt deeply. Just as Chico's words had hurt when he left and angrily pronounced that he'd married me as a ploy for a war deferment.

After I closed the door, I went to the mirror and looked closely at my eyes. Yes, looks do matter, I sighed. What can I do about the appearance ... of my eye? I wondered. I have to accept my lifelong condition or seek medical advice. Technology and surgical techniques have improved, just maybe there is hope.

That February, I forgot everything about spiritual healing as I visited the ocular plastic surgeons at Bascom Palmer Eye Institute to begin a series of CAT scans and ultrasounds in anticipation of extensive cosmetic surgery, again.

I prayed for positive test results as I waited patiently for my pupils to dilate. A team of residents assembled around me to take turns looking into my eyes. I'd become their lesson for the day. After the findings were compiled, Dr. Tsi reported the results to me with a somber look.

"Mary, additional eye surgery is not recommended. To do so would jeopardize your existing vision. It's too risky. You have already had too many operations and there is extensive scar tissue. We can't jeopardize your sight. I recommend that you see an ocularist to be fitted for a sclera shell. That should improve the symmetry of your eyes and facial features. Good luck!"

"Thanks," I said politely though I was very disappointed.

I knew that I would have to accept myself "as is" and get on with my life. I repeated the serenity prayer as I left the hospital.

The last week of April, Julius called again. His pleasant tone suggested that he had not remembered our last encounter.

"Mary, the twins were born Monday morning."

"Congratulations. How is Blossom doing?"

"She's fine. She had to have a C-section because one of the twins was coming breech."

He paused and said, "This may sound strange, but the whole time that I was in the delivery room with her, I thought about you."

"Stop, don't call or come around anymore. No more sympathy games. Go to Blossom. She needs you. The twins need you."

I envisioned a helpless marionette being dangled by the strings choking and gasping for breath. Julius had gotten trapped by his own games. There was no way out of this one. He was permanently committed to a relationship for better or worse, whether he liked it or not.

As if I could read his mind I finally said, "I can see you more clearly. You aren't really such a nice guy. You know that many women are very lonely and that some men have been very cruel or abusive to them. So you figure that you can get more conquests by playing the good guy role. Well if you keep playing that role long enough perhaps one day you will forget that you're acting," I said.

There was silence.

"Grow up! When are you going to stop playing games with people's feelings? Goodbye!"

"Mary as a facilitator at U.S. Postal's Career Awareness Conference"

For the next month, I put all of my energy into my home based tutoring service and initiated plans to conduct speech and writing improvement workshops for adults. I was rewarded by securing a contract with the United States Postal Service to facilitate a writing workshop at their annual career awareness conference. I was so excited. I called several family members and good friends to share the news, including Rosa, one of Julius's closest friends. I had grown very fond of her over the years and wanted her to know how my business was progressing.

Rosa later informed him about the conference and he used it as another opportunity to call again. Recognizing the number, I let the answering machine intercept. He recorded this message, "Mary, I want to help you in your new business venture. Remember, I have a degree in marketing. I haven't given up on you. Let me help you again. Call me!"

He's not going to ever stop calling. His actions don't make sense. Should I call Blossom to expose his game? Yes, that will stop him. As I began dialing her number, I thought of how proudly she must feel as a new mother and I identified with her plight as a single parent.

I just couldn't call her. I just couldn't be that cruel. There had to be another way to solve this conflict. All is fair in love and war, I thought as I contemplated my next move. Looking down at the telephone book, I saw Blossom's sister's name and number. That's it. I'll call Faith. She'll talk to Julius to protect her sister's interest. Blood is thicker than water.

I quickly dialed the number.

"Hello, Faith, this is Mary. I'd like for you to talk with Julius. He's refused to stop calling me. He will listen to you since you are such good friends and confidants," I said hoping for relief.

"I know that Julius is a snake and I've warned Blossom. Julius is afraid of commitment."

Faith eagerly began to tell me the other side to the Julius-Blossom saga. Julius was using me as his scapegoat. He would do or say anything to keep the pressure off of him.

Later that evening, Hope couldn't wait to tell Blossom about my call confirming that Julius was still playing games. They angrily confronted him that night. Dismayed, he angrily blamed everything on me. I was jealous and maliciously trying to mess up his relationship.

The next morning Rosa, Julius's best friend, called. Blossom had spoken with her earlier.

"Beware Mary, Blossom is like a bear protecting her cubs," Rosa warned. "Take care of yourself. I'll take care of Julius. This is the last time he's going to use me as a mediator in his affairs."

"Thanks, Rosa."

I dressed and went to work. As usual, I called home at noon to access my telephone messages and was shocked to hear Blossom's voice. In a pronounced and exaggerated Caribbean accent she roared,

"Hello Mary, this is Blossom. I know what you're trying to do but I'm telling you now that it won't work. If I hear that you call Julius or my sister again, I'll consider it a declaration of war. I know that you are an emotional weakling and are unstable. So you aren't prepared to do battle with me. I'm a formidable opponent. You will not enjoy fighting me. Believe that!"

Then the sound of crying babies consumed the additional time on the recorder. It sounded as if their mouths were purposefully placed on the speaker. They bellowed loudly.

Disappointed that my conversation with Hope had not accomplished the desired effect, I pondered my next move. I was so tired of playing this game. I'd helped both Julius and Blossom, and now they both want to harm me. "Push Mary from the ledge; hold her down and kick her; destroy her mind is their attitude. My friendship has been rejected and now my life has been threatened again," I fumed.

I clearly realized that I had chosen to learn these lessons the hard way. I had drawn another negative experience into my life. I was the ultimate writer, producer and director. I had chosen my actors, and cast them in various scenes. Julius and Blossom were just two characters who I'd selected to act out these devastating dramatic roles.

This segment of my life was a blockbuster hit full of villains, illusions and props; but now the plot thickens. The play wasn't over yet. Blossom had to be dealt with, I thought. If she could make such hostile threats then she wasn't too weak to hear the other side of the story from my perspective. She needed to learn a lesson also and she, subconsciously, had chosen me to teach her.

Apparently, Blossom was a fighter and I didn't want to appear on the six o'clock news as the victim or the criminal. What was I going to do?

When I returned home, I took 100 mg of B-complex and 1000 mg of Vitamin C to calm my nerves. I wanted this problem solved this day; with no encore or repeat performances. As I went to sleep, I programmed my mind to be receptive to a positive solution and sincerely prayed for spiritual intervention.

THE SEVENTH DAY: SUNRISE

This is the final morning of the cruise. The ship will dock in approximately three hours. The seven days have passed so quickly and I've accomplished a lot. I've been up all night writing. I quickly return to the cabin to shower and pack. I get a bite to eat and hurry down to my favorite spot and stare at the ocean and smell the breeze again. Birds are flying overhead so I know that we're nearing land. I pick up my pen to write the final reflective episode.

THE UPPER ROOM: A HIGHER ORDER OF THINKING

When I awakened, I went to the computer and began to type Blossom a letter. I wouldn't give her the satisfaction of thinking that I was afraid of her.

I wanted to tell her the details, but as I positioned my fingers over the keyboard, my body shuddered and my head buzzed. High frequency ultrasonic sounds bombarded my eardrums internally. All of the peripheral sounds of the computer's equipment instantly became mute. I felt as if a transparent glass dome had encased me in a sound proof booth. Realizing that the inner voice was attempting to get my attention in a drastic way, I stopped typing and listened.

As I became still, ideas and positive thoughts overwhelmed my mind. My attitude immediately changed. I didn't have to stoop to a low level to be effective. The scripture, "a soft answer turns away wrath," reverberated in my ears.

Suddenly, I remembered the sounds of the crying babies left on the answering machine. My mind was smoothed. Blossom had purposely recorded their cry to foment my mind. It was her childish way of saying, "I've got Julius's babies and you don't."

Though Blossom meant it for evil, God meant it for good. Now their cries sang out to my soul. The babies were the channel through which the Holy Spirit chose to provide me with a higher order of thinking.

I laughed and calmed down. My love for children was overwhelming. Remembering the hell that I had put myself and my children through, I knew that I had to be kind and respectful to both Blossom and Julius or my words and actions could negatively impact the twin's lives. I didn't want to harm anyone. I just wanted my involvement with them to end.

"But how?" I wondered. Then the solution crystallized in my mind; I am a teacher, so think of Blossom as my student. How should I present the lesson to be most effective? Yes, I'll write her a letter suggesting ways to positively redirect her negative energy so that she might become a loving parent. Great! I began to type.

Dear Blossom,
God is my strength and my support. He is my fortress and strong tower. I run into HIM and am protected. My God is a mighty warrior

also. I don't have to fight you. God does my fighting for me. What you choose to do is your business, but I suggest the following:...

Thank you for your call, it was most enlightening. May God Bless your family forever.

Mary

Rosa called a week later. "Julius intercepted the letter that you mailed when he went over to visit the twins. He read it to me; but it doesn't matter because Blossom soon realized that you were not the culprit."

"She knew it all along, but she had done as I did. I closed my eyes so that I could believe what I wanted to believe."

"Mary, how do you feel about Blossom now?" Rosa asked.

"Like me, she'll reap what she has sown. When that happens, she will reflect on this day. I surely don't envy her nor am I jealous of her."

"You should have demanded more of Julius. Blossom did and he jumped to her beat. You can't be easy with men, Mary. They don't respect you if you are weak."

"Well, I guess I'll have to remain single. You can only demand of yourself not of others. You don't own people. Rosa, I believe in demanding what I want by demonstrating love, respect, trust, and friendship, hoping that it will be appreciated and reciprocated."

"When a person feels ensnarled, they develop feelings of resentment and later express forms of hostility and revenge. A true relationship can't be established on that unhealthy foundation."

"I'm not weak at all and I don't care who perceives me as being weak anymore. I'll define myself. If Julius were meant to be with me, no force in the universe could have separated us."

Rosa remarked, "Mary, I've never heard you express yourself so vehemently and confidently."

"I'm just waking up, Rosa. I finally know who I truly am."

I hung up the phone and gathered the few gifts that Julius had given me over the years, placed them in a box and returned them to his doorstep. I didn't want anything to remind me of him and I didn't want anything to obscure my sight.

My consciousness was rising and I was ascending. I felt good about myself. I turned on the radio and heard an old familiar song that soothed my wounds and gave me hope. ***"Release Me and Let Me Love Again."*** I remembered how U-2 suggested that I listen to lyrics and thought, yes, release my mind! I sang the song over and over again.

The Seventh Day: Sunrise

I stop writing and smile. Things are going to be different when I get home. My life will be positive and productive. I will live in the glorious moment, I affirm. Now let's see if I can summarize what I've learned about myself and what issues I've resolved.

SELF ACTUALIZATION

The most important lesson I've learned is that I constantly failed to listen to and obey the "still small voice" that consistently rang out from within my soul. I rationalized, made excuses, procrastinated, and justified my every action and reaction. I was too analytical and intellectual to allow spirit to work through me effectively. Therefore, I'd subconsciously chosen all of these experiences for my soul's growth, and for my personal development.

I attracted hostile personalities into my life because of my fears of being criticized, rejected, dominated and controlled. The scripture states, "That which you are afraid of shall come upon you." So each character represented a specific challenge for me to overcome. Each one reflected some aspect of my personality that needed to be examined.

My subconscious desire to destroy the precious gift of life that the Creator had granted me was why I kept attracting those desiring to help me fulfill my death wish. The dominating men represented a cry from my soul to regain its balance. The emotive side of me had been running rampant and unchecked for eons which was the cause of my PMS; physical, mental and spiritual imbalance.

My problems were in my head, not in my body. My enemies were of my own internal household. Also, those whom I confided in kept betraying me as a lesson for me to trust in the God presence within me. And finally, I must remember that "No" means "No" if there are to be no more repeat performances of negative situations in my life.

Being satisfied with my self evaluation, I place my pen in my bag and close my journal. I realize that to continue my life in a more positive manner I would have to forgive myself since I've previously forgiven everyone else.

I relax realizing that I am no longer fearful of men or of those who are masquerading as such. I pleasantly remember a conversation that I had with Job before he returned to his island home.

"Mary, you need to trust in yourself more. You need to learn to love yourself and know that God is with you and protecting you wherever you are."

That day, Job made me stand up, took me by the hand and guided me to a mirror. He slowly undressed me.

"Look at the beautiful lady in the mirror. She is made in the image and likeness of God. Let her be your best friend, go with her on a vacation. Learn to like her. Stop tormenting her. Learn to love yourself first before you attempt to love another. Then and only then will true love find you."

I now realize that Job had been an angel placed on my path.

I quickly return to my cabin, take off my shades and stand in front of the mirror. I take a good look at myself. As if for the first time, I see a very beautiful, loving, compassionate, intelligent, strong and friendly woman with a most pleasing personality and positive outlook. "Yes! I like you," I say aloud enthusiastically.

With tears of joy in my eyes, I turn and kneel on the floor alongside the bed to say a prayer of thanksgiving. As I begin to utter, an old prayer that I used to say as a good Catholic resound in my mind. I laugh. I'd repeated that prayer daily as a child as part of the Rosary; but now I personally relate to it since my name is Mary. I chuckle then pray:

"Hail Mary full of grace the Lord is with thee. Blessed art thou among women and blessed is the fruit of thy womb.

"Yes! My children and I are so very blessed."

"I stand and say, "Mary! What a noble character. I'll have to start proudly living up to her attributes." I smile again at her in the mirror and watch her gleefully return the smile!

The flutter of butterflies that I felt in my stomach as I boarded the ship to begin this journey seven days ago are now gone. My soul is at peace. I've been given a second chance to fulfill my dreams and to find true love.

HOME: MY DEBUT

Once home, I decided to stop being so reclusive by creating a plan to go public with my home based tutoring service and by expanding the programs and workshops that I conducted with children in the inner city. I realized that working with children would be the key to my participation with other organizations.

I composed letters, created brochures and flyers, had t-shirts printed, designed a banner, and started looking for commercial office space to lease. I joined a Black History reading group at the local library and networked with a group that sponsored the Pan African Book-Fest. I was so excited. Finally, I was coming out of my self-imposed shell. It was as if I was having my debut, my formal presentation into society.

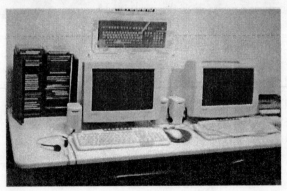

Home: My Debut

"Students presented certificates and trophies by Fireman Willie Brinson at the tutoring center"

"Students participating in Speak Easy Tutors Annual Communications Extravaganza at North Dade Regional Library"

THE COTILLION: A DREAM FULFILLED

As a twelfth grade student, I was desirous of receiving a letter from the local chapter of Delta Sigma Theta Sorority stating that I had been chosen as a debutante. Their cotillion was a big social event in the Black community that inspired pride and a sense of recognition and accomplishment in the participants and in their families. I had acceptable grades and had joined various school organizations, like the Hospitality Club, the Future Nurses of America and the Girl Advisors to demonstrate my social involvement, but my letter never came and I watched with envy the girls who had been chosen as they gleefully talked about their experiences in class.

So while attending college and contemplating choosing a sorority to join, I realized that the selection process for this grand event was basically a "who knows who." So, to ensure that my "planned" daughters would become selected, I pledged Delta then dreamed of the day that they would be presented to society. I mentally planned every detail: their gowns, the limousine, and the photos. I waited for their day; my day!

My oldest daughter Renee is a daddy's girl. She's materialistic, humorous, and peer-oriented. She seeks attention because being in the spotlight enhances her self-esteem.

In contrast, Juanita is detached, secretive, outspoken, daring and manipulative. When my mother first visited the hospital's nursery to see Juanita, she said, "That one has been here before. She has an old soul. You'll have to watch her more closely than you do Renee."

I asked, "What do you mean, Mama?"

Mama just shook her head and said, "It's in her eyes, you can just tell by looking in her eyes. Juanita has been here before and she all ready knows it."

That was a very deep statement but one which I learned to understand very quickly. As a teenager, Juanita exhausted all of my mental energy as I worked feverishly to just stay a few steps ahead of her.

Finally, when Renee became of age, though she was attending the temple's school, I submitted her name to my sorority through Dr. Vern Croskey, Renee's godmother. It was not easy for the committee to accept initially. They too were suspicious of my motives. Since I didn't actively attend meetings to hear their discussions, I responded to their questions, reservations and concerns through Vern. I was grateful that they honored my request because I wasn't going to let anyone stop or discourage me from fulfilling my dream through my daughters.

But because of our affiliation with the temple, Chico adamantly refused to be associated with the event. He declined an invitation to escort Renee at the prestigious ball at the Hyatt Regency's James L. Knight Center in downtown Miami and even refused to place a congratulatory advertisement in the souvenir book for her but was furious when Herb did. Realizing this, I honored his request and asked the sorors to spare Chico the shame of any identification with his daughter by not calling his name as father when Renee was presented. They reluctantly complied. Protocol warranted that the parents names be called even if one parent was deceased. Renee's godfather, Dr. Clyde Croskey, principal at William Turner Technical Center, proudly escorted both of us to the event.

"Renee's Cotillion"

Home: My Debut

Renee was so beautiful that night. She was a true debutante and I was sure that she was a virgin. Since she was twelve years old, she has had to see a gynecological oncologist every six months because of the diethylstilbestrol I'd taken when I was carrying her. I was so very proud of her and grateful that she has remained healthy.

The Miami Herald photographed her with two other girls and featured them in their "Best Dressed in Miami" article a few months later. I was so proud. This was the night that I'd dreamed of for twenty three years. I proudly posed with Renee and took "my cotillion" photograph.

Two years later when it was time for Juanita to be presented, I submitted her name to the sorority. Juanita was now living with Chico and attending public school. Unlike Renee, Chico allowed Juanita to date and she had become a social butterfly. She had the academic ability and the self confidence to succeed; however, she had personality traits that reminded me of Chico and I wondered how her character would develop over time.

Upon notice of Juanita's acceptance, I told her that I wanted her father to escort her with his wife, Cecilia. I unselfishly wanted him to feel the joy that I had experienced with Renee. I purposely stayed in the background allowing Cecilia to attend the parents' meetings. I didn't want anything to spoil the occasion.

However, at the final rehearsal Chico became perturbed when he heard my name being announced as Juanita's mother. He stopped the flow of practice and protested fiercely and adamantly refused to continue until the matter was settled. He wanted his wife's name to be inserted as if she were the birth mother. The announcer granted him his wish to eliminate my name but refused to insert the stepmom's in its place.

Juanita called me after they returned home from practice to share with me her embarrassment. She was crying. I comforted her by saying, "Everything is OK. Just go and enjoy the night. It's your affair, your memory, your night to be presented to the Miami audience. I will be there looking at you the whole time and if you tune into me you will be able to feel my eyes on you. Now dry your eyes so that you won't have puffs under them. I want your pictures to reflect joy and happiness."

Just as Juanita stated, my name was totally omitted from the program. I sat there and cried within. I sighed realizing how foolish our behavior as parents had been. We had set a terrible example for our children.

Later when the presentation was over and the audience was allowed on the ballroom floor to greet the debutantes, I descended the stairs to congratulate my daughter. I couldn't wait to kiss her on the cheek and take a picture.

"Juanita's Cotillion"

Drs. Clyde and Luvernice Croskey, PhD.

Chico was standing next to Juanita with his wife looking as proud as a peacock. I was happy for him. I knew how he was feeling. I too felt proud. But as I approached Juanita, Chico looked at me with disdain and quickly moved away from her hoping not to be identified with me.

I hugged my daughter, had my picture taken with my instant camera, thanked Chico's wife for assisting and walked away. Chico then proudly returned to Juanita's side and happily greeted well wishers. I looked back and captured Juanita's radiant smile in my mind as I left the building. It was her life, her cotillion, but my dream had come true.

All night long the words of the announcer rang in my ears: "Presenting debutante Lori Juanita Gilbert, daughter of Alonzo Gilbert being presented by her father and stepmother, Cecilia Gilbert."

As I relived the moments, I realized that Chico's continued animosity had nothing to do with my having attended the temple. NO! It was deeper than that. It was his own self-hatred, frustrations and disappointments gnawing away at his soul that he projected onto me. Like me, Chico had unsolved internal conflicts of a different nature when we married. Marriage compounded our problems because neither one of us had been honest about our feelings and motives. All of this was my fault because I didn't listen to the inner voice which warned me to not marry him.

However, Renee is now in college; Juanita will be entering college in the fall; and Lonnie, who transferred to public school so that he could participate in sports, will be graduating from high school in two years. They are no longer as dependent on us as parents, so I don't have any reason to communicate with Chico ever again. However, I do hope and pray that one day he recognizes that he too has internal conflicts and seeks to resolve them as I have done.

"Janice Renee, Lori Juanita and Alonzo II, "Lonnie"

BLESSINGS

MY BELOVED: THE ROCK

In the fall, my assignments changed and I was transferred to North County Elementary School. It had less adequate facilities for therapy than my former schools. I was very disappointed that I was not assigned to Joella Good, a newly constructed school that was three blocks from American Senior High, my base school. Good had been built with an office dedicated exclusively for speech therapy. After years of having to conduct therapy in the schools' clinics; on the stages in the cafeterias; and in various classrooms during teachers' planning periods, I wondered if this was my punishment because some African American women principals continued to discriminate against me and barred me from servicing their schools, as a covert form of religious persecution.

As I slowly unpacked my supplies and set up my area, I decided to take a tour of the school. As I walked to the portables, I crossed the physical education hard court. I turned to see if anyone was in its equipment office because I heard music. As I looked, the physical education teacher walked out and glanced at me; but he didn't say a word. Out of respect, I nodded my head to acknowledge him, but he did not respond.

As I returned, I crossed his path and nodded. Again, there was no response. That was it! I wouldn't give him a third chance to ignore my professional gesture. Not now, I was not going to have any more negative encounters or repeat performances. I'd learned my lesson. Also because he was a physical education teacher, like Chico had been, I quickly applied the stereotype and continued to walk toward the main building.

As the school year progressed, I began to notice him more and more. It was hard not to look at him and admire his physique. He was tall, very handsome, and had a slow sexy walk that mesmerized me. He had the most gorgeous legs and he wore the most color coordinated short sets that accented every muscular curve. Because he had a head full of dark coarse hair, I assumed that he was between thirty-five and forty years old. However, I never asked anyone about him; but as I sat in the teacher's lounge, I could hear comments about his personality and attitude. He was characterized as being unfriendly and arrogant; definitely not someone that I needed in my life; but I was curious, so I asked two of my fourth grade students about him.

"Marcus, tell me about the P.E. teacher. What is he like?"

"He tough and don't play. But he pay for some of us kids with no daddies home to play little league football and baseball. He come to our games and give us high fives; so he nice too."

"Bertram, what do you have to say about him?"

"He use to play pro basketball. He have a poster up in his office. His name use to be Armstrong. That's the name on the poster. All the kids are scared of him 'cuz he will make you run around the field if you misbehave, or he won't let you play games if you bad. He make you get on the fence and watch."

I knew from the music that he constantly played and the posters plastered on the doors and walls of his office that he was into "Black Consciousness." Malcolm X, Haile Sellasie, Marcus Garvey, Booker T. Washington, W.E.B. Dubois, Frederick Douglass, and Martin Luther King were forever staring at you as you passed his area, but like the images on the posters, he too had never, ever spoken.

After a year, he disappeared. I wondered if he had transferred to another school; but as I read the Miami Times, the Black community newspaper, I noticed his picture with an article that read: ***"Jabali Appointed Commissioner of the Miami Midnight Basketball League."*** As I read the article, I was very impressed with his achievements and wished that I had gotten to know him.

Six months later he reappeared, yet he still didn't speak and though I was still curious, I was even more determined not to speak either. However, his aura was fascinating and continued to capture my imagination. He was totally in control of his environment, very self confident and in his own world while listening to his music or reading a book. I'd glanced at the titles as I walked by him and noted that he read socially relevant and philosophical works.

One day as I crossed the court, he stepped in my path, stopped me and commanded, "Listen to these lyrics!"

I did, and when the song was over, I nodded my head in approval and continued walking. I thought, Wow! He has a strong, deep melodious voice.

Then three and a half years later it happened; he spoke. I was walking into the building and he stopped me and asked, "That sign on the front of your car that reads "God Rules" is that just a slogan or do you really live your life as if He does?"

"Oh! I live it."

"What's your name?"

That question infuriated me, so I refused to answer. I thought, "If I've been servicing this school for four years and he's not asked anyone, not even Darrick Gaye the security guard who he talks to daily, "who is that stranger?" then surely he wasn't interested in me." I blinked and walked on.

On my next rotation to North County Elementary, he approached me as I entered the building.

"Hello Mary! You're the Speech Pathologist."

"Yes, I am Mr. Jabali." I wondered who he had asked and what else had he been told about me.

"I have a question to ask you. What are your thoughts about commitment and marriage?"

I was startled. First, I was amazed that his initial comment was about the sign on the front of my car. I thought, was he a religious man? I didn't think so. Now his second question was about relationships. I took a deep breath and answered, "Commitment is good; marriage is not so good for me!"

"Are you saying that you will never get married?" He noticed that I was not wearing a wedding ring.

"Yes! I'll never get married again. Never, never ever! If I'm in a committed relationship, we'll just "jump across the broom," like our ancestors did. If the relationship doesn't work, then we'll just jump backwards and it will be over. No lawyers, courts, or judges telling me how to run my life. I cherish my freedom."

He smiled. I turned and walked to my class.

The next conversation was the following week. I was in the cafeteria and he walked up behind me and whispered in my ear, "Where do you fellowship?"

I recognized his voice, but didn't turn around. I responded with a scripture. "The temple of God dwells within. Wherever I am, God is."

"That's true but the WORD also states, "That members in Christ should fellowship together." He then slowly turned and walked away.

I was pleasingly puzzled but I was not going to tell him that I had attended the temple, nor that I was now attending Universal Truth Center.

Most evangelical, Pentecostal and devout Christians considered both to be a "sect or a cult."

We didn't speak again until the end of the school year. It was the last day of school for teachers and the administrators hosted a barbeque on the patio. Mr. Jabali was the cook. All of the staff gathered around the grill to be served. I didn't participate. When the event was over, he came to me with a plate filled with a thick beef burger and pork ribs. "Here, I saved you a plate."

"Thanks so much but I'm a strict vegetarian."

He looked disappointed. He slowly walked away and threw the plate in the nearest trash can. I didn't see him again until the next school year.

"How was your summer?"

"Great!"

"What did you do?"

I decided to let him know something about the religious path I was currently walking.

"I went to Chicago to the Johnny Coleman Institute for classes. I'm studying to become a teacher of comparative religions at the university." I slowly walked on hoping to hear a response, but he didn't comment.

Three weeks later, in September, my girlfriend Connie called. She was one of my Catholic classmates who now worked as an administrator for Miami Dade County Public Schools. She was conducting "Black Art" home parties and wanted me to host one for her.

"Mary, this is Connie. I'm calling to schedule your party."

"Connie, I don't think that I can gather enough people to attend. I'll just purchase a few paintings from you."

"No! You promised and I really want to get more parties booked from your show. That's how it works. Let me make a suggestion dear," she dotingly said. "Just print some flyers with the pertinent information on it and distribute them to co-workers, friends and family. You'll be surprised who shows up. People are curious about you. They'll come just to see where and how you live."

I laughed. "Ok! Saturday, October 8th at 12:00 noon is good."

I went to the computer and created a flyer, made copies and placed them in my briefcase to take to work.

When I arrived at North County Elementary, I began to distribute them. Mrs. Dawkins was walking her class to P.E. I handed her one as she passed in the hallway.

On the morning of the scheduled event, I cleaned the house and prepared a few food platters for my guests and waited for Connie to arrive.

I was shocked that nearly twenty quests attended. I liked entertaining and yes, I missed it. In the midst of the presentation, the door bell rang. Juanita, who was home from college for the weekend, answered the door. I could have passed out. It was Mr. Jabali. He entered the family room, took a seat and watched. He didn't speak to anyone.

As orders were being taken and guests socialized, Juanita called me into the living room and asked, "Who is that "hunk" in the family room?"

"Oh! That's the P.E. teacher at one of the schools I service."

"What's he doing here? Men don't usually attend these types of events. What does he want?"

"Oh! I hear that he's into "Black awareness" so maybe he wants to buy a painting that he can relate to. He probably read the flyer that I'd given to Ms. Dawkins."

"Uh uh uh!" she said as she rhythmically waved her pointed finger back and forth.

"Ain't no man coming to a house party on Saturday at noon unless he is scoping you."

"Him? No way!"

"Watch and see." We smiled and returned to our guests.

Three weeks later when the paintings arrived, Connie called. "Mary, I attempted to deliver Jabali's paintings but he wasn't home. He lives in an apartment in Pembroke Pines with his sister. I could have left the artwork with her since he'd paid for it, but I have a funny feeling about him. I think that you should deliver his painting personally."

"NO! I don't want to get involved. You deliver them," I said adamantly.

"OK! I will, but will you promise to call and thank him for the purchase?"

"Yes, I will."

Connie delivered the paintings and I called as promised.

As the telephone continued to ring, I was relieved that he was not home. I waited for the beep to leave a message.

"Mr. Jabali, this is Mary, the Speech Pathologist at your school. I just wanted to thank you for purchasing the paintings at my house party. I hope that you enjoy them. Have a great day."

Promise fulfilled.

Later that evening, my phone rang.

"Hello!"

"Hello, this is Jabali. Is this Mary?"

"Yes, how are you?"

"Fine! Would you like to go to the movies tonight?"

I was nearly speechless, but managed to voice a weak "Sure."

"I'll be over to pick you up at 7:30."

When he arrived, I was pleased. Other than at the art show, I'd never seen him wearing any clothing other than his physical education outfits. That night his trendy attire was very "avant-garde." He was unique in his expression, and oh my God, was he fine!

We went to the AMC on Hollywood Beach to see "**Disclosure**" starring Demi Moore. Afterwards, we walked along the coastline and talked. I was more fascinated than ever. I'd never heard him utter a full sentence so I was amazed that he was so articulate and grammatically correct; his vocabulary was far superior to mine. It was obvious too that he was well traveled internationally, and very well read as we discussed many topics.

As he drove me home, he politely thanked me for the night. At the door, he kissed me on the cheek; turned around and left. I was surprised that he didn't ask me if he could come in. If he had, I would not have objected.

Neither one of us called; therefore, we didn't speak again for two more weeks.

As I passed him on the P.E. court he handed me a cassette tape. "Listen to this and tell me if you like Al Jarreau's music."

"Thanks, I will." I put the tape in my bag and kept walking.

After listening to the music and ejecting the tape, I heard an announcement on the radio in the car that Al Jarreau would be performing at the Sunrise Musical Theater the following weekend. I wondered if Jabali knew this and was considering taking me on another date. He didn't call and I never asked. Instead I went to ticketmasters and purchased a single ticket.

Two days before the concert, Jabali approached me as I was exiting the building and asked, "Did you like the tape?"

"Yes, and thanks for the tip. I bought a ticket to see him tomorrow night. Are you going to his concert too?" Jabali's eyes widened.

"Did you purchase one ticket or two?" he inquired.

"I bought one, for myself. I often go to concerts at Sunrise alone."

He seemed annoyed and just looked down and stared at me for a moment.

"Do you want to be by yourself forever?" he asked in a most frustrating tone. Before I could answer, he turned and walked away.

I realized that I still had some fear of rejection to deal with, but was intrigued by his comment. It was the first indication that he wanted to develop a relationship with me.

"Wow!"

The next week, Juanita called from college. "Mom, how is it going with you and the hunk?"

"Nothing is going on. We went to the movies and that was it."

"Girl, you had better get with it. We are grown and will be graduating soon. We don't want you in our business when we get home. You need a life. Get with it, call him."

"Thanks for the advice, but I'll pass."

When she came home for the winter break, she asked, "Did you call him yet?"

"NO!"

"I see that I am going to have to help you out. What's his number?"

After prodding me relentlessly, I reluctantly gave her his number. She dialed and waited.

"Hello, Mr. Jabali, this is Juanita, Mary's daughter. I met you at the art show. Well, would you like to take my mom to Naples for a weekend retreat?"

"Yes, I would," he replied. Juanita looked at me and nodded her head affirmatively.

"Ok! I'll call the Registry Resort and make reservations. She likes going there to chill out. I'll call you back with the details. Thanks, I'll take care of all expenses!"

Chico, who had become financially successful after purchasing the former Jackson's Toddle Inn a childcare center in Brownsville, had purchased two identical green Mercedes 190s for both Renee and Juanita to drive back to college for their senior year. Juanita decided that I should drive her car to pick up Jabali, as if my Nissan Maxima weren't impressive enough. She filled it with gas and put my bags in the trunk.

"These are your orders," she commanded. "Talk to him! Find out if he is interested in you, and if you are interested in him, tell him. If it works, it works. If it doesn't, then you can stop playing this cat and mouse game and move on."

"OK sergeant," I said as I saluted her. I got into the car, picked up my cellular phone and dialed his number.

"Hello, this is Mary. I'm on my way to pick you up."

"Ok, I'll meet you downstairs."

As I watched him descend the stairs, I noticed that he only had a small toiletry kit. I thought, "Doesn't he understand that we will spend the weekend. Why doesn't he have a change of clothing?"

"Hello, how are you today?" he inquired as he entered the car.

"I'm fine," I said nervously.

Recognizing my tension, he lightly placed his large hand across my hands on the steering wheel and said, "You're safe with me."

We drove away. Naples was a two hour drive on I75 across Alligator Alley. As we debated hot topics, I laughed. Finally I relaxed.

We checked into the Registry Resort at 4:00 p.m. Our room was on the 11th floor facing the ocean. He placed my bag on one of the beds and his kit in the bathroom. We quickly went down to the restaurant for dinner. I ordered my favorite dish, grilled salmon. He ordered steak, well done. Afterwards we went to the movies to see *"The Client"* starring Susan Sarandon. Before returning to the hotel, we walked along the shores of the Gulf of Mexico. He held my hand. He had the softest smoothest touch.

I was very tired by the time we returned to the room, so I quickly showered and dressed for bed. I'd purchased a very conservative two piece lingerie set from Victoria's Secret. I slowly entered the sleeping area only to notice that he was out on the balcony reading a book.

I recognized the title and author. It was **"Living, Loving and Learning"** by Leo Buscaglia. I'd read a companion book in his series on relationships and often watched his lectures on public television. For the first time, I thought that Jabali might be older than I had previously thought because he was wearing reading glasses. I didn't say anything to him. I just got into bed and went to sleep.

And as is my pattern, being nocturnal, I awakened around two o'clock in the morning. The curtains were open and the light of the moon shone into the room. I looked over at the bed on which Jabali lie, and to my surprise and delight, he was lying there uncovered, on his back, sound asleep and completely nude.

I closed my eyes quickly and reopened them to see if I was dreaming. No, this was no dream. As he snored, his private part, completely enlarged and engorged, rose with every breath he took. I shamefully watched it go up and down. God, I thought that I had seen it all with Job, but Jabali was different. Job was pure Mandingo; Jabali was of mixed lineage, but obvious to me now, he had inherited his most penetrating feature from his African roots.

His chest and thighs were very hairy and his skin was a silky, flawlessly smooth even blend of mocha and cream. He was physically fit and finer than I ever imagined. Oh God! How I lusted him. I was so very horny.

I quietly got out of bed and quickly went into the bathroom. I didn't want him to awaken and catch me staring or drooling. I really wanted to undress and rush back into the room and jump on him and ravish his luscious body; but I didn't.

I needed something to calm my nerves and suppress the sexual urges that flooded my body. I pulsated like never before, my mouth salivated and I was having orgasms with the "flow" just thinking about him.

I quickly went to the mini bar, opened it and took out a wine cooler. As I sipped it, I spotted a large **Baby Ruth** candy bar. It was not the nickel sized bar that I'd purchased as a kid, it was a $1.00 sized bar. Just seeing it made me drool as I likened it to Jabali's penis. I reached in, took it out, tore off the wrapping paper and began to savor the dark chocolate nutty bar.

After I calmed down, I quietly got back into bed, and tried to go back to sleep. It was impossible, so I pulled the blanket over my head but left my eyes uncovered so that I could peek over at him. As I imagined him making love to me, I slowly fell back to sleep.

At 8:00 a.m. his cough startled me. I opened my eyes and saw him walking pass my bed. I thought, Wow! God was very happy the day that He created him. I chuckled softly.

He reached into the closet and retrieved his clothing and went into the bathroom to shower. When he finished, he came over to the bed and kissed me on the cheek and whispered in my ear, "Good Morning, this is the best date I've ever been on."

I smiled and said, "Ditto."

I never mentioned that I saw him naked, but I knew that I would have a much more positive attitude and would modify my behavior around him from that moment on. I wanted him.

The next day as we again drove across I-75's Alligator Alley through the Florida Everglades, we again debated hot topics and laughed. He was a very pleasant man; I quickly erased the negative stereotype of him completely out of my mind.

Having safely returned home, I mailed him a thank you card. Several days later, I received a Kwanzaa card which read:

```
I thought your note was a real nice
touch...I like writing out thoughts
and exchanging them...if you keep
them, it is a exellent method of
keeping track of one's growth in a
relationship as well as keeping track
of points of divergence in the minds
and ideas of those engaged in the
relationship.

I am generally impressed with you and
the way that you look at the world...
I have recently become interested in
developing a committed relationship
and I have been exploring possibilities
"in my mind".

Of course we cannot live in our minds
and the time is fast approaching that
I must step out and make some intentions
known to "somebody"..

I have several fears and hesitancies in
this regard, i.e. "baggage"...This
state of mind on my part is somewhat
paralyzing as I wonder how "somebody"
will respond over time to me and the
set of conditions and attitudes that
are my makeup....

In you however I perceive somebody with
the spiritual and intellectual abilities to
live life on life's terms and give due
respect...Here's looking forward to
love, peace and happiness in 1995
```

Let us give thanks as we celebrate this Kwanzaa season.

Jabali '94

"Kwanzaa Card"

After the New Year, he called and invited me to attend a high school basketball game. Several of the students that he mentors were playing and he was going to support them. As we sat in the bleachers, I spotted a childhood friend, Herman Bain, who was there watching his son play. We hugged and exchanged news about our families; then he introduced me to his wife Connie. She smiled and asked me about Jabali. She acted as if we were old girl friends. I whispered that I'd just met him and was hopeful of developing a relationship. Then she whispered into my ear, "You deserve to be happy. I was the anonymous caller who sent you the parcel when you filed for a divorce seventeen years ago."

My eyes widened. She continued, "Herman told me what a good person you were and I just wanted to help. I was Chico's secretary. I made the copies for you because he was such a deceitful person. He openly bragged about how naïve and trusting you were. I wanted to protect you."

I smiled and said, "Thank you. You were my guardian angel." We embraced, turned around and continued to watch the game.

As we left the gymnasium, Jabali said, "I'd like to walk along the beach tonight."

"Great! I'd like that also." As we drove east on the causeway, he placed his hand on mine and surprisingly announced, "I'm going to marry you!"

"Oh really," I chuckled. "You don't even know me that well, and we surely aren't in love."

"I'm serious. I asked the Holy Spirit to guide me in choosing a companion. I looked up one day and it's as if I saw you for the first time. I wanted to know more about you. I was scoping you, just as your daughter said. I'm pleased with you generally and am willing to go with the spirit. I've been thinking about this for a long time and have been reading books on love and relationships in preparation."

"You need preparation?"

"Yes, we all do. Don't get me wrong, I haven't had a problem getting female companionship since the eighth grade," he chuckled. "I don't even have a pickup line. I haven't needed one."

"You're very fortunate! Being handsome has its perks."

"Trust me. You will grow to love me and my love will be perfect. You will not regret being with me one day. In the past, I have been very selfish in relationships. My wants and needs came first. I want to be totally unselfish with you. I just want to learn to get along perfectly with one human being. That's my spiritual goal. I want to love and be loved intensely and unconditionally."

"Wow! What a proposal?" I joked.

"No, it's a fact."

"Have you set a date also?" I amusingly asked.

"You can set the date later. I have a few legal matters and loose ends to clear up, so be patient, but be sure. I've made up my mind."

I was completely silent. I had to absorb all that had just been so eloquently expressed.

He continued, "I want you to promise me that you won't start talking to your girlfriends or letting what you hear about my past discourage you. I've been going to church regularly for a few years. As I started on my redemptive journey, I went before the congregation to "confess with my tongue" all of my transgressions. I now want to start a new life with you."

I knew that I had not shared all of my religious experiences with him so I asked several questions to bring up the matter.

"You've been going to church? What denomination? Is your name reflective of your faith? Is it a Muslim, African or Hebrew name?"

"And if it is one or the other, what does it matter?"

"Either is Ok. I have Muslim and Hebrew Israelite friends. I'm not prejudice. I just want to know about your religion since you mentioned church. We may have conflicting beliefs!"

"On vacation with Jabali in Las Vegas' Red Rock Canyon"

"Jabali, is Swahili. It means the "Rock." I legally changed my name as a demonstration of my cultural awareness, not for religious reasons. And yes, I believe in a Higher Power but not in denominations. I attend church to fellowship. Are you all right with that?" he asked emphatically.

"Yes, as long as you know that you didn't create yourself," I retorted. "I am no longer bound by rituals, doctrines or denominations either. I just believe in a higher power and I live my life based on simple principles of truth, honesty and integrity."

And as if he could read my mind and wanted to allay my fears, he stated, "By the way, I know about your religious background and of the difficulties you had in your marriage."

He looked at me and smiled. I wanted to know who had told him but before I could ask, he said, "I'm a good friend of your neighbor Leroy Floyd. I asked him about you and his wife Joan overheard the conversation and rushed into the room to tell me every little detail about your life."

My pulse and respiration increased just hearing the sound of her name. I began to tremble knowing that Joan's remarks would be very negative and distorted. Jabali perceived my distress and quickly stated, "I've based my decision on the impression that you have made on me. I'm not easily influenced. I'm an independent thinker."

I relaxed and smiled.

Now I had to face him so that he could see my eyes. This would possibly be the greatest hurdle for him to jump and the biggest challenge for me to overcome. I would have to see how he reacted before I consented.

"Have you noticed that my eyes are different?"

"Yes, I see a physical difference, but I also see you perfectly as you are."

He placed his hand on my chin to prevent me from turning my head. His smile was reassuring.

I cheerfully said, "Yes! I'll give you a try. But you'll have to make it through a probationary period first."

"What! You are going to put me on probation?" he humorously questioned.

Before I could answer, we both started laughing.

When we reached the beach and parked, he chivalrously opened the car's door and dotingly reached for me. As I stood, he embraced me tightly and gave me the biggest, juiciest, longest lasting kiss of my life. We quietly walked along the coastline for nearly an hour, just holding hands.

"Miami Marriott Hotel: Beasley Family Reunion"

"Miami Northwestern Class of 6T6 30th Reunion"

Blessings

On our way to the Delta's "Putting on the Ritz" Dance

20 / 20 VISION

The next six months were the best. It was as if I was sixteen and dating for the first time. "Mary, I want you to create a calendar of events. Schedule activities that you want to do and places you want to go. Give me a copy to place in my planner to avoid scheduling conflicts."

"What do you like to do?" I asked.

"It doesn't matter what I like. I've traveled around the world; I've met many people and I've done almost everything that I've wanted to do. I want you to be fulfilled. I am very content, but I can tell that you still have dreams. My joy will be in watching you blossom. You're still somewhat reserved and inhibited."

"Wow! Oh you think so?" I responded but I was thinking, "Not really." He just laughed. I blushed.

"In fact I find it somewhat attractive. There aren't many women your age that have your purity of thought. Most act like they know everything and are opinionated. With you there will be lots of "wow" or shall I say teachable moments."

"Like what?" I asked.

"I'll have to find out what you know and where you've been first."

"Oh, so you're going to give me a pre-test?"

"Several!" We both laughed but I was thinking that I was going to purposefully flunk each one. I smiled.

"Ok, I'll start looking in the entertainment section of the newspaper for events. Are you sure you won't complain about my choices?"

"I'm positive."

"Well, I like classical music. So I want to go to concerts. I use to purchase season's tickets to the playhouse and treat myself to dinner afterwards, so I'll schedule some plays. And though I'm not very good at it, I like to dance. I want to go to some supper clubs."

"Great! What's first?"

"I want you to make love to me." I couldn't believe that I so boldly stated that. Was I thinking out loud?

"I will make love to you one day, but not now. You don't love me, you lust me."

I wondered if he had known that I'd seen him nude or had he purposefully displayed himself to entice me?

"Does it matter that we're not in love? We're both well over twenty-one," I joked, but my entire body was seriously pulsating.

"Yes, it matters to me. I've had sexual relations with many women but now I want to develop a lasting relationship. I want you to go into the autumn of my life with me. Be patient. Regardless of the preconceived ideas you may have about me, I'm rather simple and very conservative. If I had not played professional basketball, I would have stayed in Kansas City like my brother Greg; worked in a Ford Motors plant and be married to my high school sweetheart."

I could tell that he too had been reflecting on his life and that his comments were very sincere. Though I was very disappointed, I knew that intercourse was not appropriate at the time, but I hoped that I wouldn't have to wait much longer. I yearned to be in his arms and in his bed.

"Just how long has it been since you've had a sexual relationship?"

"Exactly two years, six months, four days, three hours and twenty seconds!" We both laughed at how quickly and precisely I responded.

"Well you won't have to wait much longer, but I must tell you that though I am not a sex addict, I do desire intercourse a minimum of four to five times a week. Can you handle that?"

"Yes! Even more if you want," I joyously replied.

"One more thing you need to know about me. I sleep in the nude and I want you to sleep that way also. When I get the urge during the night and turn over to awaken you, I don't want any barriers."

"When I get home, I'll throw away all of my lingerie and pajamas," I chuckled. When he turned his head, I looked up as if I was talking to God and whispered, "Thank you, thank you, thank you." My prayers were being answered.

Jabali is so self confident. Unlike me, he is the oldest of eleven siblings who grew up in an intact family unit with loving parents. He doesn't carry the baggage of being abandoned or unwanted. Both of my parents are finally together if only because they are elderly and under our custodial care. They live in the same room at Pearl's home. Mildred, recently retired, cares for them during the week and I rotate with Liz on the weekends.

"Ben and Mattie Beasley of Eatonton, Georgia"

I was so very proud to introduce Jabali to my parents, and of course to Liz; subconsciously I still wanted her support and approval. With much effort, I'd healed those childhood wounds and had developed a positive relationship with my father. Now I feel whole and complete and ready to give and receive love unconditionally.

Taking the Better Living classes at Universal Truth Center really helped. The course, **"*Celestine Prophecy*,"** titled after the book, really helped me to see that I had been like a semi circle, a parenthesis or the letter "C" looking for the other part of me to complete my being. After reading the text, I worked really hard at becoming an "O," mentally, financially and spiritually sound.

I was sure that I had achieved that status when Jabali stated, "Most of the women that I dated wanted me to supplement and enhance their lives. They gave little thought to my needs and wants; but your priorities are friendship and companionship and you're not selfish. You are complementary and I like that."

We continued to bond for the next few months as he straightened out his personal and legal affairs. He finally revealed that though he had been legally separated for nearly ten years, his divorce was not yet final. He had purposefully waited until his youngest child turned eighteen before proceeding. There were many moments during that time that I wanted to end the relationship; but he continually stated that if I gave up, especially because of the pressure that was beginning to surface, that I would regret it for the rest of my life. I persevered.

In May, Renee graduated from Clark Atlanta University with a degree in Business Education. In Atlanta, Renee's graduation ceremony was held in the Georgia Dome. Chico and his family sat on one side of the stadium and I sat on the other side. Renee took pictures with his family first then circled around the dome to take pictures with my family. Chico and I never saw each other.

"In Tallahassee, Fl at Juanita's graduation"

In August, Juanita graduated from FAMU with a degree in Business and Accounting. At her graduation ceremony in the Leon County Convention Center, there was only one set of doors to enter and exit.

Jabali accompanied me to the event. Though Chico had heard about our relationship, he had never seen us together. When he did, his reaction was predictable. Chico stood far away from my family as we joyously posed for photographs. Juanita went to him and asked, "Will you please take a picture with me and my mom?"

He growled and angrily voiced, "Hell no!" I saw the venom in his facial expression. He waited until Jabali and I left the area, then he and his family posed with her. I looked back at them as Jabali drove through the parking lot. Chico's rudeness no longer had an effect on me.

The girls eagerly returned home, to my house. For the first time in six years we were all together again. My joys were exceeding my sorrows and I was happy again. We laughed, shopped and cheered for Lonnie, who was playing college football, when we saw him on television on game day.

However, I wondered if they were truly "my girls" again. Had Chico succeeded in turning them against me? What poison pills had he forced them to swallow? Did they fully digest his venom or did they place the pills under their tongues and spit them out after he turned his back? Could they be fair and objective enough as adults to treat both of us with love and respect, or would they take sides? Only time would tell.

Six months later Renee, now employed as a teacher, moved into an apartment and later announced that she was pregnant. I was disappointed because she wasn't married, but I was happy because my fears of her being able to conceive were allayed. I'd occasionally reminded her of the difficulties that she might face and impressed upon her how she might regret ever having an abortion. I urged her to abstain from sex until marriage but if she couldn't then to be discriminating in her choice of partners and to protect herself against STD's.

But just because she had conceived didn't mean that she would be able to sustain the pregnancy. I asked her, "Who is your doctor and have you told him that you are a DES baby?"

"No, I have not. Stop worrying. Everything will be all right."

"I will worry until I talk with him. Give me his number." I dialed the office.

"Hello, this is Renee's mother; she is one of Dr. Hanna's patients. May I speak to him? This is not an emergency but it is urgent."

"Just one moment please. I'll see if he is available."

I waited anxiously.

"Hello this is Dr. Hanna. How can I help you?"

"Your patient is my daughter; she's a DES baby. Are you aware of the complications that that drug could have on her?"

"I studied about the effects in medical school but I've never actually encountered a patient because they banned the drug in 1971."

"I was among the last women who took the drug. Renee was born in April and the drug was banned in October of that same year."

"I understand your concern."

"I know that it is common practice to order a sonogram in the fourth month, but might you order it earlier for her?"

"Yes, I'll have her scheduled as soon as possible."

"Thank you."

The next week the sonogram was performed and as I had suspected, Renee's cervix was incompetent and beginning to open. She was immediately admitted to the hospital and Dr. Hanna performed a cerclage. Renee was confined to bed for the next seven months. I hired Kara, a relative to assist her during the day and I waited on her at night.

One evening, Chico called. "Hello, who is this?" he asked in a curious tone as if he were unsure that he'd dialed the correct number.

"I'm Renee's mother. Just one moment please."

"Renee your dad's on the line. Obviously he didn't recognize my voice because he didn't curse," I said as I handed her the phone. We both laughed. I left the bedroom so that they could have a private conversation.

Moments later, she yelled, "Mom pick up the telephone, dad wants to talk to you."

I ignored her. For the next few weeks, Chico routinely called and continued to ask to speak to me.

"Tell him to stop asking for me. I won't get involved in any game that he is playing."

But he didn't give up.

The next week Juanita was at Renee's. She answered the phone. She turned to me and said, "Dad wants to know what you want for your birthday; he remembered that it is in two weeks." I was shocked.

"I have everything that I need. Tell him no thank you."

Juanita knew that I wanted a laptop computer because I had recently become licensed as an insurance agent and wanted one to carry with me on appointments. The next week, she walked in the door with a wrapped package and said, "Happy birthday. This is from my dad."

"Is it a bomb?" I laughed.

"No, it is a laptop; top of the line too."

I opened the box to see it, but refused to take it. I remembered how Chico would buy me gifts, and then take them back when he was angry. I would not fall into that trap again twenty years later.

When he called the next night, he was so cheerful. "Hello Mary, this is Chico. How are you? Did you like your birthday present?"

"I'm sorry, but Renee is asleep. Call back later sir." I ignored his comments and responded as if I were a receptionist.

For weeks he continued to call and each time he attempted to get me to respond to his flattering comments. I continued to ignore him. Then one day before I could even say hello, he said, "You ignore me because you still love me. Jabali can't erase the memory of what I put on you."

I hung up. His seeing me with Jabali at Juanita's graduation had had an impact on him. He must have been thinking of me for months. I smiled.

Unlike he had predicted years ago, someone did want me; someone that he obviously knew of and considered to be significant. He was jealous. My smile broadened.

A few years later Chico purchased a second daycare center in South Miami. During their summer breaks from college, he had required Juanita and Renee to earn their childcare certificates and work in the business. So now with this expansion, they envisioned a family venture and positioned themselves to be fully capable of operating his businesses if needed.

I often warned them, "Do not allow Chico to coerce you into signing any legal documents. Don't even sign your name to a blank sheet of paper. He may use it illegally later. I still do not trust your dad's business ethics. I hear rumors all of the time about his behavior."

I knew that Chico had not "just quit his job as an assistant principal" but had indeed been forced to resign for consistently falsifying FTE records for federal funding. However, he appeared to be prospering in this business and had not yet been challenged by the authorities. I remembered the difficulties that I had with him about our income taxes. He always wanted to inflate the deductions to receive a higher refund. He was never satisfied. His greed ruled his behavior.

He continued to lure Renee and Juanita with false hopes and promises, "I'll purchase a Burger King franchise or a Dunkin Donuts, or an Amoco Service Station for you. Just stick with me and you'll become millionaires." He never did make a purchase; he just kept dangling the carrots, his money, vacations and gifts before them, keeping them tied to his hip for financial reward.

I was dismayed because my daughters had lost their focus and were behaving as if they were "heirs" to his wealth and acted accordingly. Though they were gainfully employed as teachers, their attitude was that they were only working because they wanted to work. Their material possessions seemed to falsely enhance their self esteem as the number of their friends increased.

I constantly warned them, "The rich have many friends, but they are not always loyal friends. You need to be more discerning. Trust me; if Chico were to die, you can take my word that he's not going to leave you anything. He believes that you will share his money with me. He wants to see me destitute. So you had better save or invest while you have the chance."

"You are too cautious. He won't do that to us," they responded naively.

"Take my advice anyway." But they continued to spend as if money grew on the trees in their backyards.

He purchased brand new cars and paid cash for them; gave the girls down payments on their homes. They splurged and didn't bother about establishing credit in their own names or saving for a rainy day. They continued to disregard my advice. However, there was a glimmer of hope for Renee; she aspired to become a school administrator and enrolled in graduate school at Nova Southeastern University to earn a master's degree in educational leadership. I was happy for her. The early intervention that I provided in elementary school had paid off. She was now competent, self motivated and highly ambitious.

Juanita continued to chase the carrot that Chico dangled before her, waiting for him to purchase a franchise instead of investing in her own enterprise. I often asked her to go into business with me but could tell that she didn't think that my venture would be as lucrative; it was obvious that she wasn't going to jeopardize her chances of getting all that she could from him first. Partnering with me, if at all, would be her last resort; but I'd vowed at her delivery that I would always be there for her.

As smart as she was, she refused to grasp the meaning of the statement that I constantly repeated when she accused me of loving Renee more. "I love you equally, I treat you differently." Each child was a unique individualized expression of God requiring a specialized set of responses. Their blueprints, like the individualized educational plan (IEP) that I created for each student that I serviced, determined my actions and mode of delivery. The love was the same; equally distributed.

However, I was quite pleased with Lonnie. I had succeeded in rearing him to be the complete opposite of his dad and had broken the cycle of the verbally abusive childhood that Chico suffered through with his father. Taking Lonnie to visit my father, Big Ben as often as possible was wise. Dad was a great mentor and Lonnie's mindset was positive because of it.

Chico did not shower Lonnie with gifts nor did he contribute to his college education. When he called the house for Lonnie, he would always ask, "Where is that weak punk son of yours? Put him on the phone."

"I'm sorry you have the wrong number. No one by that description lives here," I responded and hung up the phone.

"Coach Yanda and his staff at American Senior High School"

"Lonnie wearing NC State's shirt and cap in front of school"

Fortunately, Lonnie received a full athletic scholarship to North Carolina State, an ACC division one university and had it not been for a torn muscle incurred during the tryouts at the NFL combine in

Indianapolis, he would have been drafted in his senior year. Instead he went to the Tennessee Oilers / Titans on their practice team. In his second year, during training camp, he called.

The telephone rang. "Hello."

"Hi, Lonnie how was practice today?"

"Great! I just had an incident on the field and I had to be transported to the hospital for some tests. I want you to talk with the team's physician."

My heart began to race.

"Hello, we thought that Lonnie had developed Bell's palsy during practice. His face appeared asymmetric and his speech was slurred. After we removed his helmet the muscles quickly recovered, but a CAT scan later revealed that he had suffered a TIA on the field today. We'll have to keep him under observation for a while until he goes through a series of tests to determine the cause. I had him to call you personally so that you wouldn't be unduly alarmed."

"Thanks, I appreciate the thoughtfulness." When I hung up the phone, I realized the seriousness of Lonnie's condition and began to cry. A year earlier, mom had suffered a stroke and was still rehabilitating. Jabali heard my sobs and asked what had happened. When I told him, he embraced me until I regained my composure. Not only was he my lover, he had become my best friend.

After the tests were complete, a specific cause could not be found and because of that Lonnie was released from the team. Chico called him and said, "Come home and live with me. I'll make you a millionaire," he bragged. "Work for me. Help me run my businesses."

Lonnie reluctantly agreed and for the very first time since the age of two, Lonnie would live with his father. He packed his bags and drove from Tennessee to Chico's home. The next week, he began his apprenticeship.

Knowing that Lonnie was depressed about having lost the opportunity to ever play professional football again, Chico exploited his emotions by saying, "I know how you feel. I hated when Ken Riley was chosen over me as quarterback at FAMU and started getting all of the attention. That cost me my opportunity to be drafted; but look at me now. Though Riley played professionally for fifteen years with the Cincinnati Bengals, I have just as much money and influence as he has now. Stick with me and I'll teach you how to be the envy of your friends."

After one month, Lonnie regretted his decision and called. "Mom, he treats me like I'm still two years old. Unlike Renee and Juanita who learned operational procedures, he has me doing all of the janitorial work. I left the center to go to Bally's gym on my lunch break and he chastised me verbally in front of the staff when I returned. Now I can't leave the premises for lunch at all. When I get home tired, he denies me dinner unless I join in pray service with him. He criticizes me constantly and calls me lazy all of the time. Nothing that I do pleases him."

Knowing that Lonnie was asthmatic, I cautioned him, "Don't let Chico stress you out. If you feel that you can't tolerate him anymore, come home. You've got your college degree. Find a job and support yourself. You are a man now. Chart your own course."

During all of the years of rearing the children alone, like my mom, I never once criticized their dad. When they asked about him, I would always state, as my mother did, "One day you will get to know him for yourself and you can tell me what you think of him." This was that day. Lonnie had discerned Chico's character and he was not impressed.

One morning as Chico and Lonnie walked around the childcare facility, Chico's stepped into an open hole where a sprinkler had been removed. Chico screamed in pain, "I think I've broken my leg or twisted my knee."

"Let me help you up. I'll take you to the emergency room to have it x-rayed," Lonnie said.

After waiting for several hours, Chico became inpatient and left the hospital. "I'll just lay hands on my knee and pray for healing."

"I don't think that's wise. You should stay and see a doctor," Lonnie cautioned.

"I can see that you don't have faith in the true and living God's healing powers. Your mammy got y'all messed up thinking that that man at the temple was Jesus. Where is he now? In jail," Chico laughed. "He couldn't even save himself."

"Ok, have it your way. Let's go! I'll help you to the car."

A month later, Lonnie was allowed to answer the phones at the daycare center. A parent called and asked, "Today is my daughter's birthday. Can I bring in some cup cakes and ice cream for the kids?"

"I have to ask the director. Wait a moment." He put the caller on hold and went to inquire. He returned and said, "It is permissible, you can come in at three o'clock."

As the party was being celebrated, Chico returned to the center. "Lonnie, did you give them permission to have this party?" he angrily shouted. Before Lonnie could speak, Chico rushed into the room and grabbed some cake, crushed it and sprinkled the crumbs onto the floor and demanded that Lonnie clean it up in front of the staff, the parent and the kids.

"I want all of you to know who is in charge here. I'm the chief and you are the Indians. Do you understand? You don't do anything without my permission," he shouted.

To avoid conflict and to protect the director, Lonnie humbly cleaned up the crumbs. When he finished, he stood, looked at Chico and walked out of the door. He immediately went to the house, packed his bags and drove to Renee's home. By the time he got there he was wheezing. Renee rushed him to urgent care for a prescription.

After that, Lonnie did not speak to Chico for a year. He was saddened to know that he would never have a positive relationship with his dad. However, as time passed, Lonnie began to observe my relationship with Jabali and I was thrilled when he confided in me that he respected and admired him.

Two years later, in December, Juanita and Damon held their wedding rehearsal at the Signature Grand facility in Davie. I noticed that Chico was limping and using a cane as he walked Juanita down the aisle. As we waited for Carolyn Clarkson, the wedding directress to instruct us, Chico hobbled over to me and said, "Hey girl, you looked kinda good in that leopard print in Tallahassee. I see you really like that dress cause you wore it again to Renee's baby shower. You're beginning to gain weight. Jabali must not be hitting that thang right."

I ignored his remarks but he continued to talk.

"I know you remember how ole Chico made you groove. Can't nobody erase the memories of your first love."

I turned around and affirmed, "You're right and Jabali is my first love."

I quickly walked away, but he limped along.

"I see that you still got those big legs."

I didn't respond. He started hissing like he did in high school when he courted me.

Instinctively, I looked back. He placed his hand over his heart and said, "My heart still aches for you. Remember, you're my remedy."

I responded, "If you have a heart, it's still just as sick now as it was back then." He laughed because he had finally gotten me to respond emotionally to his antics.

I was now sure that Chico was jealous of my relationship with Jabali. I smiled more broadly as I continued to move farther away from him.

The next day after the wedding, Juanita managed to get Chico to pose with me for a family picture. They had lots of pictures with Cecilia and their dad, but not one of me with him. To my surprise, Chico eagerly complied. He appeared genuinely happy at the wedding.

"Family portrait at Juanita and Damon's wedding"

"Mary and Jabali at the wedding"

I positioned myself next to my daughter thinking that Chico would stand on the other side of the groom next to Lonnie. To my horror and amazement he stood right next to me. I froze. As he moved closer to me, I could feel his breath on my neck. He whispered into my ear, "You look very beautiful, Mrs. Jabali."

I didn't respond. I continued to ignore him during the reception, but as I danced with Jabali, I could feel Chico's eyes watching. Again I smiled.

However, it didn't take long for Chico to return to his nasty ways. A year later, when our grandson Devin was born, Chico refused to enter the hospital room or to view the baby in the nursery until I had left the area. It was as if I was wearing garlic or a religious medallion around my neck and he was Dracula. He was still vicious and full of hate.

In May of the following year, I received a phone call from Fredericker. Her friend's daughter worked for the child care enforcement office.

"Mary, I just heard that Chico closed his daycare centers and has been accused of fraud for falsifying attendance records."

"That doesn't surprise me. He's been cheating all of his life. He'll find a way to get out of trouble; he always does."

"But this is serious now. I think he is going to do some jail time for this one."

"Let me call the girls; I'll talk to you later." I hang up the phone and quickly dial my daughters and put them on the three-way mode before I tell them of the news.

After hearing the bad news they quickly drove to Chico's home. "Mom, he was so desponded," they reported. I imagined him looking defeated and scared for the first time in his life.

I thought of his scheme to use me a second time when he was confronted by school administrators about his exploitation of high school girls. I remembered the last call I received from his principals years ago.

"Hello is this Mary?"

"Yes, who's calling?"

"This is Mr. Oliver. I have Mr. Mumford, the Adult Education principal on the line."

"I'm sure that this call has to do with Chico. What kind of trouble is he in now?"

"Well we just think that it would be better if he were married. He's gotten a bit wild again and though we have talked to him repeatedly, he continues with this negative behavior. Won't you consider taking him back? He really loves you. He just doesn't know how to express it."

"Are you serious? No! I can't help him now. I listened to y'all before and do you know what happened to me? I nearly lost my sight. He's abusive. Let him get fired this time. I know that you and the other coaches who mentored him since high school meant well by helping him to move up the ranks in the school system so quickly, but y'all didn't take into account his maturity or character. Now he is constantly ego tripping."

"Mary, you are the only one who can actually help. You understand him. He loves his children and he misses them," Mumford pleaded.

"I don't believe that he is capable of loving anyone. He is irreparably broken and has sociopathic tendencies. I just didn't realize that in the beginning. You'll have to find a woman more naïve than I was to trick into marrying him. Goodbye." Click!

Six months later, Chico married Cecilia. Mr. Mumford expressed that he had introduced them through a mutual friend. I laughed when I heard of the "arrangement" and thought "if she only knew what I know." For her sake, I prayed that Chico had matured or changed; but I wondered what character trait or weakness had he recognized in her that he would exploit. With him there was always a selfish motive or hidden agenda.

As I thought of Chico's current plight, I doubted that he would be able to escape the consequences of his actions. There would be no secret calls and backroom deals to bail him out this time. He would finally have to face the music.

As the investigation progressed, Renee assisted Chico, who was now virtually crippled by the old knee injury, in gathering the documents needed for his defense. She boxed and carried them to his lawyer's office.

Having had a steady stream of income for years from Family Central for the subsidized students at his childcare centers, Chico had spent without much thought of saving for a rainy day. Funds were now scarce and bills were mounting. With time on his hands, he concocted a scheme to revive his business. He called the girls.

"Renee and Juanita I want you to lease my businesses for $30,000 a month. You can operate them under a new name."

"What! That's an impossible amount especially since the centers are closed. It would take time to reestablish the private clientele and possibly months to get a contract with Family Central again," they voiced.

"Then get me the equity out of your houses, he demanded. "Remember, I gave you the down payments. It's time for you to help me now."

They realized that he was only thinking about himself. He made them feel guilty for refusing to apply for an equity line of credit, and then reminded them of everything that he had ever done for them. He was desperate for cash and without shame.

Chico had become less mobile and was using a cane for assistance. It had been four years since the injury, and he had not yet seen a doctor to have his knee x-rayed, nor had he successfully healed himself. In fact his knee had deteriorated and he was suffering from gout. He called Liz, who he had maintained a cordial relationship with since our divorce, for advice; she suggested that he lose weight and change his diet.

Anticipating that he might face jail time, he was encouraged to seek medical treatments. He did; however, he did not tell Renee, Juanita or Lonnie that he had actually scheduled surgery.

A week after the procedure was performed and while home recuperating, Chico, who had been fitted with a cast from the ankle to the thigh, reportedly complained to Cecilia, "I feel like I'm having a gas attack. Would you make me some hot tea?"

She left the room to prepare the brew, but when she returned he was slumped over. She immediately performed CPR and quickly called 911 and the family. As the kids raced to be by his side, Juanita phoned me.

"Mom, Cecilia just called. We are on our way to the hospital. Daddy stopped breathing."

I was not optimistic. I had heard of cases where patients died from blood clots after orthopedic surgery. I prayed for him but suspected that he would not make it.

When they reached the hospital, Juanita hung up and they rushed in. Fifteen minutes later, she called. "Mom, daddy is gone."

The autopsy revealed that he died from a pulmonary embolism resulting from the surgery.

Lonnie, who graduated with a degree in Criminal Justice and worked as a child protective services investigator, took the next week off from work and quickly assumed the responsibilities for Chico's final arrangements. I was so very proud of him. He was the caring man that his father should have been.

The day of the funeral, I got up as usual and dressed for work. Jabali looked at me and asked, "Why are you leaving so soon? Isn't the funeral at 12 o'clock noon?"

"Yes, but I'm not going to the funeral."

"Oh yes you are," he ordered. "You're not going for him; you're going for your children first and second to bury Chico in your mind. As long as we have been together, you still exhibit behaviors that reflect the years of abuse. You continue to jump when startled or become emotionally immobilized when you are approached from your blind side. It takes you too much time to regain your composure. I want you completely free of fear. Your love is conditional. You're still afraid of long term commitments."

I stopped and stared at him. He continued to speak.

"As kind and loving as you are, you continue to hold back a little piece of your heart. You let go then quickly pullback. I don't think you are aware of it, but it's obvious to me. You have to stop living in his shadow. You must walk in your own light. So you're also going to this funeral for us."

As he drove to the church, I didn't speak. As we entered the sanctuary, I saw the open casket down front. I quickly sat on a pew in the back row refusing to go view the body, but Jabali gently squeezed my hand and led me down the aisle. As I stood before the casket, I slowly lowered my eyes to look. Though Chico was dead, the fear of being face to face with him brought back memories of his abusive rages. I shuddered and trembled. Jabali steadied me with an embrace. When I relaxed, he slowly released the grip on my hand and left me alone with the corpse.

As I viewed the remains, my first thought was, "Who is this fat old man laying here?" Over the twenty-five years, with the exception of Juanita's graduation and wedding, I'd only seen Chico in court. In my mind, I'd retained the image of the young athletic man that I had married. This body was not the one that I feared. This gray haired obese cadaver had not abused me. I stared and stared at him, then slowly walked away remaining void of overt emotions.

As I read through the obituary and turned the pages to see the many pictures of his family displayed, I wondered, "Where is my picture?" At that moment I understood why Jabali insisted that I attend the funeral. These are my children. This is their father. This was their moment of bereavement. I had to be there for them. I sighed, but I still didn't cry.

"Another Date Night"

A month later, as Jabali and I were driving along the highway returning home from a dance at the Miccosukee Hotel and Resort on Krome Avenue in South Miami, an old song came on the radio. As I listened, I began to cry uncontrollably. Jabali pulled to the side of the road and held me tightly. He understood. The song was the *"Second Time Around."* Chico had played it daily when he wooed me into taking him back after our divorce. That night, I finally buried my high school sweetheart.

When I regained my composure, Jabali detoured from the route home and drove to the beach to our favorite spot. We quietly walked along the shore holding hands. It was so reminiscent of the night that he proposed to me.

I turned to him and said, "I love you. Thanks for everything. You have been there for me through the most difficult times. With your support and understanding, I have slowly healed some old wounds. You have truly been a rock, a pillar of strength for me. I thank God for everyday that we've been together."

He kissed me on the cheek, then placed his hand on my bare arm and lightly touched my skin; with soft stroking motions, he gently moved his fingers up and down my arm. I smiled because I knew what that meant.

It reminded me of the first night that we made love. Knowing that I understood, he whispered, "Let's go home."

As he drove, I closed my eyes and remembered that wonderful night eight years ago.

After nearly six months of dating, on the way home from the movies, I asked Jabali to stop by Baskin Robbins for some ice cream.

"What flavor do you want?" he asked.

"Any variety that has some chocolate with nuts in it will do."

I stayed in the car while he went in for the order. I watched him as he walked away from the car. He had such a sexy walk. When he returned, he handed me the cone and I began to slowly lick it. He watched me closely.

"I can see that you really like ice cream!"

Yes, but I only eat it occasionally because I'm always watching my weight."

"I'm fascinated with the way you gently glide your tongue up and down each side of the cone. You are so graceful."

"Thank you," I replied. He commented again.

"I like the way that you turn your wrist to get to the other side of the cone. It's done with such finesse."

"You are very observant." I thought, "Why is he so fascinated with how I eat my ice cream? What is he up to?"

He continued to stare at me. I continued to lick the cone. Then he said, "I'm getting excited just seeing your head bob up and down as you make sure that you don't spill a drop."

I stopped licking, turned and looked into his eyes. He winked. Immediately, I grasped his figurative language and playfully replied, "I like hard ice cream; it melts slowly and you get to enjoy it longer."

"That's correct. I have a special flavor of ice cream that you've not tasted. Would you like to go home with me tonight and sample some?"

"Yes, I would. I just hope that it is not fattening."

We laughed.

I knew that this was the night that I had been waiting for since I'd seen him in the nude in Naples on our first date. I'd perceived his subtle message and eagerly said, "Let's go."

I wasn't disappointed. The experience was better than I had ever imagined.

Tonight however, unlike it was eight years ago, would be even better because Jabali would have me completely; mind, body and soul. Finally, I'm free!

POST SCRIPT

Moses Israel was released from prison but remained under house arrest where he died of cancer. Judith was released on probation but could not associate with any known Hebrew Israelites.

Blossom and Julius married, but a few years later she discovered that he'd had an affair during their marriage. They're now divorced.

I never saw Job again; however, he mailed me a video of an awards ceremony honoring his life's achievements. I was very proud of him.

"A Beautifully Blended Family: Mattie Pearl, Mildred, Mary Emma of Boston, MA, Elizabeth, Eurie and Me at the Beasley Family Reunion in New York City"

Everyone has a story. What's yours? What incidents can you recall that may have obscured your vision or shattered your lenses and caused you to view life differently; either positively or adversely?

A series of questions have been compiled that are based on the titles of each chapter in the book that are useful for book club discussions, workshops or for individuals interested in taking their own reflective journey.

To receive a free copy, please send an email to:
<u>marysmemoir@aol.com</u>
or
through the website:
<u>www.shattered-lens-memoir.vpweb.com</u>

My Blog:
<u>http://www.ReflectandRecreateyou.wordpress.com</u>

ABOUT THE AUTHOR

 *A native of Miami, Florida and a graduate of Northwestern High in Liberty City, Mary Alice Beasley was mentored by her college educated older sister Elizabeth to read, question, explore, dream and then strive to become all that she imagined. However, her plans were derailed when she married a high school football quarterback who became a school administrator and prosperous entrepreneur. Her life spiraled into an abyss of despair and depression. Determined to get it back on track, she searched within for the strength that she often recognized in her mother to overcome the physical scars, the suppressed emotional pain and the guilt that plagued her daily. Feeling blessed and triumphant, she now dedicates her life to tutoring and encouraging young people to become positive, powerful and productive citizens.*

She received her B.S. in Speech Corrections from Florida A&M University and her M.S. in Exceptional Student Education from Saint Thomas University while serving as an itinerant Speech and Language Pathologist in Miami Dade County Schools. She later incorporated Speak Easy Tutors, an academic tutoring and educational consulting service. To become a successful, knowledgeable, and financially literate entrepreneur, she attended Gold Coast and Eagle Schools of Insurance to obtain licensing as a life, health and annuity agent and Johnson Lipman Corporation in Boca Raton for her Series 6 credentials.

She is a charter member of the South Broward Alumnae Chapter of Delta Sigma Theta Sorority, Inc.; a member of "Sistah Girl Reading Club," a group dedicated to supporting African American authors by purchasing, reading and discussing their works, and the "Women of Promise," a local support network of positive professional woman.